Pre-Production Planning for Video, Film, and Multimedia

Steve R. Cartwright

Focal Press

Boston   Oxford   Johannesburg   Melbourne
New Delhi   Singapore

Focal Press is an imprint of Butterworth–Heinemann
Copyright © 1996 by Butterworth–Heinemann
Ⓡ A member of the Reed Elsevier group

∞ Recognizing the importance of preserving what has been written, Butterworth–Heinemann prints its books on acid-free paper whenever possible.

Library of Congress Cataloging-in-Publication Data
Cartwright, Steve R.
    Pre-production planning for video, film, and multimedia / Steve R. Cartwright.
        p.   cm.
    Includes index.
    ISBN 0-240-80271-3 (pbk. : alk. paper)
    1. Motion pictures—Production and direction—Planning.   2. Video recordings—Production and direction—Planning.   3. Multimedia systems—Planning.
    PN1995.9.P7C33   1996
    791.43′0232—dc20   96-17689
                                                             CIP

British Library Cataloguing-in-Publication Data
A catalogue record for this book is available from the British Library.

The publisher offers discounts on bulk orders of this book.
For information, please write:

Manager of Special Sales
Butterworth–Heinemann
313 Washington Street
Newton, MA 02158–1626
Tel: 617-928-2500
Fax: 617-928-2620

For information on all Focal Press publications available, contact our World Wide Web home page at: http://www.bh.com/fp

10

Printed in the United States of America

Contents

Contents

FOREWORD

- Why does it always seem to take longer and cost more than planned for media production projects?
- Why does the budget for your interactive multimedia project seem to double when you begin to produce the video and audio segments?
- Why does it always seem to take so long for graphics and animation to be created?
- Why do technical problems constantly come up during production?
- Why do clients seem to expect so much and yet are only willing to pay for so little?

Should any or all of these questions strike a familiar chord, this book is for you. These typical production problems reflect a lack of planning, and planning is the most important element for successful productions. Whether you are shooting video or film or producing an interactive multimedia project, planning is the key. In this book I provide specific production planning techniques and tips for video, film and multimedia that will save you valuable production time, help you create better looking programs and generate a higher return on your production dollars.

Too often the production of a video or training film is an afterthought, tagged on to a larger (more important) training or communications event, with little thought given to planning, budgeting and scheduling. Because of this, production usually takes longer than anticipated, costs escalate, quality suffers and tempers flare. As a result, companies become discouraged and plans to develop media further are dropped because of the "expense and time" involved. I hope that this book will strengthen the case for good production planning and provide techniques that will shorten production time, reduce costs, increase quality and open many more opportunities to effectively produce and use media.

The techniques and production tips provided in this book evolved over a twenty year career in the production business both as an in-house corporate video producer and as the owner of a training and communications development company. I have been very fortunate to have worked with some of the best artists, camera operators, lighting directors, multimedia developers, editors and directors in the industry. Through many conversations with these very gifted people, I have developed ideas and tips into (I hope) a comprehensive method for production planning.

WHO THIS BOOK IS DESIGNED FOR

This book is designed to be a practical and useful guide for the novice as well as the seasoned media professional. It is intended to cover specific planning techniques for the pre-production, production, and post-production phases of program development. It will help you become a better project manager, understand the production process and empower you to work more successfully with talent, crew and clients. In short, this book is intended to make you a better camera operator, editor, director, multimedia developer, media production manager and producer.

SCOPE OF THIS BOOK

The scope of this book covers the planning process for video, film and multimedia production from pre-production meetings to post-production editing and distribution. Although the bulk of the material presented falls within the context of video production, there are many, many, planning techniques that go beyond traditional video production into applications for film productions and multimedia development.

OVERVIEW OF THE CONTENTS

Why should you know about line, form, color, and mass for graphics production? Why is understanding camera technical operation and lighting techniques important for pre-production? Why is an understanding of audio production and video editing important for planning your next media project? Because through a better understanding of all the elements of production comes a better understanding of the pre-production planning process. To plan well you have to understand the process. This book covers numerous production techniques; the intent is to provide you with a thorough production process background so that good planning can take place around each phase of production.

The planning process from pre-production to post-production is covered with chapters dedicated to program design and scriptwriting, budgeting and contracts, multimedia development, film production, video conferencing and using computers in production.

THE FUTURE

The tools we use for production are changing rapidly. And, although I have tried not to mention specific production technologies that will continue to change over the lifetime of this book, I have referred to general technology advancements that will assist the producer in the process of planning and producing video, film and multimedia. Resources for the producer are becoming readily available on computers and on-line services. New on-line services that the producer can access, such as the International Teleproduction Society's *ITSnet* and the Independent Filmmaker's *Internet Resource Guide*, are being developed daily. This exciting resource area will continue to grow for the benefit of the producer.

ACKNOWLEDGMENTS

Like any major production, this book would not have become a reality without the contributions of many people. I wish to extend my sincere thanks to my reviewers Jerry Freund and Robert Tat, and to those who granted interviews, resources, facts, and figures: Randy Baker, Oliver Peters, Grayson Mattingly, Cecil Smith, Mark McGahan, Bill Van Nostran, Thomas Kennedy, Steve Floyd, Shara Fountain, Stan Hankin, Ed Hearn, Bill Burkett, and Robert Tregenza, and to the many manufacturers that provided photos and information about their products.

Finally, I wish to thank my editor, Ellen Lazer, for her patience in the long process of writing this book and again to my family for all of their support and encouragement. This book is dedicated to my two teenage sons, Christopher and Kevin, who have made all this hard work worthwhile.

Steve R. Cartwright
Tucson, Arizona

The Importance of
Pre-Production Planning

- Halfway into editing your program you realize that a complete scene is missing. What happened? In the heat of production you inadvertently forgot to shoot Scene Eight! Now you remember telling yourself that you would come back to that part in the script and pick up the shot later. But you obviously forgot to do so.
- Your client is trying to save money by not doing a site survey before the day of the shoot. He wants to save time by not checking out the actual shooting locations. After all, you're just doing quick interviews at the plant. "Set the interview up against a nice background and just do it. Don't worry about lighting. . . ." the client says. The shoot ends up taking a full day instead of the original two hours as planned and budgeted because of poor backgrounds (windows in the shot, moving forklifts), sound problems (a PA system close by) and power problems (surges from heavy equipment). The client ends up spending more money than planned to re-shoot the interviews.

Both situations could have been avoided through pre-production planning. Both situations created problems with the program, required re-shooting, and cost additional time and money.

With the excitement and challenge of production, often we hurry through the planning process to get to the shooting and editing. But experience tells us good planning is the key to a successful project. It is one area that you must not hurry through, skimp on or delete. Whether you are producing film, video or multimedia projects, production takes an enormous amount of resources—resources that cost money (your money, the company's money or the client's), and time (more time than we usually anticipate). Good planning will save you both time and money.

A DEFINITION

I define pre-production planning as the preparation for all the steps required to execute the production and post-production of a video/film/multimedia project. I include post-production because planning is as important for the post-production process as it is for the production process (actual shooting) in saving time and money.

My definition encompasses the planning of a project from concept through completion. As I detail later in this book, planning starts with the problem, idea or communication need and continues through the distribution of the program to the intended viewer. Planning for production involves defining the problem or communication need and selecting a vehicle that will best resolve that need. Planning involves the process of content organization, scripting and visualization, equipment, crew, and talent selection and preparation, graphics planning, planning for the actual day of the shoot and planning for the editing (post-production) process. This basic planning process will apply to video, film and multimedia development.

And the planning process doesn't stop there. Planning is also needed for the duplication and distribution of the program as well.

Pre-production planning is a craft, as is lighting, camera work, directing and editing. Good pre-production comes with knowing and practicing each craft. For every successful producer there usually is an excellent associate producer working on all the details of production. This involves the art of planning. **It is one thing to come up with a great idea to put on video, and quite another to execute it.**

Figure 1 – 1
It takes a "team" of dedicated, skilled individuals to produce media. A typical "crew" could consist of a Director, Camera Operator (Director of Photography), audio technician and Production Assistant.

When I refer to production in this book, I will generally be referring to single camera style, video production, the type of production most of us are doing either for traditional linear type programming or for multimedia. However, the basic planning process also applies to film projects.

We are usually shooting "film style" or with a single camera as opposed to multiple camera production in which the editing decisions or camera shots are selected "live" through a switcher. During single camera production, we record all the various camera shots (wide shots, medium shots and close-ups) first, usually out of sequence according to our script (if we have one). Later we edit all the shots together in the sequence called for in the script or story. We are generally using small production crews or are shooting everything ourselves and producing commercials, training and information programs for organizations we work for or for clients that have hired us to do a video program. What is discussed within these pages applies to all types of production, including marketing and sales programs, documentaries, commercials and corporate news programs.

I refer to clients as anyone for whom we are producing a program. Whether you work for an organization or are hired on contract by an organization, we all have "clients" or customers for whom we are developing programs.

WHAT THIS BOOK COVERS

This book will cover each of the steps necessary in producing video projects and the video portions of multimedia. However, most of the pre-production steps apply to film production as well, as I point out in Chapter 4.

We will cover the importance of pre-production planning, comparisons of planning for film and video and multimedia, and the major elements of the production process. We will devote a chapter to what goes into the design of a program—both instructional design and production design. Another chapter is devoted to proposals and budgets and another to the details of pre-production. Planning for post-production will be covered as well as planning for duplication and distribution. Since the computer has become such a valuable production tool I have devoted a chapter to using the computer for the planning, production and post-production process.

THE 70-30-10 RULE

As a general rule, when we are producing training and information programs, we often devote as much as 70% of our time to the pre-production process and 30% to post-production with the remaining 10% (if you work at 110% like I do) devoted to the actual shooting. But the world of video seems to stress technology. So much attention is given to the equipment (the production element), it almost seems that if we simply purchase a camera we can instantly create programs. I've seen ads in magazines that lead you to believe that the video equipment is all you need to produce award winning programs. Not quite! The equipment is only one element, and a very minor element at that, needed in the production process.

The percentages should tell you where the real work and the success of the program lie. It's not in the 10%. It's in the 70%. Pre-production represents the least expensive part of your production, in actual dollars spent, but will have the biggest impact on the overall project's cost and success! That's justification enough for devoting more time to the pre-production process.

There is only one thing that can replace good pre-production planning . . . money. Pouring money into the production can sometimes replace poor pre-production planning, but don't even count on that! Devoting only a few hours to planning a program will have a drastic effect on the outcome of the project. If we spend less time in pre-production, we will spend more time in production and post-production—the most expensive parts of the project and certainly the most mentally and physically stressful.

The time we spend in pre-production will directly affect the percentage of time we have to spend in the other more expensive phases of production. An example would be not planning for a program and perhaps spending as little as 1% of our time in pre-production. We could end up spending as much as 40% of our time in production and close to 60% of our time in post-production, trying to fix the mistakes we made in production because we didn't plan properly.

Seasoned video pro Grayson Mattingly of Mattingly Productions in Fairfax, VA, states that "99% of the problems that go wrong in production usually can be traced back to poor pre-production planning."

In summary . . .

A well planned program for which we devote more time to the pre-production process will SAVE production and editing time, saving us money in the overall production of the project. The key to successful programs is planning. Whether you are producing video, film or mulitimedia projects, the more time you spend in the planning process, the more success you will have with the program.

THE APPROVAL PROCESS

- As an in-house video manager/producer for a microelectronics manufacturing company I developed many technical training programs. When I started working for the company, I was given a technical training project and assigned a subject matter expert who provided me with very specific direction on a certain technical process. I wrote the script around the process and shot the footage. But the process I recorded was actually not being done properly, so I ended up recording a technical process that was being performed improperly according to management. This problem can be traced back to the pre-production process. The appropriate approvals were not granted to the project.

- Grayson Mattingly describes a project he had been working on for several months for a client. The client had approved the video script with several changes that affected the shooting. During the production, however, the client was transferred to another state. So his client changed, as did the approval process. The new client went on to change the script further. This left Mattingly in the position of almost having to start over, which would add a great deal of time and costs not originally planned for in the budget. What happens to the budget? Who pays the difference? Again, this problem can be traced back to pre-production. The proposal and production contract did not explain specifically how script and client changes would be handled.

- A video producer with the Air Force put together scenes to be shot during a production. The script was approved earlier, so the producer followed the script closely. However, as they shot the script, there was no approval person on the set. The production team returned with the footage and edited the program. The rough cut was shown to the client who said that the talent in the shots was not the image he wanted to project. This problem could have been avoided through better pre-production planning, having the client's desired policies and practices approved and agreed upon way in advance of the shoot. The problem could also have been avoided if the client was present on the set as the script was being shot, or by having the client approve all field footage before starting the edit.

The problems cited in these examples could have been avoided if the approval process for the projects was in place. Approval means not only final approval of the project by the big boss or client but approval on all the many steps along the way. It is very important to agree to approval points before the project begins. Forms 1, 2, and 3 show suggested video production request forms that will help the approval process.

Suggested approval points (referred to as the **21 Steps to Approval**) for a video project could include: the initial rough idea or objective of the project, often referred to as the *project proposal*, the *content outline* or what material the project entails, the *treatment* or how the material will be handled (more on this in Chapter 2), the *budget*, the *rough script*, the *final script*, *storyboard*, the *talent* to be used in the production, the *shooting locations* where the shooting will take place, *sets* to be constructed, *stock footage* to be used in the program, the *original footage* shot on location (also referred to as camera tapes), final changes on script after shooting (*edit script*), *voice narration, music selections*, the *graphics* and *animation* needed in the program which include the rough layouts (storyboards for the graphics and the final pieces of work), the *rough edit*, the *final edit*, workbook or *printed support materials*, *duplication and packaging* of the final program and the *evaluation process*.

VIDEO PRODUCTION REQUEST

WORKING TITLE _____ PROPOSED LENGTH _____

DEPARTMENT_____

DEPARTMENT MANAGER/SUPERVISOR_____

PROJECT REPRESENTATIVE_____ PHONE_____

DATE PROJECT SUGGESTED _____DESIRED COMPLETION_____

IN-BRANCH RELEASE DATE_____

1. DESCRIBE THE PROJECT BRIEFLY_____

_____

2. WHO IS THE INTENDED AUDIENCE? (POSITION AND AVERAGE AGE)_____

_____

    A. EDUCATION_____

    B. PREVIOUS KNOWLEDGE/EXP. _____

    C. INTEREST LEVEL_____

3. HOW IS THE PROGRAM TO BE VIEWED?

  ☐ LUNCHTIME/BREAKS

  ☐ CLASSROOM

  ☐ SELF DIRECTED

    A. NUMBER OF VIEWERS IN AVERAGE AUDIENCE_____

    B. NUMBER OF VIEWERS TOTAL_____

    C. HOW OFTEN WILL PROGRAM BE VIEWED?_____

    D. HOW LONG WILL PROGRAM BE USED?_____

    E. HOW MANY COPIES ARE REQUIRED?_____

4. WHY IS THE PROJECT NEEDED?_____

_____

_____

_____

5. LIST THE PROJECT GOALS SHORT TERM/LONG RANGE

_____

_____

_____

6. THE SINGLE MOST IMPORTANT IDEA TO BE CONVEYED_____

_____

_____

7. WHO IS THE CONTENT EXPERT?_____ PHONE_____

    OTHER RESOURCE INDIVIDUALS_____ PHONE_____

    _____ PHONE_____

8. CONTENT OUTLINE (ATTACH)

9. IS PROGRAM PART OF LARGER PROJECT THAT INCLUDES OTHER MEDIA?_____

10. WOULD PROGRAM REQUIRE NEW SUPPORT MATERIAL? ☐ TESTS ☐ BROCHURES

11. IS THERE ANY CONTROVERSIAL ASPECTS IN THE CONTENT OR USE?_____

_____

_____

12. DIVISION MANAGER'S APPROVAL_____ _____
                                    (Signature)   (Date)

COMMENTS

_____

_____

_____

_____

_____

_____

_____

_____

FORM II

PRODUCTION TRACKING FORM

STEP COMPLETED	ITEM	PROJECTED COMPLETION DATE	DATE
1	ORIGINATION		
2	CONSULTATION & DEVELOPMENT		
3	PROJECT COORDINATION		
4	PROJECT DEVELOPMENT A. Project Team Meeting B. Meeting Summary C. Research D. Script Outline & Treatment		
5	SCRIPT DEVELOPMENT A. First Draft B. Final Draft C. Project Team Meeting D. Final Script/Storyboard Development E. Script/Storyboard Final Approval		
6	PRODUCTION A. Pre-Production B. Production C. Post Production		
7	VIEWING & EVALUATION A. First Edit B. Final Edit		
8	PROGRAM VIEWING AND EVALUATION		
9	PROJECT COMPLETION ACTIVITY A. Final Completion Coordination B. Show(s)		
10	EVALUATION		

FORM III

PRODUCTION RECORD FORM

Week of _____   **FORMAT**_____

Project # _____   **Director or Engineer**_____

Project Name _____

Activity	Mon.	Tues.	Wed.	Thu.	Fri.	Sat.	Sun.	Total
Writer/Director Hours								
Research/Planning								
Writing								
Directing								
Editing								
Other								
Engineering Hours								
Research/Planning								
Equipment Operation								
Editing								
Duplication								
Other								
Production Hours								
Video Editing Hours								
On-Line Edit								
Off-Line Edit								
Location Hours								
Audio Room Hours								
Video Duplication Hours								
Audio Duplication Hours								

PRODUCTION ESTIMATE FOR:
DATE OF ESTIMATE:

	–Estimate–		
	RATE	HOURS	ESTIMATE TOTAL

MANPOWER CATEGORY

PROJECT MANAGER
PRODUCER
INST. DESIGNER/TECH.
CONTENT RESEARCHER
WRITER—INST. MAT'LS
WRITER—MEDIA SCRIPTS
EDITOR—PRINT
DIRECTOR—MEDIA
PRODUCTION CREW
TV ENGINEER
ARTIST/ILLUSTRATOR
ACTOR(S)
NARRATOR
OTHER

TOTAL MANPOWER COSTS

ACTIVITY CATEGORY

VIDEO—STUDIO ORIGINATION
VIDEO—FIELD ORIGINATION
VIDEO—TIME CODING & WINDOW
VIDEO EDITING—CUTS ONLY
VIDEO EDITING—ON-LINE
AUDIO—ORIGINATION & EDIT

TOTAL ACTIVITY COSTS

OTHER COSTS CATEGORY

OFFICE SUPPLIES
PRODUCTION SUPPLIES
TELEPHONE & POSTAGE
TRAVEL—LOCAL
TRAVEL—OTHER

TOTAL OTHER COSTS

OVERHEAD

FIXED FEE

TOTAL ESTIMATED COSTS

A signature of the client or person responsible for the project is needed at all approval steps. If the client is involved with all the phases of production, there will be fewer surprises and a smoother production. And it is important to identify the **KEY** person for the project, often referred to as the **YES MAN**. Often that "Yes Man" is not the same person you are working with or even the same person assigned to the project, as our earlier examples point out.

Production is a **PROCESS** that we take our clients through. It is truly a team effort, and the more involved everyone is, the more likely it will succeed. Often it turns out that the process of production is as important as the end product. We need to manage this process properly, plan for the approvals, work as a team and get it all in writing.

NEED FOR ORGANIZATION

The key to good production planning is being organized. If you are a well organized person, you will do well in production. If not, hire someone who is. Good organization means a lot of things when it comes to video production.

- Keep a *production notebook* that contains the phone numbers of everybody involved with the project, ideas that come to you at 3 a.m., script changes, storyboard, site survey notes, equipment requirements, rental notes, special crew requirements, all schedules and notes on recommended shots, names of talent, crew and key location contacts, notes on props that you will need and receipts. The production notebook should hold all notes about the shoot that will help you get through the project smoothly. I find the notebook an invaluable tool for reviewing script changes, referencing important dates and conversations about content changes and billing information.
- Develop a well thought out *schedule* of events from the first meeting through the editing process, schedule the day of the shoot hour by hour, and communicate this schedule to everyone involved—crew, talent and client.
- Develop a thorough *equipment checklist* of all needed equipment and production gear from tape to camera to tripod to extension cords. A checklist will assure you of not forgetting anything on the day of the shoot.
- *Pre-produce* the program in your head and then on paper. All facets of the program should be thought through on paper, from the shots you need to the equipment requirements to transitions between scenes to how you are going to edit the program. A good producer/director will have thought through all the aspects of the program before it goes on tape.
- Develop a well organized *script* that is broken down for the shots you need by time and location, and plan in advance for all the transitions between scenes.

Good organization means attention to *details, details, details* . . . lamps, tape, cables, location, lights, sound, background, props, talent, client relations, script, script changes, schedules, crew, engineering, coffee, food, sets, make-up. I can't stress enough how important it is to think through all the details of a production. Attention to details will avert possible production problems.

Attention to details will also affect production **quality**. In major feature film production there is always someone responsible for continuity (part of the details) to assure the director that the actor looks the same in each scene, that the props in each scene are placed properly, and that the details within a scene that the director may not notice are taken care of. This adds to production quality and smooth shooting with fewer problems to contend with in post-production.

Major Elements of the
Production Process

2

Production is usually broken down into three major phases: pre-production, production and post-production. Let's review the major steps of each phase, keeping in mind that each step will be studied further in subsequent chapters.

PRE-PRODUCTION
Needs Assessment

A needs assessment should take place before any training, communications or documentary program begins production. A good needs analysis will accurately describe the problem and the appropriate solution. It will create a statement about the need for the production. This is important because everyone involved should agree that there is a problem and that media is the solution to justify the time and expense in solving the problem. What is first needed is a clear, concise statement of the problem and the proposed solution.

Budget Development

What will the "film" cost? This is the most often asked question at the beginning of any project. New clients, who are interested in producing video but have no knowledge of the costs involved, will often insist that I answer that question before a script or even a treatment is developed. Often my response is, "What is it worth?"

As I said earlier, we must first place a value on the training in order to get a handle on costs. If indeed we are going to change the viewers' behavior, performance or skill level, what is that change worth? If we produce a program that costs $20,000 and we cannot evaluate how much money the program saved the company, earned the company, or if the program changed the company, we could easily say that it cost too much. A value must be placed on the results the program creates. By measuring the results, we can evaluate how much we should spend. Know your return on investment.

One major problem that always comes up in figuring a budget is not having a script. How can you truly know how much a program is going to cost without the actual script? The script will tell you how long the program will be, how many actors are required, how many shooting locations there are, how many camera set-ups, as well as describe lighting and sound requirements, graphics, special effects, music and many other production requirements. Each of these requirements affects the cost of doing the program. It makes a big difference in the budget if the script takes two days to shoot or four, if what you shot takes three days to edit or four. Each of the script requirements will influence the cost of production. (In Chapter 4 we will learn how to break down the script into production elements and see how these elements are budgeted.) So the best we can do in estimating the budget before the script is written is just that, estimating. We have to ask the client a series of questions about the talent, number of days of shooting, locations, graphics and music requirements and try to come up with an estimate. Not until you have an actual script or firm idea of production requirements can you actually tally the cost of production. The budgeting process is quite sophisticated and takes experience to do well. For example:

- Do you know how to estimate the length of time that it will take to shoot a scene?
- Are you using professional talent/ how many? Nonprofessional talent will usually add to the production time.
- Do you know how long it will take you to edit or how many edits there are in the program?
- Will the client be there editing with you? If so, this always adds to the editing time which affects the budget.
- How many edits can you do in an hour?
- Are you going to have a lot of special effects, graphics or animations?
- Have you pre-selected your music and sound effects?
- Are you going to do an off-line edit first? (More on this in Chapter 7.)

These are only a few of the questions that should be answered before we can get close to a budget estimate. Types of budgets, budget breakdown and bid sheets will be covered in Chapter 4.

The Design Process

Program Design

I define the design process, detailed in Chapter 3, as being the critical up-front steps necessary to create a successful video training or multimedia program. Depending upon your responsibility in the production process, you may not have to be involved in the design phase of program development (usually this phase is conducted by an instructional designer or trainer), but it is good to have a basic understanding of the process.

Program design consists of clearly identifying the problem you wish to solve through the program, setting measurable program objectives, doing a thorough audience analysis and selecting the right medium or combinations of media to reach the desired objectives. Program design should always take place in the creation of training programs, and it should take place for informational/communications programs as well. With good design, you often find out that a video or interactive multimedia program is not needed at all and that a group meeting, series of audio tapes or traditional classroom training might better respond to the problem.

Each of the design steps represents an integral part of the planning process. Program design creates the road map for the entire learning event to follow and with clear, measurable objectives allows for evaluation of the programming to take place. For educational events the video program is often only one segment of many learning elements designed to reach the overall learning objectives.

Production Design

I believe strongly in production design. Production design is the pre-planning of all visual elements and sound to enhance the program and reach the communication objective. Designing all the elements ensures a coherent, comprehensive program that has aesthetic continuity. Good production design starts with a meaningful storyboard where the visual elements are chosen and designed for the biggest impact and educational value for the viewer. The design is integrated into shooting and affects the choice of camera angles, composition, lighting, pace, movement, color and sound. In other words, aesthetic choices are planned for and designed to create a meaningful response from the message. Aesthetics become the "visual language" that we use to communicate with our viewers. A thorough understanding of this special language is critical for program success.

An excellent reference for aesthetic principles is Herbert Zettl's *Sight, Sound, Motion: Applied Media Aesthetics* published by Wadsworth Publishing Company, Inc. In his book Zettl states that the medium (video programming in our case) acts not only as the distribution tool in delivering the message to our audience but actually shapes the message:

> The media, such as television and film, are not neutral machines that represent merely a cheap, efficient, and accessible distribution device for ready-made messages. On the contrary, the media have a great influence on the shaping of the message, the way the original event is clarified and intensified. Television and film speak their very own aesthetic language; they have their very own aesthetic requirements and potentials. They are an integral part of the total communication process, not just the channel by which the communication is sent.

As media producers we have the responsibility of learning as much as we can about our aesthetic choices and the impact these choices have on our viewers. Production design becomes a conscious effort on our part to make meaningful, aesthetic choices that contribute to our message and create a clearer understanding with our viewer.

Scripting and Storyboarding

The Treatment/Concept

The *concept* is the framework or theme you choose to deliver the content to the audience. Once you have researched the content and have an understanding of the audience, you can develop the concept you want to take in delivering the information. The concept sets the parameters for production considerations. The concept may take the form of an interview, game show, documentary, case study, humorous vignette, or demonstration. It is important to create a concept that will be appropriate for the audience. What will the audience accept? Will they accept a humorous concept, interview or documentary? It is important to create a concept that will satisfy the needs of your audience.

Once you have decided on a concept or combination of concepts, a *treatment* is created. The treatment is a narrative description of how the program will appear on the screen. It includes the program objectives, audience profile and concept. It would be developed in a chronological sequence of events as you see them developing on the screen and describe major locations, actors and sights and sounds that contribute to reaching the objectives.

After the content outline is approved, the treatment is often the next step in the approval process. It is important to get everyone's agreement on the approach you are going to take. The treatment descibes the concept and sets the tone for the entire program to be produced: budgets, talent selection, music, graphics and location decisions will all be based on the treatment. It may take several treatments before you come up with the best approach for your audience, budget, resources and time constraints. The treatment will also provide the guidelines for script development. An example of a treatment is shown on the next page.

Sample Treatment

Cartwright & Associates
Video Production Treatment for . . .

PROPOSAL OBJECTIVES

This proposal is intended to frame the working responsibilities of **Cartwright & Associates** in the development of a video program and provide a payment structure so that work on the project could be scheduled. This proposal represents an approximate working budget based on **C & A's** total involvement in creation and production. This includes program design, script development, visualization, video production, computer graphics, professional voice narration, music selection, directing and editing.

PROGRAM TREATMENT/CONCEPT

The program content, concept and storyline will be developed through the scriptwriting process. The basic program concept will communicate the history, traditions and values within . . . It is important that the video program depict a sense of pride in new employees, existing employees and external audiences. The video should have a strong visual concept that emphasizes the close relationship of the company with the outdoors and a strong commitment to its customers. A storytelling approach might be incorporated that helps pass along the stories of . . . It has been suggested that individuals sitting around a campfire could tell the story while weaving in warm, outdoor shots that support the strong traditions of the company. At the same time we would include shots of satisfied customers using products revealing the tradition of quality at. . . . The overall effect of the video is that of "storytelling" to get the main points across.

Scriptwriting

Once the treatment is approved, you start the scripting process. The basic scripting process follows a series of steps that will vary depending upon your knowledge of the subject, the complexity of the production and budget. You will first develop a working *content outline* that sequences the information you have to present and frameworks the amount of information to be covered. This is an approval point.

Once you have approval on the content outline, script development or research on the content begins. As the script is being developed, visuals are being selected and the storyboard is developed.

A storyboard is a visual representation of the "shots" or "pictures" you feel are needed to tell your story. The storyboard can be simple drawings on 3×5 cards or more refined drawings on printed storyboard forms. Often rough sketches of the required shots will be enough to convey your visual thoughts.

A *rough draft* script is developed along with the appropriate visuals. Approval is given on the draft and the *final script* is written. The final script will have all the directorial elements, transitions and effects written in along with all audio effects and music cues. Once the final script and storyboard is approved, the shooting script is developed.

The *shooting script* will break down the script into major production elements of locations, scenes, major camera or talent movement. The shooting script will help you develop a shooting schedule and organize the script for the day of the shoot. Two sample script excerpts are shown below.

Sample Split-Page Script Excerpt

10 DISS to graphic/pan down to graphic to haulage level	At the haulage level ore is loaded into underground ore trains
11 DISS to live shot train pulling away CUT to rotary dumps	The underground ore trains travel to the underground ore dumps where they are unloaded
12 CUT to surface level skips as ore comes to the surface	Ore is then hoisted up to the surface via the production shafts using buckets called "skips"
13 ZOOM-out to WS service shafts DISS in graphic overlay	Several service shafts provide intake ventilation for the mine, while production shafts

---

Sample Script Excerpt

11. CUT TO PATROL OFFICER AT BURGLARY SCENE CALLING FOR K-9

12. REVEAL . . . GRAPHIC STAR, (POINT #2), TITLE **"SPECIALIZED UNITS"** FROM POINT ON STAR ZOOM-OUT K-9 UNIT RESPONDING TO CALL

> **NARRATOR:** Specialized units include: K-9 units,
> trained in the detection of narcotics and people,

13. DISSOLVE TO: SHOT OF SEARCH AND RESCUE

> **NARRATOR:** Search & Rescue,

14. DISSOLVE TO: SEVERAL HIGH IMPACT SHOTS OF SWAT

> **NARRATOR:** Special Weapons and Tactics—or SWAT.

15. DISSOLVE TO: B/W SHOTS OF TRAFFIC

> **NARRATOR:** The Traffic Unit, which investigates
> serious-injury vehicle and aircraft accidents, and
> enforces DUI laws.

16. DISSOLVE TO: SHOT OF AIR UNIT . . . FOLLOW ACTION OF UNLOADING PRISONER

> **NARRATOR:** The Air Unit, which handles such
> tasks as cross-country prisoner transports and air
> surveillance operations.

17. DISSOLVE TO: CLASSROOM SHOT OF D.A.R.E. OFFICER

Figure 2 – 1
Grayson Mattingly (far right) goes over the script with client and talent before production begins.

Logistics

The logistics phase of pre-production encompasses arranging for all the details of the shoot, such as acquiring the equipment needed for the shoot, arranging for props and getting approval to shoot at the locations. The long list of logistic considerations will be covered in more detail in Chapter 5.

PRODUCTION

The *production* itself (the 10% of our formula) usually consists of focusing our attention on the equipment operation and working with crew and talent. At this point we are focusing all our energy and resources into obtaining the best possible performance with the best possible technical quality of sound and picture. Production is where your pre-production planning pays off. Your attention to the details of the shoot, your organization efforts and attention to script come together at production so you can devote your attention to performance. If we have done our job in pre-production planning, we can now concentrate on talent performance, crew performance and getting what we want on tape; it is too late to worry about the right connector/cable/power. Details like these drain you of creative energy. **Good pre-production planning will free you of the burdensome details of production and let you concentrate on talent performance.**

In the production phase we record talent on location, record studio insert shots, produce graphic elements and slides, do voice narration, record music elements, and sound effects. In other words you place all the elements that you are going to edit onto tape.

POST-PRODUCTION

After recording all the source material on tape, post-production begins. But before you start editing, the planning process comes into play once again. Chapter 7 is devoted to preparing for post-production. Briefly, post-production involves three major steps; script re-writing and tape logging, the edit and duplication/distribution.

The post-production process will require a lot of your time. Always plan for more time than you think you will need.

Script Re-Writing and Tape Logging

Depending on what you actually shot on location, you may have to do a re-write on the script because the shots on location may turn out differently than what you had originally planned. This does not usually require a lot of time, but often "tweaking" the script before you start editing is necessary and will require new script approval.

Tape logs are notes taken during or after the production that reference footage recorded onto tape. (See example in Appendix.) Tape logs are usually detailed lists of the shots that are recorded onto tape showing the order they appear on the tape. Tape logs usually contain the scene number, shot number and take number. By using time code numbers or the footage counter on the record machine, the locations of the scenes are registered on the log. The log will help you find the material you shot during the editing process. The more accurate the logs are and the more details you have on the logs, the better the editing process will go.

After the production, often we will match the log to the footage we shot and check that the location numbers, scenes, shots and takes all match. In other words we will clean-up the logs so we can use them in the editing process.

The Edit

The editing process consists of shot selection, arrangement and timing. In editing, we arrange the shots in sequence according to the script, and in doing so we affect the pace of the program, mood and visual flow. A very creative process, editing brings all of the random, recorded shots together into a coherent story that matches the script.

We first perform a *rough edit* (often referred to as off-line edit) that basically sequences our shots to the order required by the script. The rough edit gives us the scene lengths and a rough pacing of the program. Usually in creating the rough edit we do not add graphics, music or special effects and transitions. This is merely a "working draft" of the program. The rough edit allows for approval of the scenes recorded (is the content of the scene correct?), audio/visual continuity and the sequence of the shots.

Once the rough edit is approved, the *final edit* takes place. This step is often referred to as on-line editing. During the final edit or on-line process all the transitions, graphics, special effects, sound effects and music elements are added and edited into final form according to the requirements of the script.

Duplication/Distribution

Duplication of the program is next. Getting the program ready for delivery to the viewer is usually referred to as dubbing or duplication. We should pay more attention to the planning of the duplication process because it ultimately affects what the viewer actually sees.

The duplication process involves preparing the master edited program for dubbing. Usually a dub master is recorded. This is a copy of the edited master. The dub master contains the final audio mix on two channels, a slate that identifies the program, tone and color bars. This information at the beginning of the tape allows you or the duplicator to technically set up the duplication machines.

If there are only a few copies to be duplicated, the in-house video producer usually handles the job within the production facility. This assures quality control, control over all copies and speed in delivery. More often however, the request for the program is in such numbers that it does not pay for the in-house producer to take the time to make all the copies in-house, and the dub master will be sent outside to a commercial duplicator.

A Word About Program Evaluation

It has been my experience that the video, film and multimedia industry as a whole is severely lacking in the area of program evaluation. There is no set standard for program evaluation. It is an area of program development that is just not taken very seriously. There are exceptions to the rule, but, as a whole, most organizations are just not doing a very good job of program evaluation. Once we have produced and distributed the program, we usually rush into the next project, and unless someone stomps and yells about it, the program is sent off to the hinterlands never to be heard from again.

Program evaluation should not be the last step in the process but the first, since it will assure that the program is being seen by the intended audience, that the message is getting across and that the program's goals and objectives are being met. It helps place a value on the program that should tie into budgetary considerations. In its simplest form evaluations should address how much money the program saved the organization, how much money it made the organization or what efficiencies it brought to the process.

Evaluation is not just a single step or event that takes place at the end of the program, but it is an entire process. It is an important part of needs assessment, defining the audience and developing training objectives. Video training programs should change a behavior, attitude or skill, and the evaluation process should measure this change. Evaluation begins with establishing good objectives and clearly defining the audience. If good objectives are written (based on the intended audience), the evaluation process will be made easier.

As we will learn in the next chapter on *program design*, evaluation should be an integral part of the program design process. It provides a means to measure the effectiveness of the program. Evaluation should help answer how well the program answered the need for which it was designed. Refer to Forms 4, 5, and 6 for examples of evaluation forms.

Evaluating Video Programs, Is It Worth It? by Laurel Sneed (published by Focal Press) is a good reference that covers evaluation techniques and tools and provides insight into creating evaluation methods for your training programs.

As I mentioned earlier, there are exceptions to the rule when it comes to evaluating programs. While working as the supervisor of video services at the **Phoenix Police Department**, Bill Burkett conducted video program evaluations. Burkett states, "The trick to having a good video programming feedback or evaluation system is to make it simple for

FORM IV

VIDEOTAPE EVALUATION FORM I

DATE: _____

TITLE OF PROGRAM:_____

PROGRAM COMPLETION DATE: _____

CLIENT: _____

1. Were the purpose and objectives of the program accomplished to your satisfaction? Why or why not?
    Comments:

2. Was the message presented clearly and was it easy to understand? Why or why not?
    Comments:

3. What did you like best about the show?
    Comments:

4. What did you like least about the show?
    Comments:

5. What if anything would you like us to do differently?
    Comments:

6. What is your overall opinion of the program?
   Comments:

7. Any other comments?

Please return to:

FORM V

VIDEOTAPE EVALUATION FORM II

Date: _____ Location: _____

Title: _____ Copy # _____

Date You Viewed Program: _____

Number of People Who Viewed Program with You: _____

Technical Quality:	Good	Fair	Poor
Audio:	☐	☐	☐
Video:	☐	☐	☐
Length:	O.K.	Too Short	Too Long

Rating Scale: (Circle the number on each scale that most clearly reflects your opinion)

A. How clear was the message of the program?

Very Clear	Reasonably Clear	Slightly Clear	Unclear
4	3	2	1

B. How interesting was the program?

Very Interesting	Reasonably Interesting	Slightly Interesting	Not Interesting
4	3	2	1

C. How understandable was the program?

Very Understandable	Reasonably Understandable	Slightly Understandable	Not Understandable
4	3	2	1

D. How relevant was the program to you / your work?

Very Relevant	Reasonably Relevant	Slightly Relevant	Irrelevant
4	3	2	1

E. How effective was the program in presenting the subject?

Very Effective	Reasonably Effective	Slightly Effective	Ineffective
4	3	2	1

Describe any strengths or weaknesses you saw in the program (i.e., graphic quality, performance of people in the program, music selection, etc.)

Which two main points were most effectively presented?

Describe how this program will influence your actions and attitudes toward the subject presented in the program.

Additional comments:

Signature:

Please return to:

FORM VI

VIDEO EVALUATION FOR MANAGERS

RETURN TO: _____

DUE DATE: _____

Title of Video Tape: _____ Number: _____

Number of Viewers: _____

Fill in your impression of this tape. Please be frank and specific, especially in explaining negative comments. This will help in upgrading program quality.

1. The visual quality is:

   very good   good   fair   poor

2. The audio quality is:

   very good   good   fair   poor

3. The program is:

   adequate length   too long   too short

4. The content is:

   well structured   not well structured

   clear   not clear

   all helpful   not all helpful

   realistic   not realistic

5. Will you use it again?

   Yes   No

6. How would you improve this program?

Specific Comments: (Why? How?)

_____

_____

_____

_____

_____

_____

_____

_____

Briefly describe how this program has improved your training

_____

_____

_____

_____

_____

_____

_____

_____

_____

your audiences to use and simple for you to assemble the data and evaluate it."

The training system for police officers worked through the precinct system. Each precinct had a training sergeant and the videotapes Burkett produced would go to him or her. Along with each videotape went an evaluation form that the training sergeant was to fill out after the precinct's officers had seen the program.

The form wasn't anything fancy or unique. It featured a series of questions such as, "Did this program present information you could put to use on the job today?" and "Was the information presented in an interesting manner?" Each question was accompanied with a one-to-five scale on which the training sergeant circled the appropriate number based on his observations of how the audience reacted to the program.

Those forms were then returned to the video services department. Burkett explains, "When our workload allowed, we would enter the raw numbers into a spreadsheet for analysis. The advantage of using a spreadsheet for this, beside the simple fact that the computer would handle all the calculation chores involved, was that we could analyze the data in several ways.

"For example, we could tell how a program rated overall across all precincts or on a precinct-by-precinct basis. We could analyze the specific strengths and weaknesses of a particular program. We could even gather aggregate information that told us how particular precincts rated all our programs."

If any trends developed, Burkett could follow up on them for further analysis. For example, Burkett found one precinct that consistently rated the video programs low, even when reactions from the Police Department as a whole had been quite favorable. "Further questioning uncovered the fact that the training sergeant in that precinct felt video-based training was worthless, didn't even show the tapes, and gave us low ratings. Needless to say, that problem was quickly remedied."

The Athlete's Foot is a specialty retailer of athletic footwear operating internationally, with over 700 corporate and franchise owned stores. They have a very successful video sales training series (that this author produced) called the "Greet and Seat" Selling System. It is a classic six-step selling approach that contains specific key customer service points that every sales associate is required to meet on every sale with every customer. Shara Fountain, Director of Training and Development at The Athlete's Foot, states, "'Greet and Seat' has been a tremendous success for us, as evidenced by significant increases in sales results (up to 35% in some areas!)."

The Athlete's Foot uses several program evaluation approaches. For example, both segments of the Associate Video Training Series—Certified Sales Associate and FIT Technician—require certification testing of all associates. The tests consist of four pages of intensive review of the material covered in videos and directed exercises of seven modules of instruction. Standards are high—associates are required to pass the test with a score of 90. Associates may retest, but must pass on the third attempt. Certification tests are required to be completed within 90 days of the date of hire.

All store associates sign a commitment to the "Greet and Seat" selling process. Following training, they are observed by the Store Manager, Area Training Manager (ATM) and District Manager on a regular basis to ensure that they are following the steps and key points of the selling system. These observations are documented on the ATM's Training Visit Report and on the District Manager's Store Visit Report.

Another tool used to evaluate behavior change on the job is the "Fit"ness Report Card, which was used following implementation of the video training series to ensure compliance to the new system. At first daily, then weekly, then bi-weekly and finally monthly, each associate in each store was observed and given a "Fit"ness Report Card, evaluating each step and key point of the sale. Associates observed NOT following the selling system as it was trained are given corrective action counseling.

Fountain explains further, "Our business results are tracked as well. Sales results are evaluated weekly by the Store Manager, District Manager, Regional Director and Vice President of Stores regarding specific store results (sale trends up or down, comparisons to sales results and changes in store personnel, etc.). These business results are tied directly to our training efforts. Video training has proven to be a successful business tool for us."

In summary . . .

The planning process fits into all the phases of production and post-production. Each step of the production process from needs analysis through selecting locations and talent, from setting up the equipment on the day of the shoot to the edit of the tape, requires planning. And the better planned each step is, the better program you are going to produce. Successful program results are the product of good planning and experience.

Program Design and Scriptwriting

3

The planning process starts at the very beginning of program development. As the idea for a program develops, the planning process begins. The early planning stages will affect the outcome of the entire project, so time and care should be taken. Every step along the way to program completion requires good planning. And good planning begins with **needs assessment**.

Adapted from my book, *Secrets of Successful Video Training* published by Focal Press, this chapter will highlight the major planning steps for program development and production design.

MAJOR PROGRAM DESIGN STEPS
Needs Assessment

Needs assessment is often overlooked or taken lightly in the planning of a video program, but it is critical because it will determine the types of programs that are required by the organization, the amount of money spent for the project and the estimated return on investment. Know your training or communication needs and how video can meet them before you start producing any project.

Needs assessment will determine the types of programs your organization or clients need. More importantly, it will furnish the basis for a detailed video production plan to direct your activities and expenditures regarding equipment, staff and other resources for the project as well as for future projects.

The emphasis of this plan should not be hardware but programs—programs that management, employees and/or customers need to see. Time and resources must be committed to good needs analysis. In my experience, it is the programs, not the hardware, that yields success. Many companies have failed with video because their priorities were wrong. Equipment was in place, but program resources were not; therefore, their video efforts made no impact.

When analyzing your organization's video program needs, ask the following questions:

1. What kinds of programs will meet the practical needs of your organization. (e.g., cutting costs, improving services, boosting sales and profits)? Will video programming facilitate these changes? Video programs, like other tools within the organization, should contribute to the business goals of the organization. Successful video production facilities within organizations tackle business related goals.

2. Is video the most appropriate medium to deliver this programming to your employees and customers? The best video programs have strong visuals that involve color, sound and, most important of all, movement. Consequently, a good application would be a program that must incorporate these elements to achieve the program objective. Video can create change if used properly. Video programming should take full advantage of this dynamic medium.

3. What departments and operational areas will most benefit from video programming? How many people will view the programs? Where are these people located? Are the resources in place to provide video programs to your offices or plants throughout the country or world? Is the company prepared to support such a network?

To achieve the overall training or communication goals within an organization takes good management. Video has to be managed from program development through distribution. Special management skills are needed to manage program design, program development and program distribution. The management of these specific areas should be in place before programs are produced.

4. How much time and money is the organization willing to invest in video programming? How will you calculate the return on investment? Where will you get the numbers to make this calculation?

Like any other business tool, video programs must offer some sort of financial gain; otherwise, they are a waste of time. Investment in equipment, tapes, personnel and other resources must *generate* substantial dollars, either through increased sales and profits, reduced costs or improved staff efficiency. An evaluation process to measure return on investment should be put in place.

5. What video format will be appropriate for your communication needs? Your video needs analysis should help determine your organization's specific equipment requirements. Therefore, you should be familiar with the various format standards that the video industry has established. *Format* refers to the size of the tape and the process by which it records and reproduces (plays back) images and sound. There are currently more than 15 formats, and these are divided into two groups:
   a. Popular consumer formats include 1/2-inch VHS, Super VHS, 8 mm and Hi8 mm.
   b. Industrial formats include 3/4-inch U-Matic, 3/4 U-Matic SP, MII, Betacam, Betacam SP, D-1 (digital) and D-2.

For consumers, tape and equipment size and cost are the most important considerations. They place less emphasis on image quality. In contrast, industrial or professional users typically put a higher value on quality and dependability than on price. They care about the cost, but they want systems that perform consistently well, last a long time and require little maintenance, despite heavy and widespread use. In short, industrial video users are concerned about the long-term economics of ownership rather than the immediate purchase price.

In the professional sector, 3/4-inch U-Matic and 3/4 U-Matic SP, Betacam and Beta SP are the standard production formats, while VHS is preferred for playback and program distribution networks. The widespread use of VHS by company employees and customers in their homes increases the format's acceptance in the workplace and permits a broader distribution of video programs.

However, the distribution of programming within organizations is changing rapidly and should be analyzed closely. We can no longer assume that VHS will be the most cost effective means of distribution. In particular there has been growing interest for CD-ROM distribution because of the low cost of data storage and local area computer networks, which carry more training and communications. Each organization with video training and communications requirements should invest time and resources for a thorough information distribution needs analysis and be open to newer forms of technology for distribution.

A thorough needs analysis conducted by a professional communications consultant or by qualified internal video managers can yield valuable information that will contribute to program success and long range planning. A video "business plan" should be written before the first program is produced. It should include at the very least potential users of video within the organization, audience analysis, needed resources to meet the media needs of the organization, measurement tools to estimate return on investment, equipment, budget and space requirements, and long range growth projections.

A value has to be placed on video, and a thorough needs analysis will help determine value.

Identify the Problem

Once the needs of training and communication have been thoroughly identified, you can zero in on specific problems that you feel media or more specifically video can solve.

A thorough understanding of a problem is critical. You must place a value on solving the problem, so you can calculate your return on investment. With video we will invest a lot of time and resources in developing a program, so the problem should justify the resources invested. We are after results with our programming, and we must place value on those results. The results should be closely reviewed to determine if it is worth the investment of resources.

Problem identification includes:

1. Nature of the problem to determine strategy for solutions. Will video be the most appropriate solution? Video has distinct communication advantages, but it is not a panacea for all problems. Unfortunately, because video production capabilities exist within an organization, too often video is selected to solve problems that could be solved less expensively by the use of other communication resources (print, audio, slides, teleconferencing or traditional classroom training).

2. Number of people or staff affected by the problem. Are the numbers large enough to justify the expense of producing video?

3. How will you know you have solved the problem? Are the appropriate evaluation methods in place to determine outcome and effect?

4. What is the priority of the problem? Is this a pressing business need of the organization or is it a minor glitch that would make a neat video but would be hard to actually justify?

Audience Analysis

Audience analysis is probably the single most important step in designing video programs. You must understand who it is you are communicating with. Successful programs target a specific audience, while unsuccessful programs usually try to reach too large an audience. You have to know the needs of the audience and write the program to address those needs.

Through good audience needs analysis, you can design and create a program that will have impact, create change and "move" your viewers because you will be talking to them and no one else.

Audience analysis includes knowing their age and viewing location, which will influence how we present the information, and understanding the motivation of the viewers. Why should they watch the program? What's in it for them? I like to define the viewers' "need to know level." If their perceived need to know level is very high (they understand how important the information is to them), often we can devote less resources to the production. However, if you have identified that the viewers have a low need to know level, or they are not motivated to view the program, skimping on production values will have a disastrous effect. An unmotivated audience will not watch talking heads. Audience motivation and expectations directly influence production values.

Other audience analysis issues are size and location. How many people at one time will view the program? (Video is still not the best medium for large audience display; film is better.) How will the audience actually see the program? Are the viewing locations controlled in meetings or classrooms within the organization or are they in different parts of the country? Are each of these locations equipped to view the program? Who will manage the viewing function? Will there be a facilitator to manage the viewing of the program, respond to questions and handle technical problems? Is the organization staffed and equipped to show the program to all the intended viewers? Viewing considerations are often overlooked, but pre-planning will help alleviate potential viewing problems. A complete viewing system should be in place before production begins.

For example, I recently conducted a communications needs assessment for one of my clients, a large copper mining company in Arizona. In part, the communications strategy is provided below.

Communications Strategy

A need was identified through intensive interviews and focus groups to develop a communications plan that was committed to informing the work force of the culture change transpiring within the company. This plan is in response to that need.

To complete the plan, interviews and discussions were conducted with key people, focus groups were conducted with over 150 employees and information was researched and gathered pertaining to current communications channels.

This report identifies critical success factors for implementing a communications plan, provides for a short term and long term strategy and draws specific conclusions and provides recommendations around communications within the company.

This report also identifies a number of objectives crucial to the future success of communications within the company. Chief among these objectives are 1) the coordination of all communications plans, messages to work force, methods and resources; 2) the ability to provide communications consistently throughout the organization; 3) electronic linking of Business Units, key work areas, work force common areas and corporate; and 4) the appropriate use of technology to enhance communications and training.

In meeting the business goals and communications vision the communications strategy should:

- Provide a means to exemplify and reinforce the desired new culture
- Provide a means to support/promote all employees during the change to the New Team-Based Organization
- Provide a means to build awareness and knowledge within the work force of business operations and functions
- Provide a means to encourage positive modeling of desired behaviors
- Provide a means to promote an atmosphere of trust, respect and open communications among all employees

- Provide a means to listen and respond to the communications needs of the organization
- Provide a means to encourage and support the development of all employees

SHORT TERM ACTION PLAN

The Short Term Plan recommended focusing communications resources into a unified, central source headed by an internal communications person, guided by the Executive Council and supported by both internal and external communications resources.

1. In September the Council reviewed the initial short term plan and agreed to move forward with a more comprehensive plan.
2. A communications coordinator was hired.
3. Specific messages (themes) that responded to the business goals of the organization were created.
4. Individuals and systems to carry the messages to the work force were identified.
5. Specific written communications materials were developed to support training efforts.
6. A communications hot-line was developed.

LONG TERM ACTION PLAN

As a result of the Short Term Action Plan and the approval by the Council to develop a Comprehensive Communications Plan, a Long Term Action Plan was created. This plan provided the means to assess communications needs, created a specific long range plan and provided the means to evaluate communications strategies. Specific steps in this plan have been partially initiated:

1. A communications assessment was developed consisting of questions and issues addressing communications and training that needed to be brought up to the work force.
2. The focus group concept was utilized along with key interviews to address questions and to gain valuable information around the communications and training issues within the company.
3. A technology assessment was initiated.
4. Assessment of external and customer communications was initiated.
5. Assessment of the corporate communications plans and their interface with each division was initiated.
6. Assessment of the operational business goals and communications needs was initiated.

ACTION

1. Weekly or quarterly Work Team Development up-dates/bulletins that address success
2. Business Information and up-dates through videotaped programs
3. Computer network (E-Mail) bulletins for the Executive Council, Corporate and work force
4. Computer controlled signs at key work areas that provide daily financial data, meeting schedules and Work Team related daily bulletins
5. Daily bulletin board up-dates at the work site
6. Business/Work Team communications up-dates through videotaped programs
7. Printed media on an as needed basis for training highlights and specific (long range) Work Team development goals
8. Research utilization of interactive, communications technologies to enhance the

flow of voice, data, and video images from point to point and from point to multipoint throughout the company

9. Support and enhance through interactive technologies, effective communications and training programs

The plan provides for the creation and delivery of messages that respond directly to the cultural changes within the organization. These messages respond to and support the organizational development plan, revolve around themes and respond to work force questions regarding change.

The goal of the communications plan is to provide the means to create and deliver messages that communicate culture change within the entire organization and move the company forward in achieving its vision. It is designed to support and facilitate the awareness, involvement, commitment and transformation to the new culture within the time frame specified.

The plan also includes the creation and management of limited communications systems that allow selected messages to be delivered to the work force. Systems include appropriate media such as articles, papers, training sessions, video programs, signs and other technology that effectively and efficiently carry the message to the work force.

This example provides a model for effective needs assessment. It highlights the need within an organization to respond to the communications and training needs with a variety of message delivery systems. The plan provides for a means to move the communications forward, align resources and form budgets. Once this plan is set in motion, specific objectives can be written that address individual communication and training needs.

Objective Setting

The planning process includes writing concise, clear program objectives that can be measured. All the decisions we make regarding production (lighting, camera angles, talent selection, and so on) will be based on your written (and approved) objectives. Objectives describe what the viewer should know or be able to demonstrate after viewing the program. Objective setting relates directly to creating training programs as opposed to creating informational programs. Training programs and information programs should have different outcomes.

An *information* program is designed primarily to create a better understanding of a job or to bring an awareness of a subject. It may influence a better work environment or attempt to affect morale. Information is usually helpful to know, but it is not absolutely necessary or critical to job performance. After viewing an informational program, the audience will not necessarily be held responsible for the information. Or, the viewer will not be held accountable for a specific action.

A *training* program has to generate accountability, and an action or result is expected after viewing the program. The viewer is held accountable for the content and is expected to perform differently on the job after viewing the program. The viewer is tested or audited for a specific change in performance, behavior or attitude. You should determine whether the program will be training or information, because the end result or expectation will be different for each.

Be sure everyone involved in the program agrees on the objectives of the video program, because they become the cornerstone of the entire production process. Clear objectives are vital to success and assure good evaluation. (A reading of the classic book, *Preparing Instructional Objectives* by Robert F. Mager, will help you understand how to write good, clear objectives.)

By way of example, a video training program recently produced for a large paper products manufacturer contained several training modules on shelf space management (the process of analyzing financial data for effective inventory control). One of these modules was "Working Through the Concepts" (Of Shelf Space Management). The overall learning *objective* of that particular module was: the participant will demonstrate shelf space management analysis on a sample 2 ft. by 3 ft. shelf containing consumer paper products. The learning *outcomes* were: the ability to perform shelf space management using the five step process, an understanding of the impact an analysis has on a paper section by presenting the data and recommendations and an understanding of the benefits associated with shelf management. This objective with clear learning outcomes allows the trainer to measure the results of the training program. It provides what is to be taught and how it would be determined whether the viewer had learned the process under specific conditions.

Another example of a good measurable objective for a supervisory training program is: to increase the ability of supervisors to handle employee relations. This will be demonstrated by improved ability to deal with role-playing situations (as presented on the video). Improvement will be demonstrated by observation and follow-up interviews. An increase in ability to define problem situations and to recognize relevant alternatives will be considered evidence of change.

Avoid objectives that are too general such as: provide a *feeling*, provide a *general knowledge*, *acquaint* employees, develop an *appreciation* for, teach the *importance*, to *review*, examine or gain *insight*. These objectives are hard to measure and do not provide specific learning outcomes.

Objectives should not only meet the needs of the audience but of the organization as well. Where do they fit into your organization's business and goals? Will these objectives increase profits, reduce costs, boost efficiency or improve customer service? Can they be measured against specific results? Video communication and training results should be converted into dollars and cents that mean higher profitability to the organization.

The objective writing process should include separate objectives for each program goal or module. Break the objectives down to include expected outcomes that can be measured, and expand each objective into brief descriptions of appropriate, observable behaviors. Select an evaluation method that applies to each of the specific behaviors you have listed.

Objectives should be concise, specifying results to be achieved in measurable terms. Again, good program objectives provide the basis of good evaluation methods.

SCRIPTWRITING

This section will cover treatments, content development, storyboards and the scriptwriting process. There are many, many books about scriptwriting. One of my favorite books on the subject is Bill Van

Nostran's *The Scriptwriter's Handbook*, published by Focal Press. Van Nostran's book provides good research and script planning techniques along with many examples of script formats and concepts for corporate video. John Morley's *Scriptwriting for High-Impact Videos*, published by Wadsworth Publishing, contains excellent examples of communications programs and creative approaches to corporate information delivery.

Treatment

A treatment is a narrative description of how the program will appear on the screen. It will include the objective and an audience profile, and it will describe how the information will be delivered—the concept. The treatment is usually a single page, and for some organizations it will become an actual proposal. The proposal will be presented to the client and, upon approval, the project is set in motion. It is an important step in the process because approval on the treatment means that the objective, audience and concept have been accepted. This will provide direction and clearance for the project.

Content Development

The content you have gathered now has to be organized into a logical sequence. Video scripts are often organized three ways: in a time or chronological order, a topical order and a problem-solving approach. For example, with sales training you could organize the information into a problem-solving approach. Present a problem related to sales that will get the attention of the viewer, something they can relate to. Then, through behavior modeling techniques, show several approaches to solving the problem.

The objective and concept of delivery will help in the selection and organization of the material. Remember that with the television experience, the viewer will have only one chance to receive the message (as opposed to interactive multimedia, discussed in Chapter 7). The organization of the material becomes critical for successful reception.

As the outline is developed and content is defined for the target audience, the script will start to grow into a logical chain of events that will help your audience achieve the objective. But as the script grows it is important to start asking, "What exactly does the audience need in order to achieve the objective?" Content will grow and grow and the content expert, who is very close to the subject, will keep adding information that may not be necessary for the target audience. As writers, you must continually edit content and include only what is absolutely necessary. A video program should be precise and to the point. You should respect the viewers' time and provide them with only the essential information. As pointed out earlier, videotape has the capability of condensing time. Through sharp writing and transitions you can present the required information in a very short time. Do this by honing down the information and presenting through visuals and the spoken word only the information that is needed to reach the objective.

There are two schools of thought on how to proceed at this point. One is that you write the script first and then you visualize it. The second is that you visualize the information first and then write the script. I believe in the latter. After all, you have chosen video because of its visual impact, its ability to condense time and space and its effective combination of the spoken word and pictures. Therefore, I do not believe in

Figure 3 – 1
The script is your "road map" to success for film and video production.

creating videotapes that are glorified audio tapes. Often visuals are placed into a script to support the audio, and if you turned off the video you would still receive the message. If this is the case, why not save money and just produce an audio tape?

If videotape is the chosen medium of delivery, use it to its fullest advantage. You should, therefore, think in pictures, pictures that will tell the story. In other words, think visually. To this end the writer should address exactly what it is that must be seen to tell the story effectively. I approach this by jotting down visual ideas and sketches that I feel are needed to get the message communicated to the viewer. I actually create a storyboard or a sequence of pictures that depict the training event. Then I write words that support, clarify and enhance the visual experience.

During an actual video training program I recently produced for a manufacturing company, we "visualized" the program first by photographing the process that was to be taught. Then we audio recorded the operator performing the task. With good instructional design techniques, the operation was sequenced in proper order for the viewer, then the script was written. After analyzing the audience carefully, much of the original material was deleted (placed into a second training module) and only the material needed to reach the specific training objective was presented. The visuals did the teaching while the "words" were used for reinforcement and clarity.

Whichever approach you use to create the script, remember to place yourself in the viewers' position and continually ask what they need both visually and narratively to receive the message and accomplish the objectives.

The script will be influenced by the design, audience and objective. The writer will use the concept to tie the content together and, through careful organization, will create a logical flow of information that the target audience can follow. The visuals chosen will accurately tell the story in an interesting and lively way. And the words spoken will enhance the message, direct attention and help with transitions. Bringing together the individual elements of sound, pictures, transitions and music called for by the script creates the whole. And the training tape comes to life as a viewing experience that should motivate and teach.

For reference, a double-spaced, typewritten page will equal about one minute of programming depending upon how much visualization there is. So, if you are counting, you need to type about 20 double-spaced pages for a 20-minute program. With my writing experience, it takes me about an hour to write a finished minute of programming. This includes visualization, directing notes, audio cues transitions and dialog.

Page Format

A popular page format to use for video scripts breaks the page into two sections. One third of the page, usually on the left side, is devoted to visual information and is labeled "video." The other two thirds of the page is devoted to the audio portion of the program. Label the program with a title or a series title, the client, writer, date, and project number. The date at the top of the page will change as the script goes through the approval process.

Type the words the narrator will read in upper and lower case, as if you were typing a business letter. This makes it easier for the narrator to read. All audio cues, however, such as music and sound effects, should be all upper case to separate them from the narration. This section will also be used to identify sound sources such as on- or off-camera talent, music mixes, sources of sound effects and direction of off-camera audio.

The video column contains descriptions of scenes, shots and angles. It will also contain directing cues for transitions, camera moves, lighting cues, graphics and all essential visual information that will be needed to carry out the video portion of the program.

Script Tips

- Write with emphasis on pictures. After all, we are creating a video program not an audio program.
- Use words to support and enhance the visual message.
- Don't get wordy. Let the visuals carry the message.
- Use words that the audience is familiar with. Be prepared, depending on the viewers' familiarity with the content, to define words and provide an additional glossary.
- Use an informal, conversational style. Video is a personal, one-on-one medium. Direct narration to one individual in the audience.
- Use "you" and "we" whenever possible to establish an informal one-on-one experience.
- Use plenty of pauses. Pauses are used for emphasis and for editing, and give the audience a chance to digest the information.
- Write in transitions. Transitions carry the viewer from one event to the next and become an important element in creating successful tapes that flow naturally, without visual disruptions. Transitions add to the continuity of the message and should be considered a part of the scriptwriting process.
- Read the copy aloud. That will give you a feeling for timing, transitions, information flow, conversational style and believability. The audience will hear the script, not read it, so it has to be appealing to the ear.

Script Approval

The first draft attempt becomes the "rough" script. This should be sent to the client for approval. Usually, in place of a written script I send clients an audio tape of the script with a storyboard. The final product is going to be a videotape that the audience will see and hear, so your clients should experience the script in the medium it is intended for.

Changes are common in scriptwriting, so be prepared to face them. With a personal computer and a good word processing program, the scriptwriting phase can be streamlined. Some software products (more on this in Chapter 8) on the market are specifically designed for scriptwriting (the "*Show Scape*" scriptwriting software program by Lake Compuframes, "*Power Script*" by Comprehensive Video and "*Scripting Tools*" by Morley & Associates are excellent examples).

Storyboard

The storyboard is a sequence of simply drawn pictures (or photographs) that visually represents the program. An important element,

Figure 3–2
Storyboard example.

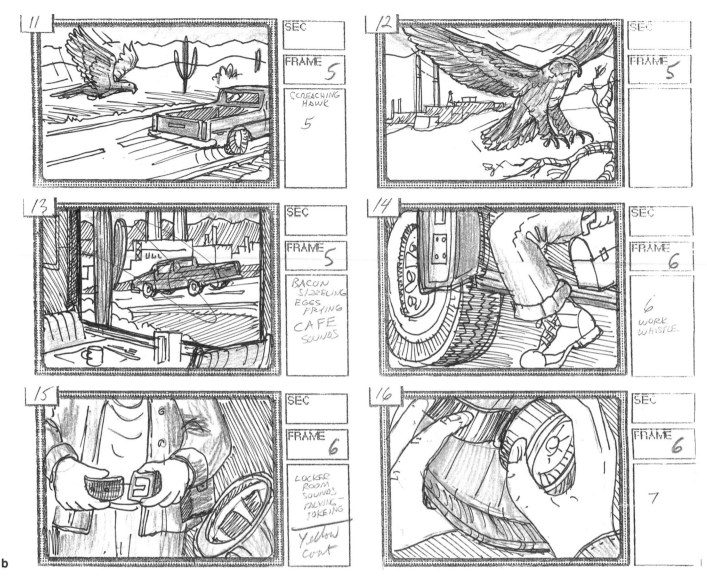

Figure 3 – 3
Storyboard example.

it allows the producer to share visual choices and creative approaches with the client, get a feeling for the pacing and timing of the program, and "edit" the program for visual continuity and clarity of message. It also allows producers to "direct" the program on paper for overall visual and oral effectiveness.

The producer, often enlisting the talents of an artist, depicts through simple drawings the script as it will appear visually on the screen, frame by frame. The audio portion of the program will be typed in under each picture. The storyboard will have a picture of each significant visual event that fairly represents the script. These events include video locations, shots, angles, graphics and transitions. The storyboard visualizes the completed program on paper. For the first time the clients "see" the visual images that tell the story. Graphics and effects can be presented to be checked for placement, clarity, and effectiveness. Location, props, scenery and talent placement can all be checked before final decisions are made.

Some approaches, such as the "talking head" or interview programs, will not require a storyboard, but more complex programs usually require at least a simple storyboard. It is best to communicate visual ideas on paper. Paper is cheaper than tape; see figure 3.3.

Production Design

4

As a communications tool, video has the potential of being more dynamic and attention getting than traditional media (still/slides/ pictures) because of its ability to display motion and sound. It is this "dynamic" quality that makes video such a special communications tool. Good video programs that move our audience into action, teach or inform take full advantage of all the special characteristics of the medium—light, sound, motion, composition and continuity. Therefore, the video producer must have a thorough understanding of these elements in order to use the medium effectively. And the video producer must plan and design these elements into the communication experience to achieve the objectives. Often these elements are referred to as the fundamental *aesthetic* elements, and working with them in developing a video program is referred to as working with the "language of video."

We must understand and plan for this special language to communicate effectively with video.

> As Herbert Zettl states in his excellent book, *Sight, Sound, Motion: Applied Media Aesthetics*, "Once you know the aesthetic characteristics and potentials of these fundamental image elements, you can combine these elements according to the medium requirements and potentials of television and film into patterns that clarify and intensify, and effectively communicate, significant experience.
>
> "Ideally, you should be able to develop a language unique to the medium of your choice—a language that will enable you to speak with optimum clarity and impact, and with personal style."

Working with the numerous aesthetic choices available in video production requires a plan or design. I describe this planning process as *production design*: the pre-planning of visual elements and sounds to enhance the message and reach the communication objective. Although it is not my intent here to provide a detailed study of aesthetics—there are volumes already in print on the subject—I would like to review some of the typical aesthetic choices we have as they apply to our planning process. For more details in planning for each video element, refer to Chapter 6.

LIGHTING

Lighting for video is used primarily to illuminate the subject so that the camera can "see" it. The video director uses light to create images that the camera will record. Light is an aesthetic element as well, because it helps in composition, creating shadow, color, texture and form. Lighting can also be used to create a mood, a psychological condition that would not naturally be present.

Television is a flat, two-dimensional medium made up of only height and width. Lighting (and staging, color and sound) can create the illusion of depth. Lighting creates this illusion by separating the subject from the background, and by giving an impression of roundness and texture. As with the other aesthetic elements, it is important to control lighting so that it does not interfere with the intended message and cause confusion to the viewer. If the scene is lit "flat" with no highlights, shadows or contrast, the viewer will have a difficult time discerning what to look at in the scene, what is or is not important in the picture. Good lighting focuses the viewer's attention, brings out picture detail and creates a realistic picture.

Figure 4 – 1
A large reflector is used for the main light source for this delicate scene involving a Red Tail Hawk. The animal was used for the opening sequence for a corporate video production.

Lighting the video program requires much advanced planning so the intended lighting objective can be accomplished with the least amount of effort and expense. The video producer/director decides in advance the "look" of the program and plans the power and lighting equipment to accomplish that "look."

Video vendors take pride in their equipment and frequently make the point that video cameras will make good pictures with practically no light. Yet it doesn't take long before the dedicated amateur looks at the footage shot with his new "low light" camera and says, "I want better looking video." The only way to improve the look of such footage is through better lighting techniques. A more costly camera is not always the answer.

Some basic facts and terms dealing with light and lighting instruments need to be understood in order to discuss even the basics of good lighting techniques. They are presented below. Two excellent references for lighting for video are Ross Lowell's book, *Matters of Light & Depth*, published by Broad Street Books and Tom LeTourneau's book, *Lighting Techniques for Video Production/The Art of Casting Shadows*, published by Focal Press. Chapter 6 discusses lighting instruments and planning considerations in more detail.

Basic Lighting Terms

Light refers to that portion of the electromagnetic spectrum that makes things visible. It does not refer to a device that projects light.

Instrument is the term for a lighting fixture. A spot is a type of instrument, not a type of light.

Lamp is the term for the source of light inside an instrument. Usually people refer to such sources as light bulbs. (Bulbs produce tulips and other plants.) The term lamp can also refer to a type of lighting instrument such as a table lamp or a floor lamp.

Color Correction Filters are glass or gel-like materials capable of converting the color temperature of natural daylight sources to the color temperature of artificial sources and vice versa. They can be placed in front of each lighting instrument or on the lens of your camera.

There are two standard **color temperatures**. Studio lights generally burn at

3200 degrees K. This is referred to as **tungsten** light. The sun is generally rated at 5600 degree K and is referred to as **daylight**. Whenever you shoot a scene lit by sources of different color temperatures, it is *mandatory* that you correct all sources to one color temperature. The two most widely used color correction filters are **85**, designed to convert daylight to tungsten, and **booster blue**, designed to convert tungsten to daylight.

When you use studio lamps on interior location sets and have to deal with daylight coming in through windows, the only way to avoid blue fleshtones on the side of your talent that is facing a window is to use sheets of 85 on the window to convert the incoming light to 3200 degrees K. This should be done whether or not the window is in the shot.

White Balance is the process of adjusting your camera's electronic circuits to the color temperature of the light you will be shooting under.

It is critical to set your white balance switch to the proper position for the type of lighting conditions involved with your shoot. Some cameras may ask you to push a white balance or "WB" button under certain conditions after you have set the white balance switch to the proper position. In some cases you may be asked to focus on something white while pushing the WB button.

Light falls into two basic **qualities**. One quality of light is **specular**. This is the type of light produced by the sun on a bright, cloudless day. The rays are parallel and produce pictures with high contrast. The side of the subject facing the sun is brightly lit, while the side of the subject away from the sun is in deep shadow. The shadows cast by objects in specular light have extremely sharp, well defined edges. The terms "hard," "harsh," or "direct," are sometimes used to define **specular** light.

The second quality of light is **diffuse**. It is the type of light produced on heavily overcast days. Under such conditions the rays of light are not parallel, but are oriented in a random fashion. Scenes lit by diffuse light have less contrast. The side of subjects facing the sun is not substantially brighter than the side turned away from the sun, and fewer shadows are created by such light. When shadows do exist, they are not as dense as those caused by specular light. Shadows produced by diffuse light have poorly defined edges. The terms "soft" or "indirect" are sometimes used to describe **diffuse** light.

The quality of light involved in any scene can fall anywhere between the highly specular end of the continuum and the diffuse end. This is true in nature as well as in artificially lit situations.

a
b

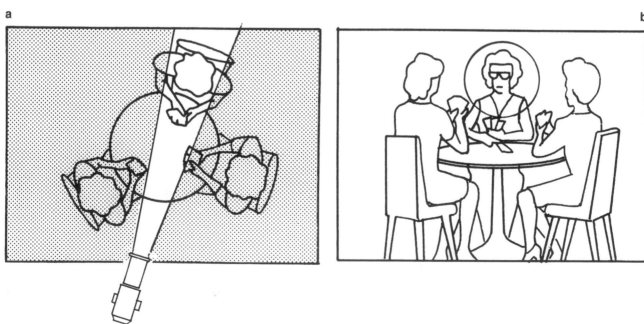

Figure 4 – 2a & b Focusing spotlight.

There are several different types of lighting instruments. They fall into three main categories. One category refers to instrument **design** or **type** such as spot, flood, etc. The second category deals with instrument **function**, or what particular job the instrument performs in any given lighting setup. The third category refers to light **output**, dealing with the quantity and quality of light produced.

There are three basic types of lighting instruments. The first and most widely used is the **spotlight** or **focusing spot**. They are designed to concentrate light into a relatively small area. These types of instruments are designed as open face units, without a lens in front of the lamp, or as Fresnel (pronounced fir NEL) units with a lens. Because of their lighter weight, lower cost and smaller size, open face spots are used more frequently for location lighting than lensed instruments. Light from these units is specular in nature.

The second basic type of instrument is the **floodlight** or **broad**. These instruments are open face and designed to provide an even coverage of light over a relatively large area. They can also produce specular or diffuse light depending on their design.

The third basic type is the **softlight**, designed to produce very diffuse light. This is accomplished by placing the lamp in a large fixture that bounces the light from the lamp onto a textured white or silvered surface that redirects it toward the subject. Unlike spots or floods, the light from a softlight is never projected directly toward the subject. This results in nearly shadowless light.

At the top of this diagram is the **backlight**. This instrument serves to separate the subject from the background and create a third dimension to the normally two dimensional television picture. It should only be bright enough to create a slight glow of light around the head and shoulders of the subject. Subjects with dark hair and clothing require more backlight than subjects with light hair and clothing.

The backlight should be placed directly behind the subject, in line with the camera. As a result, it cannot be mounted on a regular stand, since the stand would appear to grow out of the subject's head. Mount it on a boom with its base off to the side of the subject, out of the shot, or mount it on the wall or ceiling with one of the special mounting devices available for this purpose.

The most important instrument is the **key** light. It should be placed on the right or left side of the subject, depending on the location of the main light source in the room. If there is no obvious light source in the room, place the key on whatever side of the

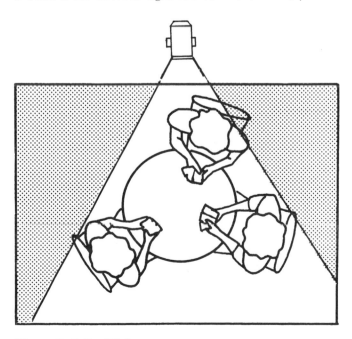

Figure 4–3 Backlight.

subject results in the most pleasing look. It should be positioned carefully above and to the side of your subject. The idea is to position the light so it casts a small shadow of the nose near the smile line of the subject's face and have it fall about midway between the nose and the upper lip.

Place your subject far enough away from the background so the shadow created by the key will fall on the floor, or outside the area of the background included in your shot. If such separation is not possible, position the key so the subject's shadow is connected to him in the shot. If there is a space between the subject and his shadow, each time he moves, the viewer's eye will be drawn away from him to his shadow. When the shadow and the subject are one mass, attention stays with the subject.

Once the key is in position, the **fill** should be placed. It could be a softlight or well diffused specular source. It should be placed on the side opposite the key. Generally, it should strike the subject from a lower angle then the key and be placed closer to the center line of the subject than the key. It should provide just enough diffused light to reduce the density of the shadow created by the key. It will also fill in some of the darker areas on the unlit side of the subject and prevent a sunken look in the eye sockets.

A low intensity fill creates a more dramatic or **low key** look. Higher intensity fill results in a less dramatic **high key** look. Under no circumstances should the fill be of equal intensity with the key and create shadows of its own.

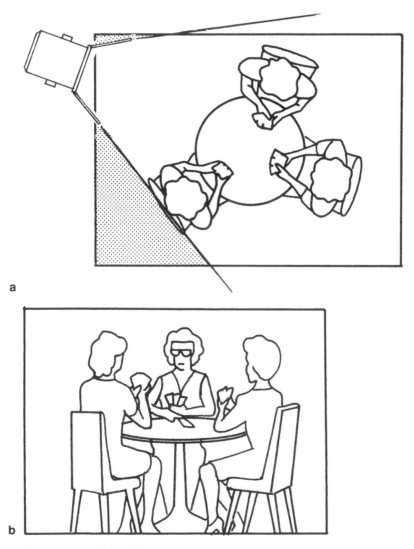

a

b

Figure 4–4a & b Fill light.

In more involved setups a fourth and fifth instrument function is added to the setup. One additional function is **background** light. Background instruments illuminate areas or objects in the **background** of a shot to give them special emphasis or bring out detail. They could also be used to add color to an otherwise blah surface. Background lights should not be confused with backlights.

In order to preserve the illusion of a single key source for your scenes, it is important that background lights are placed on the same side of your subject as the key. When this principle is not followed rigidly, the shadows created by background objects will not coincide with the shadow direction created by the key, and your viewer will be aware of multiple light sources.

The final function is that of the **effects** light, which projects a pattern of light on the background and/or the subject to create the illusion of an off stage effect such as a fire, or reinforce some visual element of the scene such as a window. The most common effect projected replicates slats of light, like those seen when sun shines through Venetian blinds. These is a tendency to project such patterns on set walls only, but placing effects light in front of the talent and allowing the projected pattern to strike the talent as well as the set will greatly enhance the realistic look and interest of your set.

SOUND

Sound is another aesthetic element that is used to shape and enhance the message. Sound can become a confusing, distracting, disorienting element in the program. It must be tightly controlled to add realism, depth and interest to the program, as well as credibility and emphasis. Good sound recording techniques should separate the voice of the main speaker from the natural background noise, add mood or emotion to the message and add to the overall rhythm and pace of the program. Sound and music also add movement to the program and smooth transitions. Often overlooked in the excitement of video production, audio contributes significantly to the overall program objectives. As with lighting for video, the process of recording good sound should be planned in advance, and most of the sound elements that are captured in the program should be designed in.

Figure 4 – 5
Audio Technician on the scene for corporate training production. The "shot gun" microphone is used on a "fish pole" to allow technician to follow the talent.

Good sound recording relies heavily on controlling the environment in which you are shooting; therefore, location scouting to check recording conditions and recording equipment and microphone selection must take place well in advance of the actual production. Control of the ambiance (natural room sounds), and dialog is a critical production responsibility, and the selection of the appropriate, believable sound effects can make or break a program. Music selection, often left until the last moment during the edit, can significantly add to the mood and credibility of the program—or it can be an added distraction.

Preparing for the audio side of video is an important step in the planning process, and sound design becomes the art of planning, recording and mixing all sound elements so that they blend naturally and complement your visual message.

Music

Music adds emotion, movement and mood to a video program and helps with transitions. Music is usually obtained from music libraries that you can own or from music studios that rent their libraries out. Video facilities that provide editing often provide music libraries as well. Good music libraries will provide you with samples of the type of music they have, assist you in setting up your library and work closely with you in making music selections. Good libraries provide extensive catalogs and have computer searches of their music. *Network Music* (800/854-2075; call them for a free CD sample) is a professional leader in the music library business. They have an excellent music library with extensive sound effects and special effects libraries as well. Their music has a creative, contemporary sound and they are always adding new sounds in production music, classical music and sound effects. A list of music libraries can be found in the appendix of this book and details on recording good sound can be found in this chapter and chapter 6.

The planning process applies to sound and music as well. Before the production begins define what you are looking for in the way of music and sound effects. Look at the script and decide where you will need sound effects and music. Look for major scene changes, transitions and movement that could be enhanced by music or effects. Music can define the dynamic nature of the setting as quiet, fast-paced or mysterious and promotes a general sense of action and movement. Also look for areas of the narration that could be reinforced or highlighted by music. If you do not use music too often, it can be used effectively to make a particular section of dialog stand out. When selecting areas of the script that sound could enhance, be sensitive to the speed or pace of the scene and how fast camera changes and transitions occur. Also be sensitive to the style of shooting during a scene and the mood the shooting style creates. The music you select will affect these aesthetic elements. Selecting the right music for the production takes time, so plan this selection process in the schedule.

In reviewing the script for sound reinforcement and music, consider adding music at the beginning of the program to set the mood and at the end to help bring the program to a conclusion. Look where sound can reinforce and draw attention to what the narrator is saying and where sound effects can add realism to the scene. But don't overdo it. Music can distract the viewer and get in the way of the pictures and narration. I've seen many good video programs ruined because the producer felt that music was needed throughout the program. This is usually the sign of an amateur production. Music helps with transitions and changes in the script. It also helps create movement on the screen, adds the element of excitement to a picture and helps with camera movement such as tracking. But like special effects, it can be over used and interfere with the message. Stopping the music behind the voice draws attention to the voice and adding sound effects or ambiance adds credibility to a scene. When people see pictures of a car moving on the scene, they expect to hear the car. Sound adds realism to your pictures and creates a presence in the scene for the viewer.

When recording narration, be sensitive to the environment. Select a very quiet room or sound studio. Pay attention to the recording levels and listen for voice pops and sibilance. You are looking for a consistency of sound throughout your program, so field recording levels and studio voice recording levels should be consistent.

Selecting the right music for your productions is another skill that is developed over time. Like lighting, scriptwriting, directing and editing, music selection and working with sound is a special craft which, if done well, will increase production value and add, not distract from the production.

The following are a few basic terms you may need to work with sound.

Basic Audio Terms

Acoustics—also referred to as **ambiance**, is the natural "sound" of a room or place. It is a good practice to record room noise (wild sound) at the location you are videotaping.

AGC—the **A**utomatic **G**ain **C**ontrol found on most video and audio recorders should be turned off during production for greater control of audio levels.

Audio Mixer—A console found in video and audio recording studios that enables the combining or mixing of more than one audio source.

Balanced Line—professional audio equipment uses cables that have a third wire to ground out unwanted noise and interference, commonly referred to as "Cannon" or "XLR" connectors.

Boom Microphone—also referred to as a **Shotgun Microphone**. A super and high-cardioid, directional production microphone that is mounted on a long horizontal boom used for on-location video scenes where lavaliere microphones are inappropriate.

EQ—short for equalization, referring to relative levels of different frequencies.

Feedback—usually an unwanted noise caused by a microphone picking up the sound from a loudspeaker.

Fishpole—a handheld pole for holding a shotgun microphone.

Gain—the amount of amplification of an audio device usually expressed in decibels.

Impedance—a measurement of electrical resistance of microphones or equipment, most professional equipment uses low impedance (or Low Z).

Lavaliere Microphone—a small, compact microphone placed on the lapel or tie.

Level—the magnitude of an audio signal, usually expressed in decibels.

Lip Sync—The synchronization of the visual and aural elements such as the voice and lips of the talent.

MIDI—stands for **M**usical **I**nstrument **D**igital **I**nterface, allows computer control of sound recording, mixing and compositioning.

Mixer—equipment used to amplify and combine the output of several audio devices.

Shock Mount—a device used to isolate a microphone from mechanical vibration often found on boom or shotgun microphones.

Sound Effects—Additional sound elements added to the audio track.

Sweetening—When audio elements are processed in post-production, it is usually referred to as the sweetening process.

Voice-Over (V.O.)—Using a narrator or talent's voice over visual material, so that the speaker is not shown on camera.

VU Meter—Audio meter that measures the intensity of sound in volume units.

Windscreen—a foam mold fitted over the microphone to reduce wind noise and distortion.

Zeppelin—a large windscreen which covers the entire shotgun microphone.

CAMERA ANGLES AND COMPOSITION

Screen composition, camera angles and depth of field are all aesthetic elements that require advanced planning. Each element affects the way in which the message is received by the viewer.

Camera angles and **composition** are usually described as the arrangement of pictorial elements within the scene. We place and move objects and talent within a scene to create the most impact for the message and viewer. You choose what to "show" the viewer with composition and angles and by placing objects and subjects at key locations within a scene or frame, we can emphasize or de-emphasize them. By moving our talent toward the camera (movement attracts the eye) and increasing the size of the image, we draw attention to the subject. Likewise, if the talent moves away from the camera, the viewer loses interest. Again, control is the key. By controlling placement and movement, we control the message we are presenting to the viewer. And the key to control is planning. We **plan and design** the scene and everything within it.

By designing and planning each scene, we remove the element of distraction. Are backgrounds such as trees, wallpaper, pictures, telephone poles or windows interfering with the foreground subject? Are backgrounds too busy so that they make viewers hunt for the important subject? There should be one center of interest within a scene. The scene should be designed so that all elements within the scene support that center of interest. The idea is to control the viewer's eye through composition. The intended message (subject) or center of interest should clearly stand out, and the viewer should not have to wade through distracting, unimportant clutter on the scene.

Composition has a language of its own with lines, forms, masses and movements all contributing to factors that affect the message. Rules and guidelines, mostly from painting and still photography, have developed audience expectations. The video producer should fully understand the impact these rules have on his project so that he can properly plan for them shot by shot.

Composition also applies to graphics creation. I have devoted a complete section on planning for graphics in Chapter 9.

Camera angles can also add to the message or distract from it. The camera angle determines the viewpoint and the area covered in the shot. You must decide what viewpoint will best depict your message and how much area of the scene the viewer must see to understand what is going on. It is not just a matter of selecting a close-up medium shot or

Figure 4 – 6
Camera angle, above talent for dramatic effect.

wide shot, you have to select the angle of view. The angle you select will determine how the audience will view the action.

Camera angles are carefully planned frame by frame. Angles are usually depicted in the storyboard where each shot and scene are carefully drawn out to assure that the best possible picture is created. This advance planning allows for experimentation on paper to test the best idea for a shot and the best composition, saving valuable time in production. Shot composition is thought through in advance so that during production we can concentrate on performance.

Carefully compose the shot selecting point of view, angle and depth of field. Especially when working with talent, the angle a director chooses can distract viewers or interrupt the message flow. A camera angle slightly above eye level, which causes the talent to look up, can imply inferiority to the viewer. Likewise, an angle below the talent eye level can imply a dominant posture to the audience. Camera angles must be carefully planned and chosen to portray the subject best under positive light and create the best viewing angle for the scene to be interpreted by the viewer.

There are two accepted points of view: **objective** and **subjective**. The **objective** camera angle places the audience as observers only. The audience doesn't see the action from within the scene or through anyone in the scene. It is as if the viewers are sitting in a theater audience, observing the play that unfolds in front of them.

The **subjective** camera angle, on the other hand, actually takes the viewers inside the scene and lets them participate in and experience the action. An objective camera angle would observe a roller coaster ride from the ground. A subjective angle would actually take the viewer for a ride and the camera would become the "eyes" of the rider!

It is difficult to effectively switch back and forth from objective to subjective camera. It can confuse the audience. Scenes should be planned so the angle chosen stays the same through a series of shots that gets your message across to the viewer.

The angle of view can also add a psychological factor to your message. If you select an angle that is low, looking up at the talent, this view can create a dominating effect on your viewer. The talent will be looking down at the viewer. If you select a higher angle, the viewer will be looking down at your talent. These effects can obviously work for you if you plan them into your shooting scheme. Let your instincts work for you in providing the viewer with the best angle that makes your message clear.

Get Personal

Remember that video is considered a "personal" medium. Close-ups and people shots work best on video. Save the massive landscape shots for still photography where the resolution (picture detail) is greater and the viewer can study the scene. Let the viewer get involved with your message by shooting with the subjective camera, shooting close-ups, capturing action and good sound. The television set is a small display device compared to the motion picture screen, slide screen or still

Figure 4 – 7
a) Camera composition too busy, tree in background distracts viewer. b) Good composition that highlights talent.

photograph. So the medium should be used for its advantages, capturing action and sound and telling stories. The viewer will get involved if he is interested in the story and if he can understand what is happening through the pictures you present. Give the viewer what he wants to see when he wants to see it.

Line of Demarcation

Demarcation refers to defining boundaries, and in shooting video we have to define boundaries for our viewer. What this means is that, by selecting an angle for shooting your subject, the view you create establishes boundaries. If you shoot two people talking, subject A will appear on the left of the screen and subject B will appear on the right. If we cross boundaries or the line of demarcation, we will switch the positions of the subjects. It is important not to cross the line of demarcation because it confuses the viewer. (This is especially bad while shooting a football game!) This line will also apply to continuity of motion or action.

Depth Staging

By utilizing foreground and background, selective focus and depth of field, we can create the illusion of depth on the screen. Television is really a very flat medium, and we have to create the illusion of depth. One way is through depth staging. By placing objects in the foreground of our shot and having those objects appear slightly out of focus with our subject in focus, the illusion of depth is created. We can arrange the scene so depth staging takes place within our frame. Place foreground objects so they are out of focus, the subject in focus and the background out of focus (depth of field).

Transitions

Transitions are used to transport the viewer from one shot to the next or from one scene of action to the next. A good transition will take the viewer from one scene to the next smoothly and logically without drawing attention to the change. The next shot will be "matched" logically and naturally with the last. A morning sunrise shot would not match naturally with an evening shot or a shot of someone in the afternoon. We try to take the viewer through a sequence of shots that go together logically, that will be easy to follow.

Smooth transitions create a professional "look" to our programs and add continuity. They need to be thought out in advance, so you know what shots to capture to create the transition.

Transition Techniques

TITLES A simple way to connect scenes or move from one sequence of action to the next is through the use of titles. By making the title "Goal Two . . . Birthday Party, June 1992" you will prepare the viewer for the action to follow. While this technique is easy to achieve, more creative approaches will make the program more interesting.

CUT The most common transition is a cut. It is an instantaneous change from one shot to the next. We can create a cut with the camera change or through editing.

The simple cut is really the best transition of all. If it is well placed, the viewer does not notice the cut, and it does not interfere with the message. A well placed cut is usually many times better, cheaper and less distracting than a special effect such as a dissolve, wipe or page turn.

DEFOCUS   By defocusing the camera on the scene and then refocusing the camera on the next scene, we can create a transition. At the end of one scene or event, defocus the camera . . . at the beginning of the next scene, bring the camera into focus. This is an interesting effect that can indicate a passage of time or "flash-back" of time.

DISSOLVE TO BLACK   Most cameras have the ability to dissolve to black at the end of the scene. A simple push of a button on the camera creates this effect.

PAN   By panning the camera off the scene you are shooting, pausing the camera, then panning the camera onto the next scene, you can create a nice transition effect.

MATCHING ACTION   This technique is created by matching the action of one shot with the next that is connected by action, motion or content. Example . . . if your subject leaves the room and goes outside, you can create a smooth transition from the inside shot to the outside shot by matching the action of the subject. Simply record the subject walking toward the door and reaching for the door knob and opening the door. Cut the camera, reposition the camera to the outside shot of the subject shutting the door (be sure the same hand is used on the doorknob) and continue the action.

You can also match similar shots to create transitions. For example, simply end the scene with a shot of a close-up of a calendar or pictures on the wall, and begin the next scene with a similar shot of a calendar or picture on the wall.

ZOOMS   By zooming in on an object at the end of a scene and then starting the next scene with a close-up of an object and zooming out to the action, you create a transition.

WIPE   Through use of a switcher a wipe replaces one scene with the next by "wiping" it on or off to create a transition.

It is a good idea to watch television shows closely, especially mini-documentaries, and see how they create smooth transitions. Remember that a good transition should not be noticed by the viewers. It should smoothly and naturally take them from one shot to the next.

COLOR

Colors evoke response and feelings. As you are shooting in video, you should become sensitive to what colors add to your message. Reds, oranges and yellows appear to be closer to the viewer and have a stimulating effect. Blues and greens appear to be distant and have a calming effect. Colors can be combined to create depth within the picture and contrast. However, if colors are too bright, they can draw attention to themselves and distract from your picture. Too many colors in a scene can also distract the viewer and become too busy. This is especially true of backgrounds. When you are shooting people talking on camera or are shooting objects, it is best to keep the background simple. And if possible, choose a background that is a nice contrast to your subject. For instance, blue and gray backgrounds are nice complements to all skin colors.

You will have to experiment shooting different colors with your camera. Different cameras react differently to colors. Some cameras will have problems recording bright reds or blues, and others will not record the true color of objects. Also remember, as mentioned in the lighting section, that objects will pick up the colors that surround them. If you are shooting objects in a room where the walls are painted orange, the objects may take on an orange appearance. This will be true for reflecting light as well.

MOTION

Video is often selected to communicate a message to an audience if the message requires motion. When deciding if video is appropriate for a particular message, I look at two requirements: is the message visual in nature and does it require motion? Unsuccessful programs often lack these two basic requirements.

The aesthetic element of motion adds a great deal of complexity to the medium of video. It is one thing to create an aesthetically pleasing still picture and quite another to create an aesthetically pleasing **moving** picture. Video should be a continuous, logical flow of visual images. It shouldn't be a collection of individual still images. Moving images combined with sound become a coherent message. By combining a series of shots, scenes and sequences, video becomes a controlled rhythm of moving images that create a whole message.

Zettl aptly describes three types of motion in his book: *Primary motion*, motion generated from the subject in front of the camera; *secondary motion*, motion generated by the camera itself through pans, tilts, zooms etc., and *tertiary motion*, or editing motion that is created in the editing of the program. This motion is described as the pace or rhythm of the program.

All the factors that affect movement—the movement of the subject, the camera movement through pans, tilts, dollies or zooms and the movement of the story through editing—must be well planned in advance, because they all help clarify, reinforce and carry the message to the viewer. Through individual shot and scene planning with storyboards, through blocking and talent direction from the director and through pacing and rhythm established by the editor, motion is controlled and presented in a manner in which the audience interprets the movement in its overall understanding of the message.

The pre-planning process through storyboards involves planning for movement on the screen. By camera placement relative to the subject, we can control screen direction. Planned camera moves and subject moves help in the editing process (Chapter 8). One of the objectives in the editing process is to create a smooth, transparent message, a logical development of shots and scenes. To create a logical flow of movement so as not to confuse the viewer, movement within a scene should be consistent.

If we were shooting a scene in which we had a wide shot of our talent getting up from a chair and walking toward a flip chart to write something, the flow of movement or action in this case could be from the left of the screen to the right of the screen.

If we were to plan to cut from the wide shot to a medium shot of the talent approaching the flip chart, the action would have to continue from left to right within our medium shot in order to make a good edit and have a consistency of motion. This is a very simple example; these decisions become more complex as the talent "moves around" within shots and scenes. Screen direction should be consistent and well thought out before you start shooting so that you have the appropriate direction of movements for the editing process. Learn to see and plan for motion in terms of its direction on the screen.

DEPTH OF FIELD

Depth of field is created by the relationship of the subject to the lens. If you shoot several objects that are different distances from the camera, some of these objects will be in focus and others will be out of focus. The area where the objects are in focus is considered "depth of field." Different lenses will have different depth of field capabilities. Also light will affect depth of field. If there is not much light on a subject and the lens has to be opened to a wide aperture, this will decrease the depth of field and "flatten" the picture out. Likewise, if the aperture setting is small, the depth of field will be increased. Depth of field is a creative tool for the camera operator because it can be used to focus attention and create the illusion of depth on the screen.

CONTINUITY/SEQUENCE

While editing a program, continuity of shots, lighting, sound and motion come to life. Through editing we start to understand the importance of continuity and planning for it. Angle changes, cuts, motion of the talent and camera, lighting and sound between scenes should all be transparent to the viewer. They should not notice the techniques you use to move the story along. A cut from a wide shot to a medium shot should be motivated by the subject and therefore not noticed by the viewer. Good continuity will create uninterrupted action; there will be no jarring jump cuts and changes in lighting intensity or sound levels between shots.

Good continuity comes from good planning. The storyboard helps you think through angles that will cut well together where the action at the beginning and end of each shot match well and provide correct screen direction eliminating jump cuts caused by missing or mismatched action between shots. Video is a continuous sequence of moving events; think in terms of sequences of shots and scenes, not individual shots. Continuity ties the shots together into sequences that flow well together. Always plan the shots to work together creating a continuous sequence of movement. Planning allows you to "pre-shoot" the sequences on paper relieving you of the task of trying to match action while you are actually shooting. Know where you are going with the shots at all times, where the edit points are and how the shots will edit together.

Continuity will be discussed further in Chapter 8 when we discuss editing techniques, but remember when you get to the edit, it is too late to change camera angles and screen direction. Plan ahead for the edit and think through continuity.

Be aware that it is easy to misuse video and cause confusion. *You must understand the power of video and its overall impact on the message and the audience.* You must use special effects, graphics and sound so that they work for you and not against you. Through good production design, we plan video to enhance the message and create a clearer understanding for our audience.

Don't get carried away with the fancy special effects video offers. Use them only when they are appropriate for the message. Don't throw in effects because they appear to make the program more professional or because you feel obligated to use your expensive special effects switcher. Think through the program objectives and plan special effects that will help you achieve these objectives. How can split screens, freeze frames, slow motion or dissolves contribute to the message? Planning creates effects that belong in the program and do not appear "tacked on" or used for "dazzle."

The dynamics of motion affect pace, rhythm and continuity of a program in the following ways:

Pace

The **pace of a program** is created by how long the scenes or shots remain on the screen. If a shot remains on the screen for a long time, it tends to slow the program down. This length is, however, affected by the length of shot in front of it and behind it. If there are a series of shots that are short in length, the program appears to move faster. The dialog, acting and motion within the shot also add to the pace or feel of the program. We pre-plan the pace of a program by expanding or shortening the shots.

Rhythm

The **rhythm** of a program is determined by the overall pace or speed of the program. All programs or sequences within programs contain a certain rhythm we consciously create based on the context of the message and the rate at which the action within the frame occurs. While we create the rhythm of the program in the editing process, however, the way we shoot a scene can affect the rhythm, so we have to plan for this rhythm in our shooting.

Continuity

If the **continuity** is wrong, if the shots don't follow a logical sequence, other than for shock value, they become confusing to the viewer. Poor continuity causes jarring jump cuts and wrong screen direction.

Therefore we plan an establishing wide shot, followed by a medium shot followed by a close-up, the logical flow of shots that the viewer expects. The wide shot creates a "point of view and an establishing location" for the viewer; often the physical surroundings in the wide shot are as important as the talent within the scene. The medium shot focuses attention to the subject (talent) and eliminates unneeded pictorial information that appeared in the wide shot. The close-up emphasizes a particular point the subject is making. Don't overuse the close-up; like the zoom it can be overused and lose its impact. Think of the close-up as an exclamation point! Save it for those occasions that are important for the viewer in understanding a phrase or procedure.

Designing production is the art of combining all the elements into a message that reaches the audience . . . light, sound, motion, continuity and composition have a direct effect on how the viewer receives the message. Planning the design of these elements must take place so the intended message is correctly received by the viewer.

Proposals, Budgets and Legal Issues

5

PROPOSALS

Proposals help define the scope of a project, the resources needed to accomplish it and provide for an estimated cost. They are essential to the planning process.

It is important to get agreement on what is to be done, how it is to be done and how much it will cost. Proposals provide a vehicle to communicate the desired work and outcomes with clients. Video production involves investing time, money and talent. A commitment is necessary to begin the project and the proposal provides the framework for this commitment.

Proposals identify the "need" for the project along with how the need is to be addressed. The proposal can provide an "approach" to the solution, but it is not the plan to carry out the treatment (the video program) nor is it a detailed answer, script or budget. It is simply a way in which the solution can be addressed. The proposal identifies the problem and suggests a solution. It justifies the commitment.

A simple proposal or request for services within an organization will usually contain a description of the problem and the audience that is affected by the problem and will describe a solution or approach in solving the problem.

Statement of Work/Request for Proposal (RFP)

Often government and business organizations provide a "statement of work" that describes the work to be performed. The statement of work usually contains the objective of the program, a description of the work to be performed with specific tasks to be done (for example, research and scripting, production, locations of shooting, editing requirements, graphics, printed support material and duplication and distribution requirements), the general requirements placed on the contractor (schedules, evaluation, deliverables) and the amount of flexibility the contractor will have to carry out the work. The statement of work can ask for a management plan that will require the contractor to describe in detail how he plans to approach the project and how it will be managed and controlled.

A statement of work usually will have:

- **General Information**, containing purpose of work, how to submit proposals, response date, evaluation procedure and information about vendor visits
- **General Requirements**, containing the award date, contract information, term of award, warranty, product ownership, confidentiality and proposal format
- **General Description** of the work to be done, goals of the project, hardware and software requirements, pilot-testing requirements and project evaluation requirements
- **Deliverables**, specific deliverable requirements of the project (script, storyboard, budget, production schedule, interactive design, master program tape, copies, etc.)
- **Samples** of work to be done, proposal certification and signature form

Thanks to Stan Hankin, executive producer with the U.S. Department of Labor, the following *planning checklist* for a statement of work provides considerations for getting the best contract with the government:

- **Determine the objective of the project.** What is the agency contracting for work hoping to achieve?
- **Determine the requirements of the project.** What are the actual products and services required? Who will use the products and services and how?
- **Standards of performance.** How will the contract (or proposal) be evaluated? How will the project and outcomes be evaluated?
- **Personnel.** What should be the qualifications/experience of the contractor? Are the tasks defined?
- **Schedule.** How long should the project take, what is the schedule for the deliverables?
- **Location.** Where should the project take place, will travel be required?

Types of Proposals

Often video projects will not require formal proposals. An informal letter of agreement or request for services will do. The request for services or letter describes the problem, audience, solution and payment structure. It creates an agreement between two parties and establishes the commitment. Both parties should sign the letter of agreement or request for services.

There are as many different proposals as there are producers. Each producer has his or her own style, legal requirements and details that he feels should go into the agreement . But usually there is a standard format that producers follow. A good proposal should have the following:

- Client name, main contact or company name.
- Producer or name of person who has the overall responsibility of getting the project done.
- Due date/final completion date of the project; this section may also contain milestones such as when the script is due, when the shooting and editing is due and deliverables (edit master format and number of copies).
- Overall length of program.
- Printed support materials requirements, such as accompanying brochures and workbooks, and due dates if different from the video dates.
- Problem identification, the audience and the recommended solution.
- Estimated final budget. This section may be broken down to budgets for pre-production, production and post-production and may have scriptwriting as a separate budget item.
- Production requirements. This section usually covers the format the program will be shot on, number of shooting and editing days allowed in the budget and music and talent considerations.
- Special considerations, usually covering travel related to the project and special shooting or special effect requirements along with distribution and delivery requirements.
- Treatment or concept. This section may cover how you intend to "tell your story." Treatment creation is a very creative process and can work for or against you. Be careful that your treatment is not

selected and then produced by a lower production bidder. Protect your creative treatment.

- Distribution and delivery requirements. If special distribution of the project is required, such as satellite distribution, it should be spelled out along with special duplication services, packaging and printing.
- Legal issues, usually covering ownership of the completed project and the working drafts, including copyright. Identify the owners, not only of the copyright but also of the material objects contained within the project such as the original footage, original photos or graphics.
- Limitations on the scope of use by the producer if the buyer retains ownership of the video, including the individual elements of the productions.
- Payment structure tied to deliveries and approval/acceptance.
- Approval process describes the person or persons responsible for approving each phase of production and describes the right of the buyer (client) to demand alterations or corrections and how additional fees, if any, are to be paid to the producer.
- Description of credits.
- Warranties and indemnifications between producer and buyer.
- Insurances to be obtained and who is responsible for those insurances.

BUDGETS

Budgeting is almost an art. It requires a lot of experience, a good script and a little luck. Every program you produce will require a budget. It is a good practice to start early in learning the budgeting process. Whether you work for a corporation or a nonprofit organization, someone will eventually ask you how much the program cost or how much it costs for you to produce video programs. There are no $100 programs. Each program you produce requires the resources and time of many people, the use of equipment and talent, and the facility for production. All these elements cost the organization money. Be prepared to list these costs in detail and justify them. The program should create a return on the investment, or it probably isn't worth doing.

People that have attended my production seminars often raise an eyebrow when I start discussing the budgeting process, because I really emphasize the importance of having a script (and storyboard if possible) before calculating the budget. This raises questions because more often than not producers are asked to define the budget before the scripting process begins. However, a budget is not realistic unless it is based on a script. How else will you know how long the program will actually be? How many production days will be required? How many editing days will be required? How many paid actors will be in the program? How many special effects, graphics and music selections? The script becomes the basis for calculating an accurate budget. Without the script we can only guess at costs and estimate a budget. And we can only do this with a certain amount of accuracy from our experience of producing similar programs.

There are many different ways in which organizations budget for video. Often a corporate video department is considered a "support service" and when it comes to budgeting, it is considered an overhead expense. The full cost of operating the video department and providing video services is estimated each year by the video manager. "Users" of video within the organization are never charged for the services used. Other organizations consider video an expense item within the operating budget like a "support service" but each department using video services is charged a percentage of the video department's total operating budget. These systems do not provide an accurate per-program cost or actual budget control. It is difficult to track actual costs, and the video manager is often at the mercy of the Chief Financial Officer in determining the video budget for the year. It is difficult for video managers operating under these budgeting systems to accurately reflect what it is costing the organization to produce programming, to fully justify the expenses involved in production and plan for growth.

In other organizations, the video unit may be considered a cost center and have a full chargeback system in place. This type of budgeting system charges "users" all of the full video services and materials used for each production. An accurate account of costs can be maintained while also providing a good resource planning system. Refer to Forms 7-10 to help organize budget and project planning.

Commercial producers and in-house video profit centers usually develop budgets on a per-project basis. The budgeting information I am providing here is for producers who are creating budgets on a per-project basis. A good, basic reference for budgeting is Michael Wiese's book, *Film & Video Budgets*, published by Michael Wiese Productions and available through Focal Press.

Program Categories

It is virtually impossible to discuss budget without first discussing program categories. There is a level of programming that is essentially a "talking head" that requires no pre-planning, design, scripting or editing. Then there is the level of programming that requires extensive design, pre-production, scripting, location shooting, special talent, effects and editing. These programs do not fit into the same category and cannot be produced for the same budget.

It is generally agreed that video productions can fit into one of four categories depending on the extent of work needed for completion. The levels established here represent guidelines only. Often, because of the complexity of production, a program will not fit neatly into a specific category but will overlap categories.

Level I

Level I, often referred to as the "talking head," requires little if any program design, pre-production and post-production. It is usually shot right at the organization in a conference room or office with minimum equipment set-up time. The talent is usually the (in-house, on-staff) subject matter expert who is familiar with the content, so there are no script requirements. Since the program is usually a simple product demonstration, speech or staff announcement, there are no location shooting requirements for inserts. This type of program does not require any special effects, graphics or editing.

Level I requires little if any creative contribution; no writer, director or technical personnel. It basically involves setting up the camera and shooting, so little staff time or pre-planning is needed. This type of

FORM VII

VIDEO PROJECT EXPENSE REPORT

DATE:_____ PROJECT #:_____

PROJECT NAME:_____

REQUESTED BY:_____ DEPT:_____

COST CENTER #:_____ PHONE:_____

	COST		**COST**

I. PREPRODUCTION

a. R&D		f. DUPLICATION	
b. SCRIPT/OUTLINE		g. PACKAGING	
c. SEC. SERVICES		h. SHIPPING	
d. PRINTING		i. MISC.	
e. GRAPHICS		**SUBTOTAL**	
f. PHOTOS/FILM/SLIDE		**IV. PERSONNEL**	
g. TAPE (AUDIO/VIDEO)		a. PROD./DIR.	
h. SETS		b. WRITER	
i. PROPS		c. CREW	
j. COSTUMES		d. TALENT	
k. MUSIC/SFX		e. EDITOR	
l. MISC.		f. OTHER	
SUBTOTAL		**SUBTOTAL**	

II. PRODUCTION — **V. EQUIPMENT**

a. STUDIO		a. STUDIO EQUIP.	
b. ON LOCATION		b. PORTABLE EQUIP.	
c. OUTSIDE FACILITIES		c. RENTAL EQUIP.	
d. MISC.		**SUBTOTAL**	
SUBTOTAL		**VI. TRAVEL**	

III. POST PRODUCTION

a. TAPE LOGGING		a. TRANSPORTATION	
b. WINDOW DUBS		b. LODGING	
c. EDITING		c. MEALS	
d. TAPE (AUDIO/VIDEO)		d. MISC.	
e. VIDEO DUBS		**SUBTOTAL**	
		GRAND TOTAL	

PROJECT WORKSHEET

PROJECT NAME _____

PROJECT REQUESTED BY _____

PRODUCTION _____

LENGTH OF PROGRAM _____ MINUTES

REQUIRED COMPLETION DATE _____

APPROVAL _____

JOB DESCRIPTION	SCHEDULED STARTING DATE	SCHEDULED COMPLETION DATE	ACTUAL COMPLETION DATE
SCRIPT:			
OUTLINE	_____	_____	_____
FIRST DRAFT	_____	_____	_____
APPROVAL	_____	_____	_____
SECOND DRAFT	_____	_____	_____
APPROVAL	_____	_____	_____
THIRD DRAFT	_____	_____	_____
APPROVAL	_____	_____	_____
SHOOTING SCRIPT	_____	_____	_____
ART:			
STORYBOARD	_____	_____	_____
TITLES, GRAPHS, ANIMATION	_____	_____	_____
SPECIAL EFFECTS	_____	_____	_____
VIDEO PRODUCTION:			
LOCATION	_____	_____	_____
STUDIO	_____	_____	_____
COPY / ANIMATION STAND	_____	_____	_____
NARRATION	_____	_____	_____
MUSIC / SOUND EFFECTS	_____	_____	_____
FILM TRANSFERS	_____	_____	_____
SOUND MIX	_____	_____	_____
MUSIC SELECTION	_____	_____	_____
EDIT	_____	_____	_____
ASSEMBLE	_____	_____	_____
DUBBING	_____	_____	_____
DELIVERY	_____	_____	_____

FORM IX

VIDEOTAPE MANPOWER PRODUCTION RECORD

VIDEOTAPE TITLE _____

TV ACTIVITY	MAN /HOUR TOTAL
MEETING	
SCRIPTING	
SCRIPT BLOCKING	
VISUALS	
REMOTE	
STUDIO	
CONTROL ROOM	
DUBBING	
PREVIEW & EVALUATION	
CUSTOMER SCRIPTING VISUALS, ETC.	
OTHER	

FORM X

PROJECT CHARGE RECORD

Project Name: _____ Cost Center: _____

Client /Contact: _____ Telephone: _____

Date	Employee	Function	Hours	Rate	Charge	Credit
_____	_____	_____	____	____	_____	_____
_____	_____	_____	____	____	_____	_____
_____	_____	_____	____	____	_____	_____
_____	_____	_____	____	____	_____	_____
_____	_____	_____	____	____	_____	_____
_____	_____	_____	____	____	_____	_____
_____	_____	_____	____	____	_____	_____
_____	_____	_____	____	____	_____	_____

Date	Material	Quantity	Rate	Charge	Credit
_____	_____	_____	____	_____	_____
_____	_____	_____	____	_____	_____
_____	_____	_____	____	_____	_____
_____	_____	_____	____	_____	_____
_____	_____	_____	____	_____	_____
_____	_____	_____	____	_____	_____
_____	_____	_____	____	_____	_____

Total Labor: _____

Total Materials: _____

Adjustments: _____

Total Charges: _____

Date _____ By _____

program is usually produced in a matter of hours, perhaps a total of one day by the time the copies are made and labeled.

Examples of Level I programming could be product introductions or demonstrations, staff announcements, informational and (video) memos, staff events (CEO announcements), speeches and recording conferences. Not much if any budget is required.

Level II

Level II also is usually delivered by a subject matter expert, but this time a partial script is developed. The partial script may include a formal introduction of the topic and presenter by an announcer, a thorough outline (for organization) for the presenter to follow and a formal closing by the announcer. This organized, researched outline requires planning time for the producer and the SME to spend in preparing for the program.

The program is shot at the company location but may require a few "insert" shots of the plant or other locations other than the conference room or office. These location "insert" shots would not have on-camera audio requirements and are usually used as background and fill shots for the narration.

Level II programs usually involve a product demonstration with insert shots of the manufacturing process or a simple training program of a new procedure. These may require a few graphics. This combination of partial scripting, narration, insert shots, on-camera talent requiring some direction and graphics demands some creativity and editing. This in turn involves planning, time, equipment and skill, all of which adds to the overall cost of the program.

Because this level requires more production involvement by artistic, skilled people (director, technician), it will involve more preproduction, production and post-production time than Level I programs. The overall production quality is increased in a Level II program. Artistic decisions about slides, graphics and location shots are required and more time is taken during production for basic talent direction. All of these elements add to the production time and, therefore, budget.

Level II programs may take about one week to produce, two days of pre-production, a day to shoot and one day to two days of editing (roughly one week to produce with approvals).

Level III

Level III programs usually require instructional design, scripting, perhaps some professional talent, voice narration, music, talent, art and editing direction, production design, location shooting, graphics, some basic effects and complex editing.

Level III programs require more pre-production time than level II programs because of research and scripting, location logistics and talent arrangements and usually involve more complex production requirements with more location shots, more insert shots and close-ups and more attention given to lighting. And because there are more complex production requirements, more extensive editing is required.

Training programs often fit into Level III, because they require extensive pre-production with research, instructional design and scripting. Instructional design with measurable objectives require the talent of trainers and the involvement of producers who have training program development experience. This, coupled with scriptwriting, talent direction, graphics and editing all add to the requirement of artistic input from experienced, talented professionals. This talent along with pre-production, production and post-production requirements add to the time and cost of Level III productions.

Level III programs take two to three weeks of dedicated time to produce. In reality, with approvals and other projects that are going on at the same time, this level of program often requires four to five weeks to produce.

Level IV

Level IV programs (THE BIG ONES!) usually involve full scripts, professional talent, complex location shooting, extensive effects, graphics, music and editing. They require the talents of directors, artists and technicians and have extended pre-production, production and post-production time requirements over Level III programs.

Level IV projects take at least four to five weeks of devoted time to produce, and often take two to three months to produce.

Interactive programs, film projects, corporate image projects, annual sales meeting motivational programs, extensive technical training programs, direct sales programs and dramatic scripts for training and marketing programs often fit into the Level IV category.

As the levels increase, the skill and talent to create the program increases as does the time and equipment resources. Often the category will reflect the production "value" as well. Usually the production value will increase as more time and talent are devoted to the project. And certainly with training programs, as the level increases so does the results.

Communication and training projects require different levels of production. Each project will usually have a desired result, and the result will be weighed against the budget and resources needed to accomplish the result. Usually the higher the value placed on the result the higher the production level. If specific, measurable results are required of the project, then a high level, well designed, well planned program will be needed to accomplish the results.

Multimedia

Interactive multimedia projects require extensive up-front planning as described in Chapter 7. They will also require capital expenditures for specialized production and program delivery equipment. Budgets for the creation of multimedia projects normally are much larger than for video projects and multimedia projects require a great deal more time to produce. This time factor is the most significant force in the increase of budgets for multimedia. Basically, multimedia budgets will vary from video project budgets only in the areas of program development and authoring (manpower time) and in the program mastering process (creating the replication master for program duplication). The scriptwriting process, graphics development, video and audio production and printed support materials costs will be similiar to traditional media production.

Budget Considerations

There are many items to consider before creating a budget that will affect the budget and your approach to the program. I have listed several important considerations that apply to forming a budget. The

Figure 5 – 1
Dolly track being set for a "tracking" shot. Adding a moving shot to your program adds production value but adds time to the production schedule that you have to plan in.

object is to prepare you for the budgeting process, not to tell you what each item will cost but to provide a guideline so that you can begin.

Audience

Your audience will often determine the budget. Their expectation level helps you determine how much should be spent on the production. Sophisticated audiences of today will not settle for a camcorder/ over-the-shoulder production when learning their jobs is at stake. Young audiences are used to the sophisticated production values of MTV, so the style of corporate television talking heads that worked several years ago will not hold the young audiences of today. Be considerate of your audience, provide the production value they expect and build your budget on these expectations. Today video/film and multimedia projects are business tools and deserve the budgets that will assure measurable results.

Objectives

What will it take to accomplish your objective? Your overall communications objective will contribute to your budgeting decisions. That is why it is so important to establish clear, reachable and measurable objectives at the beginning of the project. If the objectives are agreed upon by everyone involved, they will help you with the budget. Clear objectives help you determine audience expectations, production quality issues and program levels.

72

Distribution

How will the program be distributed? Each distribution method (VHS copies, film, broadcast transmission, videoconference network, CD-ROM) has unique production requirements for optimum distribution re sults. These production requirements for each medium will influence your budget.

Deadlines

Deadlines affect budgets. If it's a Level III program and the clients want it produced in one week, it will usually cost more because there will be overtime involved, special scheduling requirements and quick scripting, shooting and editing turnaround time. There is an old saying in the industry when it comes to video production, "*You can have it good, fast and cheap . . . pick two.*" Time, production quality and cost all interrelate in producing programs.

Script

The script is an important tool in the budgeting process. Production and post-production costs can be determined in advance by breaking the script down into production units of scenes and shots (or major location). By breaking down the script into production units, you can accurately determine production costs for talent, logistics, travel, equipment, lighting, production time and personnel. Each unit should have its own cost-out per production item, referred to as line items. This will tell you what's involved in actually producing the program. Once the script is broken into production units you can also determine editing requirements, special effects and music costs.

Common Variables Associated With Costs

There are many variables associated with production that always seem to affect the final budget. Some of these are special effects used, professional talent, field production variables and post-production costs.

For example, the client may decide at the last minute to add a flashy opening segment with special effects and animation. These effects will add costs to the program budget in a big way.

Professional talent may have an effect on the budget as well. Professional talent can save overall production time; however, the initial cost for hiring professional talent has to be planned into the budget.

Field production variables that may not have been taken into consideration in the original budget include location permits, equipment or talent transportation, meals and unexpected transportation costs.

Post-production costs may increase due to last minute changes in the script or changes in shooting requirements in the field. As production requirements change, post-production changes. Adding new shots that were not planned, making narration changes or adding graphics or effects that were not planned and budgeted for always add time and cost to post-production.

Other post-production considerations are duplication, distribution and printing. Often production budgets are created without consideration of program duplication. After the program is edited, copies must be made for approvals and audience showings. Many duplicates may be ordered to complete the project along with printing of labels, mailings and evaluation tools. These post-program costs need to be planned for in the initial budgeting process. Also consider costs for printing of student workbooks and hand-out materials that may accompany the video-tape. These items are often overlooked in the excitement of creating the production.

Contingency Expenses

Productions are complex endeavors that are always subject to unforeseen delays and problems, so it is a good idea to include a *contingency* item. The contingency figure in the budget reflects the unforeseen problems of productions. The contingency is a percentage of the total budget often calculated in the total budget or broken out into a line item. Contingency percentages often run from 5% to 20%.

Types of Budgets

I have included several types of budget examples from an informal summary to a line by line cost breakdown. In addition, standardized budget formats can be obtained from the International Television Association and the Association of Independent Commercial Producers. There are also several books that offer budgeting forms such as *Budget Forms Instantly!* by Ralph S. Singleton, Lone Eagle Publishing, and several computer software programs described in Chapter 10 can help you create budgets.

Budget Items

Since production breaks down logically into three main categories, I like to break the budget into the same three phases, pre-production, production and post production.

Typical Video and Multimedia Production Budget Items

PRE-PRODUCTION

Development stage for multimedia programming, typically budgeted by hour units:

Program needs analysis, including setting business goals for project, audience analysis, environmental analysis (delivery issues), needs/task analysis and forming program objectives

Interactive program design, preliminary design document including structure, treatment and training strategy

Creative: the creative pre-production steps can be budgeted separately, they are usually budgeted by hour units.

Concept/Treatment

Script Research

Script Development (may have 1st and 2nd drafts)

Storyboard

Multimedia applications storyboard

Production flowcharts for multimedia

Asset collection/management for multimedia

Authoring document for multimedia

Authoring Stage:

Interactive authoring

Prototype or Check Disc

Graphics plan

Text Files (plan)

Validation stage:

Develop Plan with purpose, methodology, instrument, data collection and criteria for feedback

Location Search (usually billed by the hour at 1/2 Director's fee)

Site survey (usually billed by the hour at 1/2 Director's fee)

Producer (usually billed by day rate or production)

Director (usually billed by day rate)

Production Assistant (billed at day rate)

Secretarial Services (billed at day rate)

Instructional Designer (billed at day rate)

Multimedia Developer (billed at day rate)

Stock Footage search and retain

Legal

title search

insurance/fees

copyright search and registration

permits

royalties

sub-contracts

PRODUCTION

Interactive Authoring

Check Disc or Digital Video Creation

Graphics Creation

Text Creation

Director

Lighting Director

Grip

Director of Photography

Camera Operator

Engineer

Audio Engineer

Tape Operator

Make-up

Stylist

Wardrobe Attendant

Teleprompter Operator

Talent Casting/Casting Fees

Talent

    on-camera principals

    extras

    models

    voice-over talent

Additional Personnel

Camera Package

Additional Personnel

Lighting Package

Audio Package

Dolly/Crane

Teleprompter

Walkie Talkies

Generator (quite often billed with lighting package)

Additional Rental Equipment

Tape Stock

Set Construction (including expenses, construction and materials)

Studio (billed for prep days, production and strike days plus personnel and lighting requirements)

Audio Recording Studio (often this line item will include music selection, creation, fees and voice overs)

Graphics (includes 2/D-3/D still graphics)

Animation

Location Rentals

Props

Wardrobe

Still Photography

POST-PRODUCTION

Director

Editor

Editing Facility

Film to Tape Transfers

Slide Transfers

Tape Format Transfers

Video Digitizing (for non-linear systems)

Time Coding

Window Dubs

Audio Transfers

Audio Mixing

Camera Inserts

Off-Line Editing

On-Line Editing (often includes special effects used and character generator; however, some editing facilities will bill for each piece of equipment used in editing)

Digital Video to Tape Transfers (for non-linear system)

Preview Dub

Implementation Stage for Multimedia

   site preparation

   installation and training of interactive system

   Create on-going support system/monitor results

Duplication (this might include program package design, printing, special tape mailers, hand-out materials, workbooks, cataloging, booking, invoicing and storage)

Office Expense (may include accounting fees, telephone, office supplies and insurance)

Transportation (expenses for crew and talent)

Travel

Lodging

Per diem (meals included for travel and production days)

Mileage

Miscellaneous Expenses (this item may include shipping, freight, extra meals and the many unforeseen items)

Union fees/benefits/payroll taxes/pension/welfare

Petty Cash

Contingency (5% to 20% of total)

Guidelines for Effective Budgeting

- Establish clear objectives for the program
- Clarify client expectations and level of program
- Be knowledgeable about production styles, options, costs, time and resource requirements for production
- Budget program from a completed script or program design for multimedia
- Client involvement from start to finish with appropriate approval points
- Good budget management with the use of appropriate production budgeting and tracking tools
- Quality control methods for vendor selection, talent and resource management
- Multimedia prototype created for multimedia series

INSURANCE ISSUES

Any number of things can go wrong during a shoot, things for which you may be held liable or accountable. If you are an independent producer, freelancer or owner of a small production company and offer video production services to clients, it is a wise move to protect yourself with insurance. Among the most common types are comprehensive liability, equipment loss or damage, and rental floaters.

Accidents happen, no matter how careful you or your crew may be. A camera gets dropped and the lens shatters (this happened to me in a recent project), the crash cart bumps into a wall leaving a foot-long hole, a fire starts because of overloaded circuits. You could be judged liable for thousands of dollars in damages. **Comprehensive liability** will protect you from claims filed as a result of property or bodily injury or death. You may be required to carry comprehensive liability by equipment rental companies, production houses you work for as an independent contractor or by clients who hire you to produce a film or video.

Other coverage will protect you for the damage or loss of equipment that you own or rent. Having a camera or monitor stolen or lost can set you back thousands of dollars. Be sure you are insured for this unpleasant event.

A floater, an addition to a standard insurance policy, can protect you from loss or damage of all equipment rented from a specified company at any one time. A floater, which is usually good for one year, needs to be made out to each individual or company from whom you are renting. You can also purchase insurance directly from a rental company, usually for about 10% of the rental fee.

Other types of insurance such as the producer's insurance policy can cover the entire production. This may be required if you have investors involved. Other types of insurance include specific cast, crew, set and prop insurance; and errors and omissions insurance protection. Errors and omissions insurance protects you from being sued if there is an infringement of copyright because of something you put in your final program.

If you hire freelancers often, you should be aware of the way the IRS classifies workers as either employees or independents. Failure to understand and comply with the law can result in a large outlay of back taxes. Essentially IRS guidelines seek to answer just who has the right to direct and control a worker regarding the details of when, where and how work is to be performed. If you exercise that control over the worker, then he/she can be considered an employee of yours. If you specify the desired outcome of a project but do not dictate when, where or how the necessary work will be done, then the worker is usually considered an independent contractor.

There are many more insurance issues that can be covered in detail with an insurance company experienced in video and film production. I strongly encourage you to investigate and purchase production and business policies that fit your specific needs and budget. Cohen Insurance of New York, for example, offers a booklet "What you should know about production insurance."

LEGAL ISSUES

Numerous legal details need to be worked out well in advance of a production. Producers should have a working understanding of the copyright laws and legal considerations for talent and music. Often legal departments get involved, and that may cause delays in production, editing and project delivery. If company logos are involved with opening graphics or in printed support materials, their use often has to be approved by legal departments. Be prepared in pre-production to spend extra time with legal issues.

Thanks to Ed Hearn, an attorney in Palo Alto specializing in the entertainment industry, I have provided a brief statement about the copyright law and notices that producers should be aware of. Obviously you should check with your legal counsel for more details pertaining to your specific project and with local talent unions about their requirements.

What May Be Copyrighted?

Works that can qualify for copyright must pass two tests. First, they must be original works of the author, meaning they must have been created by the author. Second, they must be fixed on a tangible medium, such as paper, videotape or film. An idea for a training program would not qualify for copyright until it was put into writing or actually produced on videotape. The various components of a video—the script, music, sound, performance, soundtrack or visuals could be separately copyrighted once they are put on paper or tape.

Ownership of Copyright

According to the Copyright Act, the copyright on a work belongs to the person who created it, in other words the author. Only the copyright owner, or the owner's agent, may register a copyright claim.

The issue of ownership becomes less clear, however, when the work represents the combined efforts of many people, as in a video or multimedia project where one person may fund the project, another may write the script, another may produce it and still others may direct, run the camera or perform in the finished tape. In such cases, each person who contributes to the work may claim to be the author and therefore the owner of the copyright, collectively if not individually. As a joint copyright owner, each of the owners may exploit the work in whatever matter he/she wishes. Each one is accountable to the other owners for his/her share of income from the video and may be held liable for any claims. It is usually best to simplify this situation by having all those who contributed to the video agree in writing who will be identified as the owner of the video.

Commissioned Works and Work for Hire

Works that are made by someone other than the actual owner or user include commissioned works and work for hire. If you are commissioned by a company to create a video, you as the maker would retain the copyright—after obtaining in writing an acknowledgment from the other contributors. For instance, if a company hired you to produce a video describing its product, and there was nothing put in writing to the contrary, you as the creator of the video would own the copyright, with the company having an exclusive license to use the video for the specific purposes for which you were asked to create it.

Work made for hire includes videos produced by an employee for a company and works that would be commissioned as part of a collective work when the parties involved sign a statement that the work will be considered "work made for hire."

Copyright Notice

Any copy of the work that is disseminated to the public should contain a copyright notice that is clearly visible to the viewer in order to prevent the work from going into the public domain and the copyright protection being lost. The notice must include: the word "copyright" or the symbol "C" in a circle, the year of publication and the name of the copyright owner.

Adding the notice does not grant the copyright, since the copyright automatically vests once the work is created. But placement of the notice is important in preventing the copyright from being lost to the public domain. Under the former Copyright Law, the omission would result in forfeiture of the copyright. The current Act, however, allows for some protection for five years.

As a producer, on behalf of the buyer of the video production, you contract with third parties to contribute material to the video production. You must make it clear in writing with those third parties who will own the work they are contributing to and whether it is a commissioned work or a "work made for hire." Your responsibility is to provide the buyer a finished product in which all rights to all elements have vested in a way that they can be transferred to the buyer for its use.

Should you not acquire outright ownership of any element in the video, you must try to obtain a perpetual and universal right for the use of the contributed element in the video in all formats and all media, so that there would be no restriction on the buyer's use of that material in the video.

Music and Clearance

Typically musical works have the same copyright protection as other works, so "borrowing" a tune from your favorite CD to set the mood for your next educational program is not recommended. Often copyright ownership belongs to the publisher which collects and shares royalties with the creators. This copyright generally covers the published sheet music, right of performance and the mechanical rights or the form of playback, such as film, tape or CDs. Producers need to obtain clearance rights for performance or synchronization license. Performance licenses are usually granted from performing-rights groups such as ASCAP, BMI and SESAC. Agencies such as the Harry Fox Agency in New York also have authority from publishers to grant producers music rights. It's very important for the producer to understand copyright and clearance issues and obtain appropriate clearance for all music used in all productions.

Arrangements Between Producer and Performer

If your production requires professional talent, you should be prepared to provide the following:

- Statement of function and role of performers.
- Compensation agreement for performers including overtime fees.
- Credits statement.
- Provisions of relevant guilds and unions.
- Clearance for the rights to use name and likeness of performer.
- Amount of time needed for the production.
- Payroll statement and time sheets required by union.

More on these issues under the "Talent and Casting" section of Chapter 8.

In summary, it is wise to become familiar with copyright and professional talent requirements. Often what starts out as a good relationship with a client or organization does not always end as a good relationship. Therefore, copyright ownership and talent issues need to be worked out in advance, so there are no surprises and disappointments at the end of the production. For example: I did a video production for a very large cruise line, which changed the "rules" at the end of the production. It was agreed (verbally) at the beginning of the project that I could use excerpts of the program for teaching purposes in the seminars that I conduct. The excerpts I wanted to use were excellent teaching examples of using video for training and good acting examples.

At the end of the production, the client decided that I couldn't use any excerpts and withheld approval of the final payment until I signed an exclusive copyright agreement, a document that was unusual and certainly not in line with industry standards. Avoid such last minute surprises and inconveniences by getting copyright agreements in writing well in advance.

A sample Letter of Agreement and Video Production Contract are shown on the following pages.

Sample Letter of Agreement
{LETTERHEAD}

Production Agreement
Re: *[name of project or working title]*

[Date]

Ms. Client
XYZ Corporation
Address
City, State ZIP

Dear Ms. Client:

This serves as a Letter of Agreement between XYZ Corporation, hereafter referred to as "Client" and Able Video Communications hereafter referred to as "Producer."

It is hereby agreed that Producer is to produce a videotape program on the subject of: *[working title or purpose of program]*.

The estimate cost for production is based upon the Client approved treatment, and is subject to Producer review of the final approved script when available. The estimated cost is complete for all scripting, pre-production, production, and post production through submitted edited master videotape. The estimate cost includes and is subject to the following specifications:

- Finished length is not to exceed 12 minutes.
- Scripting up to and including a maximum of 3 drafts, content materials to be provided by the Client.
- Producer/Director services for production prep; casting; live action production; graphics, music and narration production and post production.
- One (1) day of studio production on a sound stage, including all associated crew and facilities and set up time.
- One (1) day of remote production at location(s) to be provided by·the Client, including all associated crew and facilities.
- Professional talent at AFTRA union scale for voice over narration and on camera roles.
- Production music, including all clearances.
- Animated graphics (logos, etc.) and charts required.
- Off-line approval edit for client review.
- On-line final edit on Betacam SP or equivalent quality.
- Please Note: No duplication is included in this agreement.

The estimated cost for production (contract price) is *$41,350* and is not to exceed $45,485. ($41,350 plus a 10% contingency of $4,235) without prior Client approval. This estimate is itemized in the attached Production Budget, which is a part of this Letter of Agreement. The contract price is based upon the production parameters listed above (as suggested by the approved treatment), and is subject to Producer review of the final, approved script when available.

Terms of payment are One-Third upon awarding of contract; One-Third at commencement of principal photography; and One-Third upon delivery of submitted master.

Producer reserves the right to assign or sub-contract any portion of this project.

Producer is being retained by Client as an independent contractor. All work performed under this agreement shall be deemed works made for hire, in accordance with the federal copyright laws. Completed videotapes shall be owned outright by the Client.

Client acknowledges that Producer may refer to Client's name in promotion of Producer's future business. Client also agrees that Producer will receive one (1) copy of the completed production and may thereafter use the program in the promotion of Producer's further business.

Either party shall have the right to cancel or postpone this agreement prior to completion of the agreement. In the event Client initiates such cancellation or postponement, Client agrees to pay Producer cancellation/postponement fees to be negotiated based upon services performed, schedules already committed, and sub-contractors already engaged up to and including the date on which written notice of postponement or termination is received by Producer.

If you acknowledge and agree to the above terms, please sign and date this Letter of Agreement, retain a copy, and return an executive copy to Producer. We look forward to working with you.

Very Sincerely Yours,

[Producer]

The above terms are agreed to and acknowledged.
Able Video Communications

By _____

Date _____

XYZ Corporation

By _____

Date _____

* * * *

SAMPLE VIDEO PRODUCTION CONTRACT

Video Production Proposal for . . .

Proposal Objectives

This proposal is intended to frame the working responsibilities of **Cartwright & Associates** in the development of a video program and provide a payment structure so that work on the project can be scheduled. This proposal represents an approximate working budget based on **C & A's** total involvement in creation and production. This includes program design, script development, visualization, video production, computer graphics, professional voice narration, music selection, directing and editing.

Production

The primary goal of this project is to produce a 10 minute video program that captures the history, heritage and traditions of . . .

The videotape to be produced will be broadcast quality, untilizing on-location footage, music, professional narrations and computer graphics.

Program Concept

The program content, concept and storyline will be developed through the scriptwriting process. The basic program concept will communicate the history, traditions and values within . . . It is important that the video program depict a sense of pride in new employees, existing employees and external audiences. The video should have a strong visual concept that emphasizes the close relationship of the company with the outdoors and a strong commitment to its customers.

Cost Estimate

1. *Pre-production:* ***Cartwright & Associates*** will provide producer services, assistance in content development, concept development, scriptwriting, visualization, graphics design, production management, pre-production logistics and meetings, and shooting script, approx: 10 days.

The tentative production schedule has been determined by . . . with the final post production phase scheduled for early October.

2. *Production:* ***Cartwright & Associates*** will provide location video recording, lighting, talent preparation, talent direction, sound recording, and tape for all location shooting requirements at the . . . property, approx. 5 days.

3. *Post production:* ***Cartwright & Associates*** will provide professional voice narration, music selection, music/sound mix, logging and indexing of footage, computer graphics and animation (if required), rough edit, final edit, master digital tape; approx: 6 days.

APPROXIMATE TOTAL PROJECT COST . . . $18,000

Payment Schedule

Estimated budget represents ***Cartwright & Associates*** total involvement in production and consultation:

1/4 of total estimated budget due at project start
1/4 of total due at script approval
1/4 of total due at production
1/4 of total due at delivery of finished program

Cartwright & Associates will provide a final, edited, digital master.

Approval

. . . will provide approval on the content outline, rough script, final script, original footage, rough edit, music selection, graphics and talent.

Pre-Production
Considerations

6

After we have gone through the major design steps, understand the audience, objective, budget, and have a script, we conduct our first actual "production" meeting with the key people. This will be the first of a series of meetings that will define the deadlines, resources, production approach or "look" of the program, special logistics, schedules, crew information, talent arrangements and special shooting, lighting and sound requirements. We will review the script (if it is complete) with the production team, and review schedules.

It is important to communicate as much about these elements as you can to your team. The team may consist of you alone (the producer/ director/ videographer/artist/lighting director and sound recorder) or, if you are from a larger facility or have a larger budget, there may be several people doing these jobs. But the team should be notified of as many elements affecting the production as can be communicated.

DEADLINES

Most projects will have specific deadlines, and the production meeting should detail the deadlines for each phase of the production. Deadlines have a rippling effect. If one deadline is missed, it will affect all the other deadlines along the way to completion. Everyone should be made aware of the deadlines and be prepared to meet them.

RESOURCES

The initial pre-production meeting will also identify resources. Resources are the skills involved in the production of the program (producer/director, lighting, sound, artwork/graphic art, engineering and make-up). These production resources (your team) have to be lined up and selected. Resources also include the equipment needed for the production, sets, props, location arrangements, talent arrangements and graphics. These resources have to be identified and secured. The pre-production meeting spells out what resources are readily available and which will need to be obtained through outside resources, contracting, purchase, or rental.

If a subject matter expert (SME) from the client or your organization will be involved, a commitment of time will have to be agreed upon. I have run into many problems with SMEs because the organization did not realize how much time the SME would have to devote to the project. Be sure to secure this commitment up front before the project begins.

When lining up resources, decide if there is talent in-house to handle the project, and if the talent has the time and ability to participate. As a producer, I have worked for organizations that had video production services in-house, but they were not available for the project. On other projects, the client did not want to use the in-house services because they were looking for a "fresh" approach to a problem. Often in-house services fall into the trap of providing the same video solutions to all problems, perhaps because of limited budget, equipment or talent.

Using Outside Resources

How can you save money by using outside production resources? By providing specific production skills and techniques required by the project and by providing the kind of production efficiencies that are hard to duplicate in-house. As a producer who has worked on both sides of the fence for more than 20 years—I have hired outside production resources while working as a corporate video manager, and now I provide production services to corporate clients—I can attest to the fact that video managers can save money on projects by turning to outside production resources. Video managers face production barriers everyday—insufficient funding for staff, equipment and maintenance; scheduling conflicts; unrealistic deadlines; and lack of expertise in technical, production and content areas required for specific projects. Outside resources fill in the gaps in these important areas. They can supply fresh, creative approaches to projects, supply the specific technical and production expertise needed and allow the corporate producer to use state-of-the-art technology without a long term financial investment. The video manager only has to commit to the resources needed to accomplish the objectives of the project.

Most corporations are open to using outside resources. They often use outside consultants and vendors and have the system in place to tap into these resources. If the video manager has done his or her homework and can show the corporation how the program will effect change and save the corporation money, justifying outside services is not an issue. What the manager goes for is producing a cost-effective program that will achieve specific objectives. Hiring outside resources can help the video manager achieve these goals.

Companies call upon outside production resources to solve a specific problem, such as consulting on the viability of using video, creating a concept and script, providing specialized production services or helping with the evaluation process. By hiring outside resources they expect to meet those needs. In almost every case, they will save money by bringing in the expertise they need.

Corporate video managers will also turn to outside production facilities when there is a scheduling problem with their own equipment or staff, if they are looking for a particular effect or shooting technique that they do not have or if the program demands a special talent. Solving these problems by hiring outside resources can be cost-effective. In order for production facilities to be competitive, they have to stay current with technology and have the most efficient tools. Although they may have a higher hourly rate than what is reflected in-house, they may get there faster in terms of the finished program. This efficiency is reflected in dollars saved. The final cost of a project is not always the bottom line or hourly rate.

I have found that most facilities specialize in some aspect of video. They may have good remote production capabilities but may be lacking in post-production, or they may have all the latest equipment but do not have staff instructional designers and writers to create complex corporate training or communications programs. Few facilities in the country have all the skills and talent needed to carry an industrial program through from concept to completion. That is why managers hire outside independent producers. An independent producer can secure the appropriate facility and talent needed to accomplish the program objectives.

Video managers know that more time (safe estimates are up to 70%) is devoted to the pre-production phase of a program than to any other phase. For programs that are produced in-house, the staff will devote most of its time to pre-production, program design, scripting, visualization and pre-planning. The smart manager will start devoting more time and resources to this phase of program development and de-emphasize the production and equipment phase. He or she will then start realizing the value of contracting outside resources for this small percentage of program development. People, not equipment, create programs.

Outside production companies offer vast production experience and can draw from similar experiences with past clients and bring you new ideas that will enhance the production. This experience can become very valuable to the in-house producer. The bottom line shouldn't be the only factor when deciding to go outside. You should also consider the experience, creativity and technology that you get and how those elements will enhance your production.

With the trend in downsizing of large corporations today, reviewing the benefits of using outside resources is a serious exercise for in-house, corporate video managers. Video managers have to more than ever justify their production capabilities and smart managers are turning to outside resources to economically produce their video segments. It makes good *cents* to provide good, creative design, writing and producing capabilities in-house and turn to outside production resources, when they are needed, on a per-project basis. Below is a summary of the items you need to plan for when using outside resources.

Using Outside Resources

1. Write down a clear statement of the purpose of your program.
2. State your concept in writing.
3. Identify the intended audience.
4. Make clear statements of the program's objectives.
5. Identify the quality of production required.
6. List all special requirements: extensive graphics, special effects or computer graphics.
7. Identify all locations and studio/set requirements.
8. Identify the special tone, mood and look.
9. State optimal program length.
10. State target date for completion.
11. State available budget (or estimate).

To conclude, the rational for using out-of-house production is as follows:

- Production houses maintain state-of-the-art equipment, upgrading and replacing as the marketplace demands.
- The client does not have to commit its financial, plant and personnel assets on a long-term basis to developing a production facility for which it does not have a long-term need. It can abandon production at any time without enormous write-downs and layoffs.
- Out-of-house production is cost effective: you pay only for what you need. Conversely, the client's staff will be motivated to secure the best qualified service organization(s) for each stage of production.
- A corporation's limited staff can concentrate on each project without worrying about technical or operational problems. They can focus

on the area that makes the program successful—pre-production and creative scripts.

- Savings on staff and equipment can be put on the screen where it shows to the in-house producer's best advantage.

THE LOOK OF THE PROGRAM

The "look" of the program should be communicated to all involved at the first production meeting. This gives everyone direction to follow, helps with planning for lighting and camera work, sound design and graphics or artwork creation. I like to provide sample tapes or photos to show the "look" I am after. For example, in doing a public relations image program for a company, I wanted to project an early morning, warm look to the program. I found photos of the "feel" I was after and shared them with the crew. This allowed the gaffer to start planning for colored gels or reflectors for the scenes. It allowed the camera operator to plan for filters. Everyone was clued into the look I was after, so plans could start being made to achieve the look. Based on this look, shooting schedules were drawn up to best take advantage of the light for early morning or late afternoon shots. We planned our indoor shots during the middle of the day and the outside shots early in the morning or at sunset.

There have been times when I didn't communicate my ideas to the crew early enough, and they came to the shoot saying, "If I had only known what you were trying to do, I would have brought . . ." or, "If I had known you were trying to get this type of a shot I would have brought a dolly." Communicate your ideas early, and let everyone start thinking about requirements BEFORE the day of the shoot.

It's not just the crew you need to communicate with about the look of the program. Be sure the SME or your location contact knows what you are trying to achieve. They may have to prepare props and people well in advance of the shoot so everything is ready for you when you arrive. There is nothing more frustrating than arriving at the location to shoot, the talent and crew are ready but the computer (prop needed in the shot) has to be set up for the shot, or the people in the scene have not been told what you are doing and have to be prepared. That takes extra production time.

The importance of pre-production planning was painfully driven home—and actually provided the motivation for completing this book—with a recent experience I had producing a video training series. I truly hope this book will help save other producers from similar nightmares, for just about every conceivable production problem was encountered during this project, and each problem could easily be traced back to poor production planning.

The company that hired me was a large cruise line. The budget for the project was well below industry standard for the amount of video they needed (isn't that often the case?), but the allure of shooting on a cruise ship sailing the Caribbean was too hard to resist. My desire to go on a cruise clouded my judgement. I ignored many of the essential planning steps, including the need for close client involvement. As a result, my twenty years of video production experience was tested to the maximum.

I should have suspected trouble at the beginning when our client contact, the training director, kept delaying and cancelling critical planning meetings. We had agreed on a strict shooting schedule and deadline (based on the cruise that we were booked on), but the look of the program, storyboard and script were never really agreed to in detail before shooting began. Lacking these critical planning steps, we encountered a great deal of grief while shooting and editing and much higher costs than originally planned.

As the shooting dates approached, we still had not received any feedback on the scripts from our client. The real nightmare began after we boarded the ship and started shooting the program. Our client had not made any arrangements for shooting in specific areas of the ship nor had she made full arrangements with the cruise line employees to appear in the programs. Needless to say this created a great deal of lost production time (increasing the production shooting schedule from 10-hour to 18-hour days) and a great deal of stress for both crew and talent. Our client never really looked at the scripts until we started to shoot each scene. Only then did she step in and begin changing the scenes and rewriting the narration. As we left the port of Miami, my crew and I quickly realized that this was turning into the "client from hell" and there was no turning back.

Get agreement up front on the "look" of the program, so each scene can be visualized. Insist on final approval for the script and storyboard before the shoot begins and be certain all shooting arrangements have been made far in advance of the actual production date. Each of these critical planning factors greatly affects production time and budget. Do not let the excitement of doing your first video (or the allure of a Caribbean cruise) deter you from good production planning.

LOGISTICS

For shooting on location, preparing the location shooting scene, props, transportation, and food for crew breaks are all details I call *logistics*. All the details of the logistics need to be pre-planned and brought up in the pre-production meeting. Someone, such as a production assistant, has to follow through with the important details—and all details of production are important.

Some of these location details include:

- equipment and crew transportation to the location
- parking
- location site maps for talent and crew
- security clearance for talent, crew and equipment
- loading and unloading arrangements at location
- location shooting clearance and permits
- special safety issues at the location, such as special jackets, outerwear or long sleeves, hard hats, safety glasses and I.D. badges
- meal arrangements for talent and crew
- security issues for equipment and storage of equipment if it is an overnight production
- telephone access, communications, bathrooms and changing facilities for talent
- traffic control for exterior shots
- special union requirements or restrictions at the location

Often the person responsible for the details of the logistics is the production assistant (PA). The PA assumes the responsibility of managing transportation, parking considerations, food or lunch breaks, props, special talent arrangements and a million other details that can make or break the shoot. I've always said that if you are good with details, you will do well in video production. If you are not good with details, hire someone who is.

During the actual shoot, the PA may also assume responsibility for labeling tapes and keeping logs of the shoot, helping with continuity notes and generally assisting the director with talent, crew, equipment, location and client details.

Logistics usually fall within several categories that include talent, crew and location. Talent arrangements often include rehearsals, scripts, releases, contracts, union requirements, wardrobe and makeup.

Crew arrangements involve transportation arrangements, especially if there is out of town travel, loading and unloading equipment, call-out time (when to have crew arrive at the set in the morning), lunch or food arrangements, contracts for outside services, time sheets, W-2 forms and insurance.

Location arrangements often include approvals to shoot on location, releases for locations, permits, location contacts, security, traffic control, parking and equipment logistics and equipment staging arrangements for the day of the shoot. Location arrangements must be made for the appropriate props and talent to be available for the day of the shoot, appropriate power and audio arrangements for the day of the shoot and safety considerations for crew and talent.

Location Shooting

Location shooting offers many advantages (and disadvantages) over shooting in the studio. One advantage is credibility. Location shooting allows the viewer to experience the actual "visual feel" of the location whether it be a meeting room, manufacturing area, hospital operating suite or external scene. Scenes shot on location add a certain amount of credibility to the script.

We do very little studio shooting anymore for corporate television. With the portability of video equipment today, film-style, single camera shooting is the choice of most professional video producers. However, this choice does create many logistical considerations for crew, talent and equipment. Shooting on location requires good problem solving skills. The problems of location noise, lighting and environmental conditions should always be addressed during the pre-production process. Time spent in solving as many of these problems as you possibly can will always pay off in time saved during production. Think of as many things as you possibly can that could go wrong on the day of the shoot and address these potential problems during pre-production.

Site Survey

Most producers will agree that one of the most important considerations for location production is the location site survey. The site survey will provide invaluable logistical information for the crew and director, and for the script as well. Often after the site survey has taken place, script changes occur. Once on location you can determine if the camera angles called for in the script are possible, if talent movement, backgrounds and lighting are appropriate for the conditions of the scene and if the script audio requirements are possible. Notes are taken (and photos if possible) on power, lighting and sound considerations as well as equipment and crew logistics and what special location problems need to be solved before the day of the shoot.

The site survey allows you or the assigned director to actually "see" the scenes, action and shooting logistics required by the script. The director can enhance the script based on what he or she experiences on the location (sites and sounds that may not appear in the script, such as interesting background highlights and lighting conditions). The director will walk through the script scene by scene, shot by shot to determine shooting feasibility, camera positions and special lighting requirements, then make notes on camera placement in each scene, talent and camera movements, special audio conditions and changes in the script based on site logistics.

The director, director of photography or lighting director will "visualize" the scene and determine what lights will be needed to achieve the "look" called for by the script. Requirements for lighting the principal areas will be considered and notes taken for special lighting instruments and grip equipment (gels for windows, reflectors, extra power for larger lights, special lighting effects) and time needed to set up the lights for each scene. Talent movement will be considered as well as background, foreground and set lighting requirements. Ceiling height, overall room brightness, color, texture and reflective surfaces within the setting all have to be considered to make appropriate lighting decisions and equipment selections.

The site survey also allows the director to properly block the script, schedule the shooting based on best shooting conditions for each scene, and determine equipment set-up and movement. Equipment placement will be determined along with audio recording considerations (mic placement and ambient noise). The site survey will allow the director to make the proper location contacts and start the location problem solving process.

Location Scouting

For larger productions a **Location Scout** is hired to locate, preview and help select locations for the production and check out shooting requirements for the director.

There are companies throughout the country that specialize in location scouting and arrangements; another good source for location information is the local city, county or state film bureau or office. The film office can become a valuable resource for finding local talent, crews and equipment, assisting with city shooting permits and paperwork and providing information about local union arrangements and requirements. A listing of each state's film office is located in Appendix D.

Location Scouting Tips

- Bring to the survey a note pad for room diagrams and lighting plots, light meter (if appropriate), tape measure to measure windows for gels and room sizes, a compass for sun and shadow direction and still camera.
- To determine which outlets are on which circuits, take along a circuit tester or nite light, and contact the building engineer for building plans to help you identify power placement, room locations and traffic patterns.
- Shoot photos or camcorder footage during the scout.

- Be sure everything is put back in its proper place after the shoot.
- Visit each location at the time scheduled for the actual shooting, so you can experience lighting, sound and traffic conditions. Find out what other activities are scheduled at the time of the shoot (such as shift change, a retirement party in the next office or building cleaning and maintenance).
- Check access to locations for equipment movement. Are the doors big enough for easy equipment movement for dollies and carts? Is there easy access for crew and talent?
- Check the ceiling height at each shooting location for lighting requirements. Can you hang backlights? Do you need ladders, lifts or scaffolding to hang lights? Are there ceiling sprinklers that may create a problem when you turn on the production lights? Are there ceiling alarms that may create a problem with lights and sets?
- Check room noise (ambiance) for air-conditioner noise, fluorescent light hum, background music, outside traffic noise, hallway noise, elevator and soda machine noise and extra noise at shift changes and rooms above the location.
- Check the wall colors and reflective surfaces within the scene that may affect your lighting.
- Check room lighting conditions. Are there windows in the scene? Can they be gelled so they match the color temperature of your lights? What will be your predominant lighting source? Are there other lighting sources or mixed lighting sources that will affect your lighting requirements? Can the fluorescents be turned off? Do the lighting conditions change throughout the day?
- If shooting exteriors, check the sun's position in the sky at the scheduled time of the shoot for reflections and shadows; exteriors may require extra lighting and reflector equipment.
- What are the power limitations? Will there be sufficient power for the lights and equipment? Will you need to make an electrical tap? Check distances for electrical cables from power sources.
- Create a room plan and lighting diagram for each scene for furniture placement, lighting, equipment and camera placement and power outlets.
- Use the location checklist and contact sheet and be sure office managers and supervisors, building engineers, electricians, shop stewards and security are listed.
  Refer to Form 11, Form 12 and Form 13 for survey checklists.

Technical Logistical Considerations

The following section is made possible thanks to Mr. Coleman Cecil Smith and his excellent technical reference, *Mastering Television Technology, A Cure for the Common Video*, published by Newman-Smith Publishing Company, Inc.

Power

Each electrical circuit is designed to provide a maximum amount of electrical current. To make sure that a circuit will not overheat and catch fire, a fuse or circuit breaker is installed in the circuit. The fuse or circuit breaker is designed to break the circuit if the designed maximum current draw is exceeded. Once tripped, a "blown" fuse must be replaced or a "tripped" circuit breaker must be manually reset.

To make sure that the current flowing through a circuit is not interrupted during production, some calculations during location scouting are appropriate. The following procedure should be followed:

FORM XI

REMOTE SURVEY CHECKLIST

Program:_____

Location: _____

Date: _____ Time: _____

Contact People: _____

Power Available:

Additional Lighting Needed:

Possible Shots:

Special Arrangements:

SCOUTING REPORT

Project Name: _____

Address of Location: _____ Shot #: _____

    Interior: _____

    Exterior: _____

    Scouting Date: _____

1. Describe activity. How many people on camera?

2. How much space involved?

3. Light level   Source of light

4. Will the action be shot from the same location?
   If not, describe camera position(s)

5. Recording Sound: Sync or wild?

6. Special equipment needed at this location?

FORM XIII

REMOTE SURVEY CHECK

Date of Survey: _____

Location: _____
            (street)   (city)

_____
            (county)   (state)   (apt. #)

_____
            (room)   (floor)   (misc.)

DAY OF SHOOT: _____
                        (date)   (time)

PRODUCTION CONTACT: _____
                                        (name)

_____
            (phone)   (position)

ELECTRICIAN/JANITOR/MAINTENANCE: _____
                                                    (name)

_____
            (phone)   (location)

AC OUTLETS: _____ (see attached diagram)
                (quantity)

AMPS: _____ _____
            (#)   (problems)

REFLECTION INTERFERENCES:

OBSTRUCTIONS BLOCKING CAMERA VIEW:

SPRINKLER SYSTEM:

SUN LOCATION:

VIEW FROM INSIDE LOOKING OUT:

SURROUNDINGS:

EXTENSION CORDS: _____
(how many)   (length)

TYPE OF FLOOR:

CEILING HEIGHT:

WIDTH OF HALLWAYS:

WIDTH OF DOORS:
(for room dimensions, door and window locations, see attached)

PERMITS/CLEARANCES: ☐ POLICE   ☐ PARKING   ☐ FIRE DEPT.
     PASSES

NAME OF CONTACTS FOR PERMITS/CLEARANCES:

SPECIAL PROPS NEEDED:

MISC. INFORMATION ATTACHED?   ☐ YES   ☐ NO

1. Decide which wall outlets will be most convenient to power equipment and lighting.
2. Determine to which circuit each desired wall outlet is connected.
3. Determine which circuit breaker or fuse is in each desired circuit and the designed maximum current load for that circuit. The electrical current (in Amps) that the circuit is designed to safely carry is printed on the fuse or circuit breaker in that circuit. 15 Amp, 20 Amp and 30 Amp circuit breakers are the most commonly found sizes.
4. Determine which other wall outlets (and connected equipment and lights) are on the same desired circuits. Determine the total load (in Amps or Watts) of all other equipment and lights on the desired circuits that will be operating during the production. This should be printed on the equipment, frequently on the back or bottom. If there is no printed information, look for a fuse or circuit breaker size. In North America, you may convert Watts to Amps with the following formula:
5. Current (Amps) = Lamp Power (Watts)/110 (Volts)
6. The total amount of current available to power television equipment and lighting on each circuit is the designed maximum current load minus the load of other equipment connected to the circuit that will be operating during production.
7. The total amount of current consumed by equipment and lighting is the production current load. Look at the load printed on each piece of equipment and the load of the lamp in each fixture and add them together to determine the production current load.

Production Equipment Power

Basic television production equipment requires approximately the following amount of power for proper operation (at 110V power):

Television camera	0.2 Amps
VTR	0.1 Amps
Camcorder	0.2 Amps
Picture monitor	1.0 Amps
Waveform monitor	1.0 Amps

The exact amount of power drawn by an individual piece of equipment is printed on the equipment, in the service manual or on the manufacturer's specification sheet.

Lighting Equipment Power

The lighting of the scene is the most important factor in improving the quality of the picture. The amount of current required to operate lighting instruments may be determined with the same Watts-to-Amps conversion formula above. For quick reference common lamp Wattages converted to current demands (at 110 Volts) are as follows:

100 Watts demands	0.9 Amps
250 Watts demands	2.3 Amps
500 Watts demands	4.5 Amps

600 Watts demands	5.5 Amps
750 Watts demands	6.8 Amps
1000 Watts demands	9.1 Amps
2000 Watts demands	18.2 Amps

The total load on a given circuit must not exceed the maximum designed load for that circuit. If it does, the circuit will eventually be interrupted. The interruption may not come immediately, depending on the amount of overcurrent demand, but it will eventually occur.

Power Extension Cords

Extension cords are frequently used in portable production to provide temporary power. In general, the larger the load, the larger the conductors within any extension cord should be. In addition, the longer the extension cord, the larger the conductors within the extension cord should be. Extension cords that have conductors that are too small for the application pose a serious fire hazard.

Two-wire consumer extension cords should be avoided entirely. Three-wire (with a long grounding pin on the plug) rated for "heavy-duty" use should be used.

Extension cords are designed to be used only for portable applications. Permanent installation of outlets to fulfill frequent power demands should be completed by a competent electrician.

Environmental Logistics

Physical factors that will affect the quality of the picture and sound must be carefully considered for a potential production location. The two primary areas in which problems may be encountered are picture and sound.

Picture

The primary factor affecting picture quality is lighting. The amount of lighting, the placement of lighting sources, and the quality of lighting all affect the picture.

Quantity of Light

A potential production location must be scouted for too much or too little lighting to achieve the desired depth-of-focus in a given scene. In most situations, the lighting must also be balanced in such a way that the desired objects in the scene are brighter than undesired scene objects. Both of these considerations involve the amount of light, an increase in which requires an increase in current through the circuits providing power.

When estimating the amount of light required, remember that varying times of day, varying weather conditions and varying distances from large reflective objects (like white or mirrored buildings) will have a significant impact on the quantity of natural light available during production.

Quality of Light

The quality of light is a very important factor when evaluating a potential production location. Television cameras see things differently than the human eye; different colors are seen with different intensities. To achieve a natural-looking television scene, the camera must be "color balanced" to match the characteristics of the human eye under similar lighting conditions.

Color balance is coarsely adjusted with colored filters between the lens and the camera's imaging devices (tubes or "chips"). Fine adjustment of color balance is performed with electronic "white balance" and "black balance" circuits in the camera. To make sure that a camera is properly adjusted for a particular scene, it should be balanced immediately before the production is to be taped.

Mixing several types of light creates mixed results in the picture. In general, only one type of light source (tungsten, sunlight, quartz-halogen, etc.) should be used in any given scene. Fluorescent light sources should be avoided. If there is a mixture of light source, it is usually best to try to overpower with light from one source. In office production environments, it is common practice to place large gels on windows and overpower fluorescent lighting with quartz-halogen lamps.

When considering the quality of light in a given scene, remember that varying times of day, varying weather conditions and varying distances from large reflecting objects will have a significant impact on the quality of light available during production. Nearby colored objects will reflect colored light onto objects in the scene.

Light Intrusions

Short-term lighting variations may be introduced by nearby automobile traffic, rapidly moving clouds, diesel exhaust or any of a number of other moving objects. It may be desirable to place light-blocking material between the production area and traffic or other such measures in an attempt to reduce the influence of short-term lighting variations.

Sound

Quantity of Sound

In most productions, the perceived amount of sound coming from the desired source must be higher than the amount of sound coming from any undesired source. This may be controlled by selecting a different microphone (a "shotgun" instead of a lavaliere) or it may be controlled by increasing the amount of desired sound (louder talent) or it may be controlled by decreasing the amount of undesired sound (with baffles, etc.). The final result is to increase the volume of the desired sound while reducing the volume of the undesired sound.

In investigating potential production locations, look for loud noise generators like pedestrian, automobile, train and aircraft traffic and fans. Remember that there are daily variations in the amount of sound from these and other source—it may be most desirable to shoot on a weekend or at other non-business times.

Quality of Sound

The quality of the desired sound is an important consideration in evaluating a production location. Microphone placement and technique must be carefully evaluated for the particular scene. In general, the closer the microphone is to the desired sound source, the better; conversely, the farther away the microphone is from the desired source, the louder other sounds will seem.

Beware of locations that impart an echo to the sound. There is no practical way in which a "barrel sound" or other reflective sound distortion can be corrected. Some sound distortions may be corrected with equalization and "sweetening" during post-production, but getting the best possible quality during production is critical for consistently good results.

Sound Intrusions

There will always be short-term intrusions into the desired sound that are created by outside sources. Emergency sirens, noisy aircraft, noisy automobiles and noisy crowds are common sources of undesired noise.

To reduce the quantity of some of these undesired noise sources, dial out on telephones, employ crowd control, shoot on weekends or in the dead of night, shoot when the wind is from a particular direction (near airports) or employ other sound-stopping measures.

Equipment Logistics

The quality of equipment used during production is usually secondary to the environmental considerations of a potential production location. Under certain circumstances, however, the quality of the equipment will drive the quality of the released product. In most situations, the quality of the equipment is driven by the quality of maintenance performed on that equipment.

Production Equipment

Production equipment should be checked from stem to stern to try to make sure that it will operate in the field. Some of the things to check are as follows:

Lenses

Check a zoom lens for smooth operation from wide-angle to telephoto. Make sure that the lens is clean. Use a brush and bulb blower (or compressed air) to remove granular particles. Use moistened lens cleaning tissue to remove filmy residues (like fingerprints). Check for installation of a clear filter on the front of the lens. This will protect the expensive front lens element from getting scratched.

Popular lens filters to have to handle production demands are:

- *Neutral Density* filter, used for exposure control in bright light situations
- *Conversion* filters, used for converting various light sources such as fluorescent lighting into daylight
- *UV Haze* filter, reduces excess blue caused by haze and ultraviolet rays
- *Softnet* filter, used to create a soft focus effect
- *Polarizer* filter, outdoor color filter reduces glare and saturates colors

Check with the **Tiffen Manufacturing Corporation** (Hauppauge, NY) for detail listing of filters used for special production requirements. They also have a helpful videotape available entitled "Which Filter Should I Use."

Cameras

- Check the viewfinder for proper operation.
- Check registration on a tube-type camera. Confirm the operation of any "auto registration" or "auto shift" circuits. Confirm proper registration across the entire picture (particularly in the corners).
- Check color bars and live picture for proper colorimetry. Confirm the operation of any "white balance" or "black balance" circuits.
- Check the condition of all cables and connectors.
- Have a technician adjust the camera or make any repairs necessary for proper operation.

Videotape Recorder (or recorder circuits in a Camcorder)

- Record and play back a test recording to make sure that the recorder circuits are operating properly.
- If available, play back an "alignment tape" to make sure that the recorder is still in "interchange."
- Have a technician adjust the recorder if there is any sign of a tracking (flashing horizontal lines in the picture) or skew error (with a top that is bent over).

Picture Monitors

- Confirm operation and adjust for proper display of color bars.
- Check framing for overscan (normal) operation. Have a technician adjust if the picture is not centered or geometrically distorted in any way.

Waveform Monitors

A waveform monitor is a test device that provides an accurate picture of the video signal coming from the camera. The waveform monitor is used to measure the timing and amplitude of vertical and horizontal lines and includes measurements of horizontal blanking, horizontal sync, burst, vertical blanking, vertical sync and special tests for differential gain, frequency response and chrominance to luminance gain. It is an advantage to have a waveform monitor on location shoots to ensure that the color camera is set up and operating correctly and providing the best possible picture under the shooting conditions.

- Use only with a precision 75-Ohm termination.
- Confirm calibration to the internally generated calibration signal.
- Have a technician check and calibrate the unit every eighteen months.

Support Equipment and Supplies

Cables

Do not crimp, tightly bend or flatten cable. Confirm reliable continuity of cable and connectors. Regularly replace cable that is frequently used under harsh conditions, and immediately replace power cables that have frayed, cracked, or damaged insulation.

Tripods

Keep clean and check for smooth operation of the head.

Lamps

Never touch a lamp (cold or hot) with bare fingers.

Batteries

Maintain according to manufacturer's recommendations. (NiCad batteries are usually kept charged.) Keep away from heat.

Videotape

Repack (fast forward to the end, then rewind to the beginning) fresh tape before initial use. Keep away from strong magnetic fields. Store and use at a constant temperature and humidity. Do not touch, stretch or fold the tape.

Ditty Bag

Another film term applied to the video world, the *ditty bag* (a little dis and a little dat) is another important item to take along. The ditty bag contains all of the items you wished you would have brought along:

- extra lamps
- gaffer tape
- extra video tape
- small make-up kit
- clothes pins and special fasteners for lights that are often found at your local hardware store
- string, rope, rubber bands, masking tape and knife
- small kit of tools
- flashlight and batteries (also batteries for mics)
- clipboard for logs and script
- extra production forms and talent release forms
- pens, pencils and markers
- small first-aid kit
- camera filters and lens cleaning kit
- and every conceivable technical adapter you can think of

EQUIPMENT

There are many equipment considerations on a shoot. The most important ones include:

- a shooting equipment check-out list to ensure that you bring everything you need to the production
- equipment operation check-out list, to ensure that all of your equipment is operating correctly
- arrangements need to be made in advance for transportation of equipment
- advance arrangements for loading and unloading equipment at the location
- staging of equipment at the location, appropriate space for unloading, setting up and checking out the equipment before it is taken to the set
- hauling equipment to the actual site; usually a large dolly or hand truck is needed to transport the equipment to the staging area and to the shooting locations
- advance arrangements to secure the equipment

Refer to Form 14, Form 15, Form 16 for examples of remote production checklists that will help organize equipment for a remote shoot.

REMOTE SHOOT CHECKLIST

Camera and Accessories
☐ Camera(s): _____

☐ Camera batteries   ☐ AC adapter-battery charger

☐ Video cable (camera-to-recorder) ☐ BNC-to-BNC (for emergencies)

☐ White card   ☐ Registration card

☐ Tripod & plate   ☐ Screwdriver (small standard "tweaker")

Recorder and Accessories
☐ Recorder(s): _____

☐ AC adapter/charger   ☐ Power supply-to-wall cord

☐ Power supply-to-recorder cord   ☐ Recorder batteries

☐ Tool kit   ☐ Cassettes

Monitor and Accessories
☐ Monitor(s):   ☐ Color   ☐ B/W

☐ Video BNC-to-BNC   ☐ Battery/AC cord

☐ Audio cable 3-pronged to mini

Microphones and Accessories
☐ Mics (specify number/type): _____

☐ Batteries   ☐ Head set w/ adapters

☐ Wind screens   ☐ Table stands

☐ Tie clips   ☐ Audio cable

☐ Adapter box

Lights and Accessories
☐ Light kit # _____   ☐ Gloves

☐ Diffusion material   ☐ Extra lamps

☐ Clips   ☐ Light stands

Miscellaneous
☐ Masking tape   ☐ Power Mate reels & drop cords

☐ Duct tape   ☐ Labels, pen

☐ Cue cards   ☐ Extra scripts

FORM XV

VIDEO PRODUCTION CHECKLIST

Format
Location

- ☐ 1"
- ☐ Studio
- ☐ 3/4"
- ☐ H.O.
- ☐ BetaCam/BetaCam SP
- ☐ Location

CAMERA

Type (specify) _____   ☐ Electrical Ext.

Cords _____   ☐ Tripod

Mode
- ☐ EFP   ☐ Shoulder Mount
- ☐ ENG
- ☐ Studio   ☐ Monitor,
- ☐ Camera Cable   Size _____

Power
Connectors   ☐ Filters
- ☐ AC Adapter   ☐ Spare Video
- ☐ Battery (full charge)
- ☐ Recharger   ☐ Tools

VTR

☐ Studio VTR   Power
-     ☐ AC
☐ Portable VTR   ☐ Battery

☐ Adapter
Electrical Ext. Cords
(full charge)

AUDIO

Microphone(s)   ☐ Mixer
- ☐ Shotgun
- ☐ Conference Mic.   ☐ Headphones
- ☐ Audio Ext. Cables (3 feet)

    Mic. Stand

Other _____   ☐ Floor
    ☐ Table

FIELD EQUIPMENT CHECKLIST

☐ CAMERA ☐ LENS TISSUE ☐ BATTERIES

☐ TRIPOD ☐ DOLLY/TRACK ☐ RECORDER

☐ BATTERIES ☐ HEAD CLEANING SUPPLIES

MICROPHONES

☐ LAV ☐ SHOTGUN ☐ HAND HELD ☐ BATTERIES

☐ BOOM ☐ MOUNT ☐ BOOM ADAPTER

☐ MIC MIXER ☐ MIC CABLES & ADAPTERS

☐ COAX CABLE EXTENSIONS

☐ HEADPHONES

☐ VIDEO MONITOR ☐ CABLE TO VTR ☐ BATTERIES

☐ LIGHTS ☐ LIGHT METER ☐ STANDS & CLAMPS

☐ SPARE LAMPS ☐ DULLING SPRAY ☐ SAND BAGS

☐ SCRIM ☐ REFLECTORS

☐ GELS – DAYLIGHT ☐ OTHER _____

☐ N.D.

☐ FOAM CORE ☐ BLACK MATERIAL

☐ POWER BAR

☐ AC POWER CABLES ☐ 3 PRONG ADAPTERS

☐ GAFF TAPE ☐ WHITE TAPE ☐ BLACK TAPE

☐ LADDER ☐ SCISSORS ☐ STAPLE GUN

☐ C-CLAMPS ☐ MAKE-UP KIT

☐ STRING ☐ ROPE ☐ BLACK CORD

☐ TOOL KIT ☐ PLASTIC TO COVER EQUIPMENT

☐ VIDEO TAPE ☐ SLATE ☐ LOG SHEETS

Figure 6 – 1
Equipment check-out and logistics planning will help assure a successful field production.

Often productions require the rental of special equipment such as special filters or lenses for the camera, tripods and mounts for the camera, dolly sound equipment and lighting equipment. As corporations downsize, equipment rental is becoming more and more important. Why have equipment that will be outdated in a year? Rent just what you need when you need it. And of course do not forget tape stock. Figure how many tapes you will need by your shooting schedule (more on that later) and add two.

CREW

In the pre-production meeting communicate the concept and "look" of the program. Each crew member will have contributions in each of his/her areas of expertise. It's also important to deal with individual crew concerns at this time and walk the crew through a typical shooting day for this production. If overtime is expected, be sure to communicate that up front so individual arrangements can be made. Also briefly "pre-direct" the program by communicating your directing style (if you are to direct the program) and letting the crew know what you expect of each of them. Give the crew a feeling for the client, the program objective, the viewing audience and the hoped for results of the program. A good crew is as concerned as you are about producing a good program that will communicate clearly to the audience, so give each member as much background information as possible regarding the program. This will allow them to contribute their best effort to the production.

The pre-production meeting will also determine crew assignments and whether outside resources are needed. Communicate the schedule to the crew, discuss special situations and anticipated problems. This meeting is used to start building the "team." The team will spend lots of time together during production. A smooth production will happen if the team is working together, anticipating needs and problems and contributing his/her area of expertise.

Figure 6 – 2
Each member of the crew will have excellent, creative contributions for production. Plan time in pre-production to discuss projects with each crew member.

To look at different assignments or roles during a production it is best to look at each assignment in detail. Often one person may wear several hats such as a producer/writer/director/director of photography and production assistant. In this instance, one person really produces, writes, shoots, gets the coffee and edits the entire production alone. Obviously, this type of situation can create problems in scheduling and creativity because few people have all the talents it really takes to entirely produce a program from idea to duplication.

However, for larger productions or facilities, specific skills in the writing and design area are used as are specific skills in lighting, directing, shooting, technical support and editing. Obviously the larger the budget or the larger the facility the more specialized you can get with the talents and skills needed for production. The skills listed below are specialized within themselves and require much schooling and practice to achieve an acceptable performance. Television production requires the skills of many.

SKILLS USED IN TELEVISION PRODUCTION

Producer/Project Manager: The Producer is usually responsible for the entire project from concept to distribution. A good manager of people and resources, the producer will control the finances and have the resources to achieve the end result (a program). The producer is also responsible for the project's success. Often the producer will act as the project manager.

Director: The director implements the producer's idea by assigning tasks to other members of the production team. He or she must plan and explain set designs, shooting requirements, staging, lighting, audio and technical video requirements. The director is usually responsible for the aesthetic or artistic direction and "look" the program takes, and communicating this direction to talent and crew. The director is responsible for working with the talent and crew to record on tape the action the script requires or interpreting the action to best take advantage of the medium. There should be only one director on the set in charge of the production crew.

Production Assistant (Assistant Director): In a complex program there may be countless things that need to be coordinated, such as talent, locations, props, travel, insurance forms, union forms, etc. The production assistant, working closely with the director, will coordinate these important details. The PA will provide on-set problem solving, preparing all of the shooting elements in advance so that the director can concentrate on directing.

Director of Photography: Responsible for the camerawork and lighting, the director of photography brings an artistic talent to the production and executes the aesthetic and technical demands of the script and director. Skilled in camerawork and lighting, the director of photography captures the pictures, moods and aesthetic requirements of the director and contributes years of experience to the overall program "look." As a director, it is a joy to work with a talented director of photography, because you know the aesthetic "look" you want is being achieved technically, and you can concentrate on talent performance and client relations.

Engineer/Technician/Tape Operator: The engineer or technician is responsible for checking the equipment before the shoot and assuring the director of technical quality during the shoot. If a malfunction of equipment (it always seems to happen during an imprint shoot) comes up, the technician can fix or replace the problem gear. The technician is good insurance to have for the equipment on a large shoot.

Sound Recorder (Audio Engineer): Responsible for sound quality, the audio engineer selects proper microphones and placement, sets and monitors sound levels, often operates shotgun microphones attached to "fish poles," and works with wireless mics. In addition, the audio engineer may select sound effects and music for the production. A good audio engineer can contribute significantly to the overall audio quality of the production, assure consistent sound and troubleshoot audio problems during the shoot.

Lighting Director: The lighting director designs the lighting "look" based on the script and director's requirements. He or she selects the proper lighting instruments to accomplish the lighting objective and works closely with the video engineer to ensure that the quality of light selected will adequately expose the scene to the cameras.

Gaffer: Often a technical position, the gaffer (on some shoots this position is referred to as the electrician) will tap into building power for proper current for the production, set lights required by the lighting director and generally assist in accomplishing the lighting objective.

Key Grip: On larger shoots, especially film shoots, the key grip will create lighting effects and handle the scrims and gels that go in front of the lighting instruments for special lighting requirements.

Make-up/Stylist: Responsible for the make-up and hairstyle of performers, a trained make-up artist keeps the talent looking good in front of the camera. Food stylists are responsible for food shots and scenes.

Scriptwriter: Interpreting content material into the language of television is the scriptwriter's job. It takes a special talent to write for video, and this talent usually shows up on the screen. The single most important element of the entire production process is the script. If it is a good one that engages the audience all other production elements are secondary. The scriptwriter writes dialog and creates images that bring the message to the audience in the medium of television.

Continuity/Script Supervisor: Rarely do we have the luxury of continuity in video productions made for corporations. But continuity is a position always found in feature films and large commercial productions. Continuity is responsible for the continuity of the program. Continuity tracks changes in the script during production and keeps notes of any deviations from the script. Continuity also keeps track of the camera angles used for each shot, camera and talent movement and staging, lighting set-ups and talent costumes, assuring that all of these elements stay in harmony so problems do not arise in editing.

Wardrobe/Props: In large productions there are people responsible for wardrobe for the talent and props used on the set. These are specialized skills that greatly contribute to the overall success of the program.

A tip for good pre-production planning is to know the jobs of each crew member and prepare work for them in advance. Know what *you* want in advance, so that you can communicate these requirements to the crew. The crew can immediately spot an ill-prepared director. Not being prepared puts an extra burden on everyone involved. Being prepared helps the production go smoothly, helps morale and creates efficiencies of production.

SCHEDULING

This section is possible thanks to conversations with Tom Kennedy and his book, *Directing Video*, about directing.

Once you have the script complete with the script breakout and shot list, a production schedule can be created. To do this the director will assign specific amounts of time for each shot. Shooting logistics will require different amounts of time for specific shots. When special shooting requirements such as a dolly move, a unique lighting set-up or a difficult move with the camera and talent is required, more time will be allotted for the shot. Once you have assigned time for each shot, group the shots into hourly or time frames based on the eight-hour working day. Group shots by early morning shots, mid-morning, early afternoon and afternoon. Relate the grouped shots to the hours available in the day. This will tell you how many actual days of production are needed to record all required shots. If budget doesn't allow for this new production schedule, negotiations begin with the client to shave down production time by better grouping shots, allowing less time for some shots, decreasing the shot requirement (such as not using a dolly shot that was called for in the script) or eliminating some shots altogether.

Be realistic in your shot breakout and in allocating time for shooting. It almost always takes longer than you first imagine to shoot the scenes. Experience will help you get an edge on the time it takes to shoot a particular scene, but at first be cautious and allow plenty of time for shooting.

Once this time breakout is created, a production schedule emerges. This schedule details hour for hour the production day; based on this schedule a final overall production schedule can be created. This final schedule will include:

- arrival time for the crew at the location
- additional arrival times for other crew members such as make-up or rental equipment
- talent and client arrival time
- set-up time for the first shot
- meal breaks

- special times during the production day when extra talent or experts are to arrive
- time breakouts for each new location, when the crew is to arrive at each location and the time of the first set-up at that location
- finish time and breakdown and travel time for each location
- release time for talent and crew

Production Notebook

As I mentioned in Chapter 1, I find it helpful to start a notebook with each production. The notebook helps me with all the details of production (logistics, talent, crew schedules and equipment) from script changes to site survey notes to important telophone numbers related to the shoot. The notebook keeps things together where I can find them and helps me get organized for the shoot. The production notebook starts on the first day with the names of key people involved with the project and telephone numbers, notes I've taken at the first development meeting and lists of things I will need at the next meeting. From there the notebook goes to the second and third development meeting and finally has the storyboard and script. The notebook goes with me on the site survey, and I jot down special shooting requirements for the location (power, sound and logistics problems) and travels with me to the first pre-production meeting I have with the production team, where I refer to all my notes and discuss the various site problems. The notebook is an indispensable tool that I constantly refer to at all hours of the day.

There are many computer programs that assist with the details of production. I cover some of these programs in more detail in Chapter 10. These computer programs help the video producer with everything from scheduling to scripting to logging to editing. They are very valuable tools for the producer.

TALENT

The next section under our pre-production meeting is arranging for talent. If you are working with in-house talent, the most important thing you will discuss with them will be the schedule. Let them know in advance when you are planning to rehearse and shoot the program. Be realistic with them and let them know how much actual time it will take to do the shooting. In-house talent are usually unfamiliar with the production process and do not realize how long it actually takes to shoot a five-minute scene. If good front-end communication doesn't take place, problems can arise at the scene when the talent is not prepared for the hour it will actually take.

Also be sure to communicate the importance of keeping to schedules with crew and talent. If the first scene takes more time than planned to shoot, it will throw the rest of the schedule off and cause problems throughout the day. If talent shows up late or has to stop in the middle of shooting to attend a quick meeting or make a call, this will affect the schedule and cause problems with other departments as you show up late at their locations. It is difficult to shift the schedule even by half an hour when so many elements are involved (talent, departments expecting you at a certain time, product or props being readied for a certain time, lunch being moved back, making the crew grouchy and extending crew times into overtime) These problems occur when the schedule changes. It is the producer/director's responsibility to stay on time if possible. If he sees the schedule slipping, special arrangements must be made ahead of time with the next location. The client should be informed that the shooting schedule may be extended and the budget may be affected because of overtime or extended shooting days.

While shooting a training video for a large mining company in Arizona, my production company experienced several production delays that added to the overall cost of the program. The delays were a result of having to shoot a few scenes near the highway where the company is located. Our client assured us that since we were on or near their property, there would be no problem shooting the scenes. However, because we were near the road, we found out at the last minute, that traffic control was required by the police. It took us several hours to arrange for a police officer to be present on the scene. A simple call to the local police department before the shoot could have saved hours of down time. Assume nothing.

Talent Release Forms

When a person's image or voice appears in a video program, to be able to use that image the person needs to release the "rights" or permission to use the images. The talent release form allows the producer (or sponsor, client or company producing the program) to record (or capture the voice and image of) any talent used in the program. It provides the permission to use the images and allows the producer to own the images. The releases describe the extent and nature of the permitted uses of the talent's appearance in the program and if they received compensation for the release. Producers should **always** obtain release forms from all talent used in the program whether they are professional talent or in-house talent. Corporations should keep a blanket release form in the personnel files of all employees so the producer does not have to get a release every time an employee is used in a video, ad or voice narration.

CASTING

I would like to thank Rob Tat for contributing to this section.

Another element in the pre-production phase of working with talent is the auditioning and casting of professional talent. The casting process starts with the script. The writer, as part of the scripting process, writes *character descriptions* for the various parts or the client will request certain "characters" to be included in the program.

Each character description would include information such as personality characteristics and particular physical type or look that would be important to the script. Often times these character descriptions can be rather fun and amusing. I once produced a training series for a large consumer products company, and the client wanted to show how *not* to make a sales call. I wrote the incorrect approach and "modeled" this approach by writing in a character who portrayed the competition. We had fun with this character, having him do all the wrong things at a sales call. We used professional talent for this one character (all the others in the program were in-house talent), so there would be no repercussions after the program was produced. The audience could identify with the talent but could not recognize him being on staff. This approach added credibility to the program.

Figure 6 – 3
Producer/Director Robert Tat (far right in picture) discusses scene with talent on location for corporate video production.

Talent and Casting Agencies

Once the characters have been written into the script, you will proceed to fill the roles. Usually you will contact a talent agency or casting director. A talent agency is a business that represents talent. They earn their money on a commission basis by booking talent. Actors go to them, make a presentation and try to get represented by an agency. If the agency feels they can successfully book that talent and earn enough money to make the association worthwhile, they will take them on.

Sometimes talent agencies are exclusive with an individual talent and other times they are not. In smaller or medium sized markets, there may be just a few agencies and talent may be booked with more than one agent. In larger markets, the agencies become much more specialized and talent would generally become exclusive with a particular agency. In large markets like Los Angeles, Chicago or New York there are hundreds, maybe thousands of talent agencies, and they are very specialized. There will be a talent agency that will specialize just in kids for commercials, or kids under five for commercials. Or they may specialize in voice work or talent for comedic commercials. An actor will generally be exclusive with an agency with a particular specialty in L.A.

Casting directors do not represent individual talent. Their job is to do the casting process for a director. If you were to submit a script and the character descriptions to a casting director, he would choose from all the different sources of talent he has available to him from the various agencies and put together selections for you. (In a larger market, it would be impossible to cast without a casting director. You would have to call hundreds of agencies to cast for a roll because of the exclusivity of the arrangement there. In a smaller market where you have just a few agencies, you could ask the major agencies to submit talent to you and then cast through them all).

Working without a casting director requires the director to do all the casting work him/herself. The casting director would find people for you, audition them on videotape, show you the selected few, and then you would make the decision. It's nice to be able to work with a casting director. They save the director time, and it draws in a level of expertise

113

and knowledge about the availability of individual people that the director probably does not have, since the director does not deal with the casting problem every day as the casting agents do.

The casting agents of course make it their job to know talent, to know who's out there, to know what they can do, and who's good, so they are equipped to help the director make an informed choice.

We have the script, and we have the character description. Now we're going to submit these to either the agencies or the casting director with whatever other guidelines we might have for the talent. For example, for a project I just worked on, there were considerable lines to learn, so I needed actors who could memorize lines. I needed experienced actors. I was not willing to go with less experienced people. A lot of the agencies have models who can sort of act, and they're okay if they need to just do a line or two, but you wouldn't want to use them in a major role.

Based on the character descriptions the agent sends *composites*. These are photographs of the talent, head shots. They are called composites because usually on the back of the photo there will be a montage of four or five photographs of the same actor in different kinds of looks or in different costumes showing the range of their "look" and their style. Attached to that is the resume. When the agencies send these composites to you, these are referred to as submissions.

When you receive the composites, you'll go through them and pick people who have the basic look that the script calls for or what your client has in mind for a character. As you review the photos, look carefully at the resume. You'll want to know if the people you're choosing for the first "cut" have the experience (in acting for video) you need. You'll want to see what kind of training they've had. Have they been to acting school, have they had industrial roles or have they just "modeled" for still photos?

Talent will often list acting credits in feature films, but they may only be as background or "extras." If they've only done stage work, it might be difficult working with them in a video environment. They may not understand some of the intricacies of working single camera productions, continuity issues between different shots, different angles, the necessity to repeat the same body language and the same read on the different takes, as well as some of the issues around shooting film style. These are some of the things you can tell from reading the *resumes*. Resumes will generally list education and experience—industrial, film, stage or feature film experience—and these items need to be scrutinized.

So now you've culled down the submissions to a few people that you want to audition. Be sure that you have an ample number of people to audition, because no matter how good people look on the resumes, sometimes when you audition them they are not what you are looking for. So you want to have several choices. Forms 17 and 18 will help you in the resource selection process. Forms 19, 20 and 21 are examples of release forms.

Auditions

The next step in the process is setting up an *audition*. This could be at the agency, at the casting director's office, at your own office or wherever you want to do it. What you need is a waiting area for the talent and a separate room where you can hold the auditions. You want to videotape the auditions to see what the talent looks like on screen, if they

FORM XVII

FREELANCE REFERENCE DATA INPUT

1. NAME: _____

2. PHONE NUMBER: _____

3. SOCIAL SECURITY NUMBER: _____

4. PRIMARY SERVICE CODE: (circle as many as apply)

1. Artist	9. TelePrompTer Operator
2. Camera Operator	10. Video Editor
3. Film Editor	11. Writer
4. Floor Manager	12. Video/Film Production Houses
5. Lighting Consultant	13. Producer Services
6. Maint./Production Engineer	14. Photographic Processing
7. Producer/Director	15. Set Const. & Design
8. Talent	16. Other

5. NAME, FIRM, OR AGENCY PAYABLE: _____

6. FEDERAL ID#: _____ 7. PHONE NUMBER: _____

8. STREET ADDRESS: _____

9. CITY: _____ 10. STATE: _____ 11. ZIP: _____

12. COMMENTS: (describe "other" if circled)

FORM XVIII

TALENT AUDITION SHEET

Applicant's Name: _____ Phone #: _____

Address: _____

_____ Zip: _____

Agent's Name: _____

Please give details of past acting experience:

Will you be available during the weeks of   ?

Can you drive a car (automatic transmission)?

Can you memorize large segments of script at a time?

Interests:

Comments:

Are you a current member of AFTRA and / or SAG?

FORM XIX

RELEASE and AUTHORIZATION to
PHOTOGRAPH or OTHERWISE RECORD

I, the undersigned, do hereby consent to being photographed or otherwise recorded by

_____ , or any of its affiliates, and I also give

_____ permission to put the finished

photographs, films, or videotapes, to any legitimate uses it may deem proper. Further, I

hereby relinquish and give to _____   _____ all right,

title and interest I may have in the finished pictures, negatives, reproductions and copies of

the original prints and negatives, and further grant _____

the right to give, sell, transfer and exhibit the negatives, original prints or copies and

facsimiles thereof to any individual, business firm, or publication or to any of their assignees

and to circulate the same for any and all purposes and in any manner, including

publications and advertisements of all kinds in all media.

I, the undersigned, do hereby further agree and acknowledge that I have not, and

will not claim to have, either under this agreement or otherwise, any right, copyright, title, or

interest of any kind or nature whatsoever, in and to any program of films or videotapes

taken by _____ in which I appear, including

but not limited to the scripts, title, copyright, ideas, names, theses and / or the other

characteristics and incidents of any such program of _____ ;

and such rights are recognized to be in _____ ,

its successors, agents, licenses, customers and assigns.

I further hereby release _____ , its

associates, successors and assignees, from any and all claims for damages for libel,

slander, invasion of the right of privacy, or any other claim based on the use of said

material.

This release is made on behalf of myself, my heirs, executors, administrators and

assigns, and is to be governed by the laws of the State of _____ .

_____
Signature

_____
Date

_____
Witness

117

FORM XX

RELEASE I

For valuable consideration received, I hereby grant to _____ _____ , its successors and assignees and those acting under its permission or upon its authority, the unqualified and unconditional right and permission to use all videotape productions in which I have and will be involved, and hereby release any and all property I may have therein.

Executed at _____ on the
                               (city)

_____day of _____ 19 ____.

_____   _____
           Witness   Signature

FORM XXI

RELEASE II

The undersigned does hereby consent to the photographing of the undersigned, together with any subject matter owned by the undersigned, and does hereby authorize

_____ and its successors and assignees, to cause the resulting photographs to be sold, exhibited or otherwise used, for purposes of advertising, trade or otherwise, as still photographs, transparencies, motion pictures, television or other media or means of reproduction, transmission or exhibition. The under-signed does hereby release _____ , its employees, agents, associates, successors and assignees, from any and all claims for damages or compensation or libel, slander, invasion of the right to privacy, or any other claim based on the use or sale of said material. The undersigned does hereby waive any right to inspect, approve or edit said material or any descriptive or advertising material used in connection therewith.

_____
Date

_____
Signature

_____
Witness

can project their personality onto the screen. When you're auditioning, watch the monitor to see how they're coming across on screen.

Another reason for videotaping is to watch the auditions again, get another sense of what they were like, and compare them. In the case of industrials, you also want to be able to show your client who the selected talent are, so the client can take part in the decision.

Generally the talent is scheduled at ten or 15-minute intervals. If there are two people reading together in a script, you might want to schedule them simultaneously, so they can read in pairs. Have the parts marked in the script, so when they arrive they can start to study the part. Some agents like to have you send scripts out in advance to the talent so they have more time to become familiar with the material.

When you call them in, tell them a little about the program and the role, the type or style of the character you're looking for. The actors will do a first or cold read. Videotape that, then ask them to do it again and provide some direction this time. This will show how well they take direction and if they're able to build it into the performance.

There are other ways to audition talent, which are a little bit more creative. Some feature directors won't have the talent read actual lines. They'll have them come in and do some kind of improvisation. They want to see how good they are at getting into a character. They might ask the actor to give them an idea of what they think the subtext would be of this character or have them do an acting exercise. But that's a bit of a luxury, because the industrial scripts don't have that much character development built into them, and you generally don't have the time to spend.

Another thing to be aware of in the auditioning process is that the actors have just a limited time with the script, so it's basically a "cold" read—and some actors are very good at cold reads while others are not. I've seen actors do a very impressive cold read, then when you hire them and get them on the set, they're terrible. All of their talent is in spontaneity. I've also seen actors who have done a very poor read, but I felt they had the talent I was looking for, and they could be developed. Once they were hired and had time to internalize the script, they were excellent. So it's often hard to know when you audition somebody whether they'll be good on the set. You just have to go with your gut feeling.

Try to have an assistant do the actual videotaping, so you can concentrate on the performance. I usually make notes and score the talent on a scale of one to five. By the end of the audition, you'll usually have a sense of who your picks are or who the top two are for each role. Go back and watch the tape again, usually with the client, showing them your selections. Then make a decision or do a call back.

A *call back* is when you bring selected actors back to audition again, for example if you're not sure about someone's ability. They may have seemed right for the part but were a little bit weak during the reading. You might ask them to do it again after you work with them a little. If you're selecting people in pairs, you might want to call back two people who had not read together, so you can see how they work with each other.

Be sure to check with local talent unions and guilds about rules and regulations that pertain to the casting, audition and booking process. Often with union actors, you will not have to pay for an audition unless you keep the actor for more than an hour. Once you book them for a shooting date, you cannot cancel the date without having to pay them. So it's a good idea to check with the unions to find out fee structures, payment schedules and insurance rules.

Booking the Talent

After you *select the talent*, you book them. This would be done through the agent that represents the talent. Casting is ultimately the responsibility of the director. It's a crucial responsibility, and the success of the program rides heavily on the selection of the proper talent for the role.

Once the talent is booked, ask the talent agent to have them call you directly. Send them full scripts marked with their roles highlighted, with a copy of the character description. Also send them a copy of the shooting schedule, so they know how they fit into the schedule. When the talent calls you discuss:

- The role, answer any questions they may have, and talk about character development.
- Logistics, where the shooting will take place (location) travel, meals and parking.
- Wardrobe. If they're supplying their own, ask them to bring several color options, so you have choices about which looks best on camera or how the wardrobe looks against the other talent.
- Prompter. If you're using a TelePrompter, you still want them to become familiar with the script and not to depend on the prompter.
- Shooting style. If you are going to shoot out of sequence, explain which sections you'll be shooting first, so they can work on the lines in proper order.
- Make-up. Will there be a make-up artist or stylist on the set or should they come to the set with their own make-up? If you are planning to have a stylist or make-up artist on the set, be sure to allow time for the talent to be made-up. Make the talent morning call with make-up preparation in mind. The make-up artist will need an area away from the set to put on the make-up, it should be well lighted and comfortable for the talent. Once the make-up is on, the make-up artists and you will check it in front of the lights and camera. Once the make-up artist has made-up all the talent, the artist can either stay around for the duration of the shooting for make-up "touch-up" or be released.

Unions

If you work with professional talent through an agency, you will encounter talent unions. Talent may belong to either the Screen Actors Guild (SAG) or the American Federation of Television and Radio Artists (AFTRA). These unions provide talent contracts that provide for standard union working hours, rates, conditions, etc. Members will have formal, standard union paperwork for you to fill in and sign (W-4 forms, payroll, time cards, forms such as citizenship status, vouchers for travel, etc.) at the beginning and end of the production. As a producer you should become familiar with union contracts and talent agreements.

Pre-Production Planning
for Film, Multimedia and
Video Conferences

7

There is very little difference in the pre-production process for film, interactive multimedia development, teleconferencing and video. Whether you are in pre-production for a film or the video segments of an interactive program, the planning and pre-production is very similar to traditional video production. The elements of pre-production that we have discussed thus far will crossover well into film, interactive multimedia and teleconferencing. Yet there are a few differences that should be explained.

PRE-PRODUCTION FOR FILM

With a shooting ratio of 100 to 1 (that is, for every foot of film used in the final edited version at least 100 feet are shot in production) planning is paramount in film production. Often it is more important than in video, because it generally costs more to produce in film. Since you can't see what you shoot in film until after it is processed (unless you have video assist), a problem with a shot can require a re-shoot several days or months later. However there are only a few things that are different in the pre-production of film compared to pre-production of video.

Film producer/director Rob Tregenza of the Baltimore Film Factory in Baltimore, MD, assisted with this section. In a conversation with Tregenza he stated

> "Pre-production for film is not a lot different than it is for video. Obviously we have to plan for film stock, camera and lighting, but the planning stages are quite similar. We start with the concept, storyboard and script. From there we go to location surveys, equipment and talent arrangements, as we do with video shoots. It is advisable to order the film we are to use early and do a 'scratch' test with the camera to see if there are any camera problems. You should also schedule the processing lab early so they are prepared in advance for your film processing. But generally we cover the same planning steps as we do for video projects."

Often on film projects there are more detailed storyboards than with video. Again, we need to take more care because we do not have the luxury of instant playback in the field, unless the director of photography (DP) is using video assist. Video assist is a video camera attached to the film camera with a similar lens. The video camera image (similar to the film camera image) is recorded during the scene as the film camera is running. This video recording can be used to check continuity of action, camera angles, lighting and a host of settings the Director or DP can use for technical and aesthetic decisions. A shooting ratio of 7-1 is often quoted as an accepted ratio for video production as opposed to 100 to 1 with film. One reason this shooting ratio is less is the advantage of having video playback in the field. We can check our footage as we shoot it (however, it adds to production time and the possibility of recording over scenes you have already shot). Instant playback allows us to check the shots and correct errors before we leave the location or get to the editing process. Film on the other hand has to be processed before we see our images, so we tend to shoot at a much higher ratio covering all angles.

Tips for pre-production for film

How to Select a Lab

Be sure that the lab can offer a full line of services including video/film transfer. Often post-production of film used for broadcast is done through video editing. The film shot is transferred to video and edited through traditional video editing technology. With the introduction of the new *Kodak T* grain film, designed for film to tape transfer, the trend for high-end corporate information production is swinging back to film as the medium of choice for producers because of film's excellent quality.

Types of Film Stock and Selection

Both *Fuji* and *Eastman* have developed stock for video post-production. Select a stock that gives you as much speed as possible, so your lighting and grip package will cost less. But as with most production considerations, there is a trade-off. The faster the film, the more grain. If you have a limited budget and want 16 mm to look like 35 mm, you must shoot the finest grain 16 mm you can find.

Selection of Film Camera and Lenses

The trend today for film producers in film camera selection is to use cameras that can record time code on the film and the sound tape at the same time. This speeds up the sync process in post-production. Film is considered *double system sound*; sound is recorded on a separate recording device that may be a *DAT* (Digital Audio Tape) recorder or a 1/4" *Nagra* audio tape recorder. Most new 16 mm cameras also have a video assist which lets you record a videotape for editing off the film camera. 35 mm feature film camera design drives the 16 mm camera development as broadcast cameras drive the corporate video camera market.

Sound Considerations for Film Shooting

Recording sound for film is moving quickly to DAT. A thorough understanding of the sound recording process and how to obtain quality sound recording is even more important now because of the exceptional sound recording quality of DAT. DAT recording technology places emphasis on good recording techniques like mic placement, sensitivity to levels and background noises. As with video production, knowing how to operate the equipment is just the beginning. Applying good recording principles and creative techniques are the keys to success.

Directing Style for Film

There really isn't a different "style" for directing for film compared to directing for video other than video multi-camera set-up situations. Once you are shooting single camera video, you are directing in the "film" style. Most film post is moving to video editing and often to non-linear editing systems which is very close to film style editing.

PRE-PRODUCTION FOR INTERACTIVE MULTIMEDIA

Defining interactive multimedia is not an easy task. It is both a process and a solution. It is software programming and delivery technology. It is a development process and a presentation process. As Steve Floyd, author of the excellent book, *The IBM Multimedia Handbook*, states: "Think of multimedia computing as combining the emotional impact of broadcast media with the computer's processing power and the rich knowledge base of publishing."

Thanks to the computer, multimedia has highly interactive capabilities that are combined with high resolution color graphics, stereo sound, digitized images, full-motion video, animation and text to provide presentation and entertainment impact. Interactive multimedia applications range from computer-based presentations to computer games, from video conferencing to corporate training. Interactive multimedia can be delivered on desktop computers, in-store kiosks or corporate computer networks. It offers an abundance of training, communications and entertainment opportunities and video production is at the heart of successful multimedia applications.

New technologies that incorporate interactive capabilities influence the way we receive information and learn. Some of the numerous advantages of interactive technology for training and communications are:

ADVANTAGES OF INTERACTIVE TECHNOLOGY FOR TRAINING AND COMMUNICATION

- The process of interaction with content material provides strong learning reinforcement that significantly increases content retention.
- Interaction with material creates involvement with the learning.
- Students are learning at their own pace and control the sequence of learning.
- They are in control of the curriculum and direction the content takes and the amount of information they receive.

Time
- Interactive learning creates reduced learning time by an average of 50%. This can be attributed to:
  1. Interactivity creates the most efficient path to content mastering.
  2. The power of visuals and audio for clearer understanding.
  3. Good interactive programs provide constant, positive, highly effective reinforcement.
  4. Interactive learning provides for and accommodates different learning styles to maximize student training efficiency.

Consistency
- Provides consistent, reliable training delivery; does not vary in quality.

126

Reduced Costs
- Saves instructor time and student time because it takes less time to teach concepts.
- Reduces delivery costs (compared to classroom training when large numbers of students are involved and the training is repeated for many students), travel costs and time away from the job.
- Immediacy of training, bringing the training on-line when and where it is needed to decrease downtime.

In the seminars that I provide on interactive multimedia development, I present the concept of multimedia by introducing four areas of consideration, technology, development, production and delivery. Each area influences the other.

TECHNOLOGY

The use of interactive multimedia continues to grow in the training and education field. Technology choice is a reflection of audience demands, budget, equipment (platform) compatibility and multimedia program development resources. The training goals and audience demands should play a key role in the selection of technology.

The **PC** is a popular technology choice in the business environment and is the standard delivery technology in the training world. The **Macintosh** platform is popular in the multimedia development world. And there are also **dedicated** multimedia delivery technologies.

Two examples of dedicated delivery systems would be **CD-I** and **VIS. CD-I (C**ompact **D**isc-Interactive) is a low cost, self-contained interactive information delivery system based on a world standard and developed by Philips and Sony. It plays CD-I discs (full-motion, interactive video with CD quality audio), CD-Audio discs, Photo CD and CD-ROM-XA. CD-I has a computer on board with 1 megabyte of RAM, allowing interactive response and training management. CD-I hooks to any TV in the world. The Video CD format was written by Philips in conjunction with JVC and supported by Sony and Matsushita. **Video CD** is a similiar system that can be played back through a normal television set.

However, clearly the most popular delivery technology is CD-ROM, a good choice for now and into the future. **C**ompact **D**isc-**R**ead **O**nly **M**emory is an economical storage medium (650 MB of storage capacity) and has been a publishing and distribution medium for text, database, photo, graphics and video. CD-ROM can be fully integrated into a computer providing computer-based, interactive multimedia programming. Full-motion, digital video and CD quality audio coupled with interactive capabilities create a great future for the CD-ROM.

Technology choices affect multimedia development and delivery. Often we try to develop the program on the same platform that it will be delivered on as it simplifies the development and distribution process. However, this is becoming less of a concern with new authoring programs that allow you to develop on one platform (like the popular Macintosh) and deliver the multimedia program on the PC platform (also called multi-platform development). Corporate computer networks are also starting to handle the delivery of multimedia training and communications. Graphic enhancement cards, sound cards, video boards, storage capabilities and input devices all add to technology choices. Like setting up an effective video production system, multimedia technology requires professional analysis and consultation at an early stage of system development.

Interactive Multimedia Development

The development of interactive multimedia is a highly complex, sophisticated process incorporating diverse and varied disciplines of instructional design, scriptwriting, graphics and video production and computer programming. With its powerful interactive capabilities and its visual and aural impact, interactive multimedia development requires many skills and achieves many tasks. While it is beyond the scope of this book to go into the process of interactive multimedia development, there are a few pre-production steps that should be reviewed. As video producers you may be called upon to get involved with an interactive multimedia project.

The actual development of a multimedia project, like that of video, happens in phases. The phases appear to be similar to developing linear programs, classroom instruction, computer-based instruction or film projects. However, the world of interactive multimedia development is many times as complex as traditional media development.

The first phase is the front-end analysis or needs assessment. As I described in Chapter 2, for any media-based project, you have to thoroughly define the problem, the objectives and the audience. Once the problem has been defined, an approach to solving the problem is created. This I refer to as the program design. The program design is the road map (developmental guidelines) which the interactive program will follow in achieving its goals. Such factors as the scope of the project, interactive models, user requirements, environmental factors and viewing conditions, evaluation considerations and operating assumptions contribute to the program design.

The next step in the development cycle is creative design. I refer to this phase as the Production Design. Production Design encompasses all of the elements of navigation, moving easily between topics and exercises, screen layout and design conventions and flowcharts. Once the design is created, the creative development (production) begins; this is the creation of graphics, video/animation and sound elements.

The creative design process also includes crucial decisions in screen layout and design, text selection, colors, icon design and placement and many, many other considerations that are specific to the interactive process. When designing graphics and screens for interactivity, you are not just creating images that enhance the learning process but you are creating navigational devices, images to help the viewer navigate through the program. These graphics become tools for interactivity. Tools that allow the process of learning to happen.

Production

Production includes the management, design, acquisition and creation of production scripts, text elements, screen layout, graphics, audio, animation and video sequences. Production will also include authoring, prototype disc creation and mastering.

One big difference between planning for linear programming (traditional videotape productions) and interactive productions is the authoring process, needed because the program participant interacts with computers and input devices to advance within the program. Authoring brings together all of the elements that the user interfaces with to advance through a program. Some of these elements are video, graphics, animation, still frames, digitized images, text copy, voice and music. The user also interfaces with devices like the mouse, touchscreen, keyboard or joystick. All of these elements and devices along with feedback mechanisms, user controls, menus, course maps, help triggers and glossaries have to work together and are orchestrated through the authoring program built into the operating software.

There are many good multimedia authoring programs available commercially such as *Action! Authorware Professional* by Macromedia, Inc., *IconAuthor* by AimTech Corp., *Multimedia Toolbook* by Asymtrix Corp. and *Quest* by Allen Communications. Or, if you are versed in computer languages, you can write your own authoring software using multimedia software development tools for traditional programming languages. When selecting authoring software consider:

- The minimum system requirements—will the authoring software create programs for your delivery platform and equipment specifications?
- Scripting language—is the authoring language easy to follow and intuitive and does it allow for easy media integration for incorporating data, text, graphics, animation, sound and digital video?
- Authoring features—does the program allow for flexible and multiple branching capabilities, easy navigational linking, and offer security capabilities?
- Files—does the program allow for easy file manipulation, data management and retrieval and on-line help?
- Licensing arrangements—many authoring packages require runtime costs above the purchase price. Find out the costs of runtime versions and distribution licensing.

The authoring phase of multimedia development is a sophisticated process that usually requires the skills of a programmer adept at computer software languages. Each individual element of the interactive process has to be planned and thought through in detail to identify branching options, feedback for users, and any actions on the screen like graphic reveals, animation sequences and instructions for accessing the elements from storage devices. As you can see, interactive multimedia development is a complex process that takes tremendous amounts of planning.

Design Elements

Most multimedia projects share a few common elements. The **Title Page** sets the opening tone of your project. The **Table of Contents** provides a text-based overview of how your project is organized. A **Map** gives a quick, visual overview of how different parts of a project relate to each other. **Navigation Systems** provide a way to move from screen to screen, to return to the beginning of the project, to open the map, glossary and so on. The **Content** of a project includes the text, graphics, animation, video and sound. **Index or browsing capabilities** provide a means to search for information and provide for a glossary. And **Training management capabilities** enable students to control features, testing and evaluation.

Video Production for Multimedia

Special care should be taken in creating video for use in computer-based, multimedia applications. Analog video is digitized and stored on the computer hard drive for editing and insertion into multimedia programs. The video segment becomes a computer file as does audio, graphics and text. As video is digitized, it is compressed to reduce storage requirements and de-compressed for viewing from media such as CD-ROM. This compression/decompression factor affects video in many ways. The rule here is to produce your video segments on the highest quality recording format possible. If you digitize a grainy, low quality VHS or 8 mm video signal, the result will be a very low quality digitized video file.

Planning video production for use in multimedia programs involves considerations such as lighting approaches that do not add contrast to the picture that will affect image quality, and good sound recording techniques that reduce unwanted noise. Video and audio compression techniques often amplify picture noise from lighting conditions and poor sound recording. Busy backgrounds should be avoided, as they will add unwanted digital "noise" to the picture and drastically increase the data rate of the digital file. The compression process treats all picture elements as information, so busy backgrounds with much detail can over load memory and create "blocking" or choppy pictures. Motion in your shots, even camera movement, can create the same problem as well, slowing the compression process down and affecting picture quality. Plan slow, even camera moves, low contrast lighting and simple backgrounds for the best results for multimedia. Figure 7.1 is a sample multimedia program design from Authorware Professionals.

There are several good references that focus on video production considerations for multimedia development. One of the better books available is *Multimedia, Making It Work* by Tay Vaughan published by Osborne McGraw-Hill, Berkeley, CA. An excellent trade magazine that covers digital video production for multimedia is *Digital Video Magazine* published by TechMedia Publishing, Inc.

Creating a Prototype

It is important when producing interactive multimedia projects to create a prototype or sample working segment of the project. Certain authoring programs allow you to create sample flowcharts, screen designs and interactive branching designs that provide feedback into the usability of your designs. A prototype CD-ROM (often called "one-offs" or Beta check discs) can be created on CD-R, or Compact Disc Recorders. These low cost recording devices allow the user to burn sample CD-ROMs for test purposes. The prototype becomes a working model of a segmant of your program and allows everyone on the team to "test" the design early in the development phase before too much work has been done. The prototype provides an excellent "approval" tool for the project manager.

Mastering

In the last phase of production, the **mastering process**, the coded data of your multimedia computer program is placed onto a master

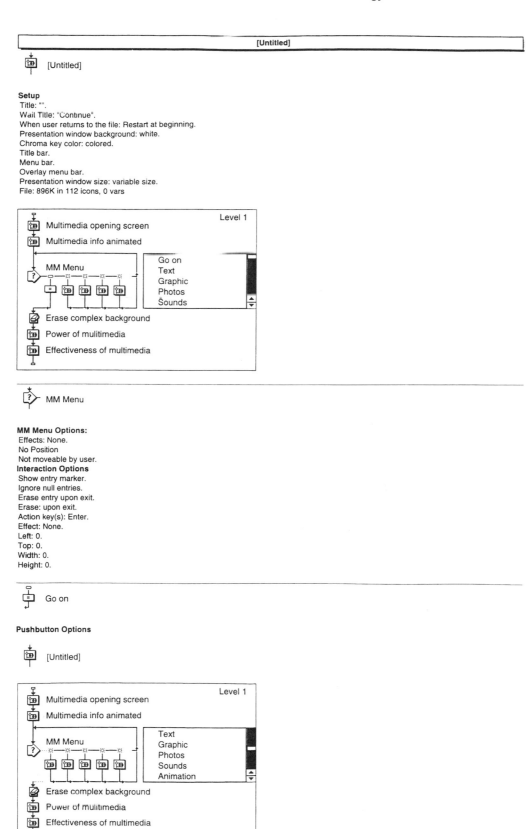

Figure 7 – 1
A sample multimedia program design from Authorware Professionals.

glass disc for replication onto a video disc or CD-ROM. The first step in the process is pre-mastering. The data is prepared to go onto the master disc and original media from a hard drive is transferred to a storage medium such as computer tape. This data is then placed onto the master glass disc that will eventually be used to create a plastic mold. The CD-ROMs will be "stamped" or replicated from this mold. After the disc is stamped it can be screen printed.

Since multimedia represents an interactive process, the student controls the pace, sequence and amount of information he wants to receive. The information (graphics, sound, video) is stored differently on the storage medium. It does not have to be stored in linear fashion (such as videotape or film) or in sequence according to the script. So storyboards become an important part of the flowcharting and authoring process. The multimedia storyboard is much more detailed than the traditional video or film storyboard because specific instructions on the boards direct authoring.

Packaging is next and you'll need to plan far in advance of this final step. The disc printing, packaging artwork, disc packages and collateral printed materials have to be ready for manufacturing and in the right channels at the right time. There are several companies that offer disc mastering and replication services. **3M Optical Recording** in St. Paul, MN, and **Disc Manufacturing Inc.** of Wilmington, DE, both have mastering facilities. **Disc Manufacturing** offers two good references that explain CD-ROM mastering and production and provide terminology. *Compact Disc Terminology* and *An Overview of Multimedia CD-ROM Production* can be obtained at no cost.

Delivery

The delivery phase of training technology development includes not only the technology choice and program delivery but also includes the student interface with the technology (computer, touch screen, mouse, keyboard, kiosk etc.). How will the student interface (interact) with the technology? Often overlooked, the interface issue is a real key to successful multimedia training delivery. Delivery considerations also include media storage, media platform compatibility, student interface, training management, networking and the evaluation process.

As Steve Floyd states, "Regardless of the visual treatment, motion video, still photo, graphics symbol, or text highlights, the goal remains the same—to improve a participant's understanding and to enhance his experience of the application.

"These twin goals of increasing understanding and enhancing the context of the experience are the roles of the program designer (understanding) and the art director (continuity and context). By working together, these two professionals can ensure that the design has a gestalt that pulls the elements of the interface together, making them more intuitive and giving them greater meaning. As a result, decisions about the graphics look—realistic versus abstract, or text versus icon, along with details such as font selections, sizing, placement and color combinations contribute to the participant's understanding. Otherwise the lack of visual continuity significantly undermines the integrated look of the program.

"In multimedia, the visual design of the interface is often the only cohesive force that can pull together so many seemingly unrelated elements. The visual interface establishes user conventions and reinforces the structure's intuitive nature. That's why it is so important to make sure that color selections complement the palette, that text is used in ways that are compatible with the other visual elements and that the background treatment is not too busy or distracting. Each of these factors represents unique solutions that should be transparent to the casual user. They should focus attention rather than compete with the message. When the navigation controls and message create a truly intuitive experience for the participant, you have achieved the right balance."

The development process is summarized below.

The interactive multimedia application development process

Development Model

Needs Analysis

Program Design

Program Development

Media Production

Interactive Authoring

Program Validation

Implementation

Process Review

In the application development process the **team approach is recommended.** The team usually consists of :

Project Manager: the person responsible for the overall management of the project and team.

Subject Matter Expert: the person responsible for the content of the program.

Design Team: usually consisting of an instructional designer (trainer), multimedia designer and computer programmer.

Production Team: usually consists of the graphics designer, audio and video producer and scriptwriter.

Development Process

Analysis Stage

Business goals

Audience analysis

Technology analysis

Needs/task analysis

General objectives

Team roles

Approval process

Design Stage

Preliminary program design document

Program structure

Treatment

Program delivery strategies

Budget, project plan and schedule

Development Stage

Content Development

Application Storyboards

Production Flowcharts

Video Storyboards

Audio Scripts

Asset Collection/Management

Graphic Roughs

Authoring Documentation

Production Stage

Audio, music selection, narration

Video, production elements

Graphics/animation creation

Documentation (printed support materials)

Production schedule

Post production, editing elements

Interactive authoring

Prototype

Quality check and test

Mastering

Duplication

Packaging

Validation Stage

Development plan for validation process

Purpose of validation

Methodology of validation

Validation instrument creation

Data collection

Criteria/feedback

Implementation Stage

Site preparation

Installation/training

On-going support

Updates (maintenance)

Process Review Stage

Review all stages

Determine how it could be done better

Document process check

Monitor results

PRE-PRODUCTION PLANNING FOR TELECONFERENCES

Definition

Teleconferencing has changed rapidly over the last few years and specific definitions are hard to come by. Teleconferencing generally applies to an electronic gathering of three or more individuals at two or more locations with a transmission of electronic information from point to point or point to multi-point. Teleconferencing is usually referred to as a variety of technologies to enhance distant communications including audio conferencing, video conferencing and business television. With newer types of electronic devices such as desktop computer teleconferencing, voice mail and fax machines, these types of technologies will affect how we define teleconferencing. However, for the purpose of this book I would like teleconferencing to refer to a non-entertainment application utilizing audio and video to facilitate the meeting of groups over a distance rather than one-on-one communications. Our definition here represents larger teleconference events and will not include new desktop computer teleconferencing.

Benefits

Traditional teleconferencing as we know it provides the following benefits:

1.   Reduced travel time and the costs associated with travel are often the first benefits associated with teleconferencing. But people soon realize that there are many more benefits as well.

2.   Presentations that are given once allowing everyone to hear the same information represent an efficient use of time. Getting current information out in a timely fashion is an important benefit of teleconferencing. New product introductions and legal or critical procedural changes that affect company-wide procedures are good examples.

3.   Access to broader resources or technical expertise for discussions around critical issues. Through teleconferencing this expert knowledge becomes available to decision makers no matter where they are. And technical information can become available to or be received from customers and suppliers as well.

4.   Increased communications frequency. Organizations that have teleconferencing capabilities in place tend to use them with increased frequency, thus increasing internal and external communication efforts.

135

5. Teleconferencing also tends to reduce the amount of time it takes to implement new projects or products. Being able to reach expert technical staff and out-based facilities increases productivity, reducing overall project development time and product development time. Increased productivity translates to faster decision making, better quality of decisions with more key decision makers involved and more resources available. With less time and travel involved in the project, cost efficiencies can be realized.

Changing business conditions and the global market has created the need for a worldwide communications strategy. To become successful companies have to compete in a global market, placing stress on internal and external communications. Teleconferencing allows a cost effective response to the new demands placed by global communications. Linking worldwide, diverse markets, employees and customers, teleconferencing facilitates change in the way corporations do business, and who they do business with. With geographically spread out businesses, manufacturing facilities and customers, teleconferencing allows a cost effective response.

Applications

Business Television

1. Business television usually refers to a corporate television network that uses satellites to distribute analog, full-motion video programming. Often the program is uplinked (transmitted to the satellite) at the corporate facility and downlinked (received) on small earth stations at distant locations. Business television networks usually involve the use of their own television facilities or rental facilities to generate, broadcast and receive the programs. Interactivity through telephone, fax, data response systems or electronic mail makes business television a limited two-way communications system from point to multipoint. Business television exists in many forms such as private networks in corporations and government agencies (there are over 150 dedicated private networks worldwide) or subscription networks to provide programming for specific industry segments.

Business television often broadcasts information vital to the ongoing business activities of the corporations and are often broadcast several times a month or, in the case of the Federal Express Corporation business network, daily. The information is often confidential and can involve productivity reports, market research data, financial data or production/manufacturing data that can be utilized by the organization to maintain its competitive advantage in the market place. Some of the activities that fall within this type of application could be board meetings, executive round tables, stockholder meetings, corporate strategy meetings, product development strategy and technical resource sharing for product development.

A large application of business television is training and education for staff and customers. Often business networks provide training and educational opportunities for a large and widely dispersed audience. Internal training programs can be distributed via teleconferencing or external programming can be accessed through larger networks and provided to internal and outbased staff. There are hundreds of business

Figure 7 – 2
Satellite dish used for business
television network application at
Tuscon Medical Center in Tuscon,
AZ.

networks utilizing the latest videoconference technology for training and
education.

Distance Learning

Distance Learning is the fastest growing application of teleconferencing. Virtually every university is involved in some form of distance
learning. Distance learning usually refers to the delivery of interactive
educational programming utilizing several forms of teleconferencing technology but generally incorporating analog, full-motion video with audio.

Many colleges and universities offer college credit courses that
extend beyond the campus through forms of teleconferencing. Stanford
University offers engineering courses via telecommunications throughout
the country. And many universities have their own educational networks;
the Educational Management Group, Indian School Road Complex in
Scottsdale, maintains an active educational center, including satellite
uplinks, fiber optic interconnects, and fixed microwave systems, between
schools. They operate three studios full time producing interactive learning opportunities for K–12 students nationwide.

Video Conferencing

Video conferencing is a growing area that is generally described
as a digital based form of teleconferencing. Video conferencing involves
technology that handles the input of video and audio utilizing digital
compression and is often linked with computers for graphics and
interactive activities. Generally video conferencing is used for group

conferences, as is business television, but is fast becoming the platform for desktop teleconferencing.

Pre-Production Planning

Before the teleconference begins much pre-production planning must take place. Areas of pre-production include the meeting planning and logistics, talent preparation, equipment and broadcast facility arrangements, site location arrangements and production of insert elements.

Establish the Objective

An important first step in planning for a teleconference is to establish the communications objective. Identify the communication needs and write (in several paragraphs) objectives that will meet those needs. The objective helps you keep focused and will not let the technology or vendor facility lead you off course. Often without a clear communications objective you can create a situation where you have a technology looking for a problem, and this can lead to ineffective technology use and inappropriate costs.

Establish a Team

Establishing a program task force should be next on your pre-production list. This can be a small group of two or three people up to a larger group of nine or ten, depending on the nature of the conference. The task force will tackle the technology issues and the applications issues. The task force could be split so the technology people could start addressing the technical considerations of the conference and the applications people could start addressing the content, presenters and delivery issues. However, the two groups will work together eventually to discuss applications and technology approaches.

A good teleconference team could be composed of a program or project manager/coordinator responsible for the execution of the entire event, meeting and task force logistics. Often the project manager will be responsible for marketing and promoting the program as well. (Promotion of teleconferences is often overlooked.)

In addition, a content specialist should be available to the team. A network coordinator works with the sites and site facilitators as the program is developed. Site coordinators are responsible for arranging the conference meeting rooms, registration, local promotion, logistics and management of printed support materials and local contact and management of reception equipment.

Another on-site key individual that is necessary for successful coordination and videoconference set-up is the satellite or equipment technician. If you are using in-house staff, a logical person to assume this role would be the audio-visual technician, media coordinator or video producer. This person assumes the responsibilities of aligning the reception antenna (if you are using established in-house resources) on the satellite prior to each program, channel reception and maintaining good reception during the conference. If you are using an outside resource for this function, the facility should provide site coordination of equipment.

A budget coordinator, often someone from the financial services department, can be helpful in number crunching for cost justification and to help the project stay on budget. A video producer will be responsible for the video or visual elements of the conference including graphics, animations, video inserts, teleconference production equipment and recording equipment. And if the video portion of the conference will be compressed to a digital format for delivery over a computer network, it is advisable to have a computer specialist involved with the project.

As the task force is formed, schedules and timeframes are shared. The teleconference is made up of multiple tasks that are happening simultaneously, so schedules and timeframes should be established and shared with all. Some of these major schedules include video production of insert elements, graphics production, broadcast logistics, site coordination time frames, promotion schedules, content development schedules and printed support materials development. As with video production deadlines, you can set the teleconference broadcast date and then work backwards in setting what has to be done within that time frame. It is important to set realistic dates. Teleconference planning and execution takes time. Allow enough time to accomplish the objectives in realistic terms.

Hold an In-Service Meeting

After the curriculum has been put together and most of the tasks completed by the task force, get together for an in-service session. Bring in the site coordinators, faculty, production people, the people that have developed the program, will deliver the program and will be coordinating the reception of the program. This in-service will allow for the site coordinators to be trained in their responsibilities at the reception sites. They will understand what will happen and what is expected of them. They will learn how to interact with the equipment, how to coordinate the printed support materials and how to provide feedback for the session. The in-service also allows the presenters and the production people to "rehearse" the teleconference and walk through the production. Rehearse the slides and graphics, video inserts and sequence of presenters. This is a great help in avoiding problems on the day of the broadcast. Work through and discuss the possible problems in advance. It's also a good idea, if possible, to actually visit the sites before the conference.

Teleconference Equipment Planning and Arrangements

Teleconference equipment planning and arrangements are similar to that of video production. Selecting a vendor that has the equipment you need, doing a thorough site selection, writing a thorough, detailed contract for services are familiar steps for any kind of production. There are, however, a few important planning details that revolve mostly around teleconference site selection:

Arranging for Site Selection

- Have clear objectives of what it is you want to accomplish with the teleconference. Providing clear objectives for everyone involved helps accomplish the goals you are after.
- Speak to others in your field who have done teleconferences with similar goals. Ask for vendor recommendations, site coordinators, existing networks that can carry your conference and problems they ran into along the way. Speaking to others will greatly increase your

chances of a successful conference. Also try to sit in on a teleconference and see the technology and procedures used.

- Determine well in advance how many receive sites you will need for the conference and have each site (city) clearly identified. Know what your conference (the program) will look like, so you can communicate the objectives to all of the selected sites.
- The site survey should assure you of clear reception and broadcast. There should be no structures, power lines, hills or mountains that might interfere with reception. Find out if downlinks have been used at the site before and with what success.
- As you sub-contract for site (reception) coordination with a vendor, find out how they will deal with the actual program. Will they use their own people to coordinate the site or will they use sub-contractors? The vendor you select for site coordination should provide consistency for each site and have specific site procedures for conferences. If the vendor will sub-contract, how will he/she assure quality control for each site? The site coordinator should assist you with the site survey.
- Be sure you have redundancy at the sites. Does the site have back-up equipment? The contract with the vendor should include redundancy considerations and "liabilities" for teleconference delivery failures.
- The selected vendor will help you with your site selection and coordination, technology selection, provide up- and downlinks and "space" or conference time for broadcasting your conference. He or she can assist with the downlink site survey, for actual placement of the equipment and cabling and provide an actual test to assure that the reception equipment will work at that site. The vendor will assist you with the overall coordination of your conference and ease the problems at the site with its teleconference experience, written guidelines and procedures and professional equipment and technical expertise. This will allow you to focus on the content, program coordination and talent.
- Consider if you are going to hire a crew and equipment to broadcast your conference or whether your in-house staff will cover the event. How will you handle the telephone interactive system? Will you hire on-site coordinators to handle the phones, attendance, meals and room arrangements?
- The vendor will also assist with the selection of the satellite to carry your conference to assure the best scheduling and technology for your particular audiences.

Teleconference Production

Teleconferencing production differs from taped video production in several ways. These differences affect the way we need to plan for the event.

Use of Multiple Cameras

Teleconferences are usually produced with multiple cameras, in a studio or dedicated, controlled environment. Multiple cameras mean larger amounts of equipment that have to be rented or scheduled through a teleconference or production facility. The studio space or dedicated area will have to be scheduled and secured for the desired teleconference date. And if the event will be broadcast over a satellite (as opposed to telephone lines) broadcast and reception have to be arranged.

Shooting multiple camera productions (much like shooting live television or a live news show originating in the studio) requires expertise in directing the talent, cameras and crew and the technical switching of the cameras becomes a critical issue. Since the event is live, the director delivers the message or content through the selection of cameras. Camera angles, speakers and graphics are technically delivered through the switching of cameras as opposed to the editing process in single camera production.

A Large Project Team

Since the teleconference is a "live" event shot with multiple cameras, a larger production crew is required. More camera operators are required and usually a more technical crew is required. Add a graphics operator, TelePrompter operators, floor director, technical director, lighting director and several production assistants, and you have a much larger crew to schedule and manage. This takes planning and managing by the producer. But it doesn't stop there. Often there is a script involved, and if it is a training conference, trainers and instructional designers are involved. Once the teleconference is designed, a survey may be sent to the proposed audience to generate questions or further topics that could be open for discussion during the event.

A moderator and subject matter experts for the panel have to be selected as well as local on-site coordinators. Graphics and printed materials need to be created. Each local reception site will require facilitators, technical assistance and promotion. Facilitators have to be hired or trained for the event.

Inserts Must Be Ready

Graphics, slides and on-camera examples must be produced in advance. Sets may have to be designed and constructed as well as tables, platforms and backdrops prepared for the panel.

Video Tape Inserts

Often a live teleconference will require video tape inserts, often referred to as "B" rolls. These videotape segments have to be "rolled in" during the event and have to be planned, written, shot and edited much like any taped program. Opening titles, logos, segment "bumpers" and closing graphics will have to be planned and produced well in advance.

Rehearsals

Larger teleconferences will require two rehearsals. One rehearsal is scheduled for content and one for technical issues. A content rehearsal allows the talent and director to rehearse topics to be discussed, so an understanding of the content can be reviewed by everyone participating in the event and the script can be adjusted for the panel. A technical rehearsal is scheduled so the camera positions can be established, inserts rehearsed, the set readied, and the crew has a good idea of the happenings of the event. A "dry" technical run will assure a smooth live show with few if any surprises.

Plan for Interactive Participation

Plans must be made for audience participation through the design of the script and through technical logistics. Segment time in the program should be allowed. The talent and crew should be alerted to audience participation and the mechanics of handling the participation. Local receive sites need to be readied for participation through phone lines, and the logistics and mechanics of "call-in" participation worked out in advance. People have to be trained to handle the phone call-in questions and the technical switching planned to insert the calls "on-the-air."

Local On-site Arrangements

Since there are multiple receive sites for teleconferences, the local arrangements have to made well in advance. These arrangements include meeting scheduling, invitations to the events, room or receive site scheduling, local sign-in or registration, lunch or coffee break arrangements and local arrangements for reception. This could be done through a local teleconference facility, consultant or telephone company.

Materials Development

Content materials (hand-outs, further reading, tests, slides) are often made available at the local receive site. The preparation, printing and mailing of these materials have to be planned well in advance. Once the materials are received at the local site, arrangements must be made for the participants to get them. Often these materials need to be controlled during the teleconference and explained. Local arrangements for this control need to be planned. After the conference evaluation should take place and thought should be given to awarding certification of completion.

Duplication, Delivery and Marketing for Film, Multimedia, and Video Conferences

The work doesn't end at fade to black. Duplication and delivery is an important step in the program development process whether for film, multimedia or traditional video productions. The audience won't see the master tape. They'll see a duplicated copy, and there are many technical quality issues that will affect what that copy will look like to the audience. The quality of this copy will affect the viewers' reaction to the program.

Making a good copy of the program doesn't start at the duplication facility. It starts at production. By being sure that you have a good quality, technically correct edited master, the copy has a much higher chance of looking good to the viewer. For a quality duplication, audio and video recording levels should be consistent throughout the program. There should be as few technical glitches on the tape as possible, with few drop outs and no timing errors that affect picture quality. The audio track should be clean and consistent throughout the program. The duplication process usually just adds to the technical problems you may have on your tape, so a continuing check on the technical quality of your edited master is important to assure good copies. Remember, your audience will see the dub, not the master.

And before the dub is made, there is planning to be done. Consider: are you making the dubs or will you contract for this service with a commercial duplication facility? How many copies will you need? Will they need to be labeled and packaged? Mailed? Returned after viewing? Who will manage the mailing, return, scheduling and copy quality check?

The duplication program delivery effort will be addressed in more detail in Chapter 9.

Marketing and selling have two different goals. Marketing is the process of determining a "market" or viewing audience and developing a "product" or program that meets the needs of that audience. Selling on the other hand, is the act of convincing the audience that they need the program.

Good program design entails marketing. As the problem is being identified, audience identified and the solution resolved (with a video program), we are developing a marketing plan. The next step is to sell the program to the audience. If the need has accurately been addressed, then the "selling" will be easy. It becomes a delivery process—getting the needed program to the audience.

Most internally developed programs for organizations do need a certain amount of selling to assure an audience. This can be accomplished through cafeteria tent cards, a program catalog, mail, memos, staff meetings and general internal advertising. Each of these selling mechanisms requires planning. One of the first questions I ask any client is, "How will the audience see the program?" This question answers not only the delivery requirement but the selling requirement. It is our responsibility as producers to see the project through to viewing. And in doing so, this requires planning.

It is the video manager's or producer's responsibility to see that a marketing plan and selling plan is in place for the program being produced. Not only will a plan help place the program in front of the right audience, but it will assist in management needs. The value of the program and the value of the video service can be tracked through a good marketing plan. The tracking of the viewing audience, the value the company received from the program and the costs involved in reaching that value all contribute to staff, facility and resource justification. Budgets and future resources can be justified if a plan is in place to track value of programming. The service that video provides through programming should have measurable value for the organization. The programs we produce should save the organization money, improve revenues or add efficiency to the business. A marketing and selling plan will help us measure that value.

The goal of the plan should include identifying potential "customers" or viewers of your programming, researching a value to be placed on the program, and a vehicle (through advertising) to reach the intended viewer and projected "sales".

Likewise, a plan should be developed to sell the programs to the potential audience.

The object here is to get the program seen. The best produced program is no good unless it is seen by the appropriate audience. The key is that both marketing and selling require planning—planning that needs to take place prior to production.

The Day of the Shoot

If your pre-production has been done thoroughly, on the day of the shoot you should be able to focus your attention on one thing . . . getting the best possible performance from the talent.

This chapter addresses logistical, equipment and talent considerations that should be planned for the day of the shoot.

LOGISTICS

Transportation

Local Travel Arrangements

On the day of the shoot, when everyone is due at the set at 7 a.m., it's too late to start worrying about transportation, parking and security for vehicles and equipment. Once again, advanced planning is in order. Do all of the crew and talent have appropriate transportation to the scene? Has getting through the security gate been arranged for everyone? Has parking been taken care of? Did you draw maps for everyone, so they can find their way to the scene? Did you mail out the maps? Did you arrange for security for the vehicles and equipment?

Local shoots do not usually present too much of a transportation problem. However, if you are shooting in the city, you need to think about parking for unloading the equipment, and security becomes an important issue.

I remember a production I was on in New York City. At the end of the day, the local production assistant I had hired had to leave early. He left me to get the equipment (lights, camera, recorder and my baggage) down to a cab so I could make a mad dash for the airport. The problem was that I couldn't carry everything at once and had to make several trips in an elevator from the 31st floor of a high-rise to the street level where I hoped I could flag a cab. Think about that. Since I couldn't carry it all, I had to leave some equipment upstairs in an office and some downstairs in a cab. I didn't want to leave my $20,000 camera with the cab driver, so I had to ask the person at the front desk in the office to go wait with the equipment while I hauled the rest of the stuff down. A small problem, but one that caused much frustration at the time.

When you do your site survey, be sure to check out the loading dock or a convenient area for the crew to unload equipment. Think about security, and make arrangements for parking, tolls and tips.

Out of Town and International Travel Arrangements

Shooting out of town always brings complications to the production. Traveling with equipment has to be planned out and arrangements have to be made well in advance for the crew. For example:

- Arrange for a LARGE rental car that can handle the crew, luggage and equipment. Check that your insurance covers your equipment and rentals out of town or out of the country.
- Arrange flights well in advance for the best price and to ensure flights that will work best for your schedule. Be prepared to pay when you go over the limit with baggage.
- Pack the equipment well for air travel. Use an equipment checklist. A battery on the shelf at your office doesn't do much good out on location in the middle of a corn field. Check and double-check what you pack. Try to break the equipment package up and separate items,

so all of the camera gear isn't in one case and all of the recording gear in another. Separating gear will help if a piece of luggage is lost; you will at least have one camera or recorder to use. Mark the equipment boxes, so you know what is in each one, and count all the baggage, so you know at each stop how many pieces you should have. Be sure your name is in each box/bag. Some airlines have specific regulations for packing electronic gear, so always check with the airline before traveling. If you hand-carry the camera, recorder or computer, security usually asks you to turn on the equipment. Therefore be sure you have batteries or you may not make it through security.

- Have a back-up of each item, if possible, when you go on a long shoot far from home. Usually you travel on a tight schedule, and unscheduled repair can ruin the best plan.

- Arrange for ground floor rooms in hotels or motels if possible, so you do not have to carry equipment upstairs or depend on elevators.

- Research local resources. When traveling to cities you are not familiar with, always bring the telephone numbers of equipment rental houses, other production houses, the local electronics store near your shooting location, a tape source and local talent resources. And try to get maps in advance of the locations you are traveling to. State and city film offices are good resources.

- Remember that traveling with crew and equipment always takes longer than traveling solo. Allow plenty of time for checking in at the airport, car rental and hotels. Moving, loading and re-packing equipment takes extra time, so plan the schedule accordingly.

Traveling Abroad

Traveling abroad with crew and equipment presents additional unique challenges. A first step in relieving some anxieties would be to contact the host country for specific guidelines for traveling with crew and equipment. Try to obtain written guidelines for production, travel and dealing with customs. Other helpful resources for international travel are the Association of Independent Video and Filmmakers (AIVF) in New York, the Royal Television Society, RTS North America at Arizona State University and the National Association of Broadcasters (NAB) in Washington, DC.

Following are a few considerations for international travel:

- Your existing insurance policies usually do not cover international travel. If you are in the air, in the water or traveling abroad, you and your equipment may not be covered. Check with your insurance carrier. You may have to purchase an additional travel rider to your policy.

- Send for the U.S. Customs forms in advance so you can fill them out and provide the equipment details (model and serial numbers) that are required. Always have an additional detailed equipment list with proof of ownership.

- Send for customs forms from the countries you will be traveling to. They will require proof of ownership along with detailed lists of specific equipment you are bringing into their country.

- For travel between countries, you will need a "carnet" for international passage (for information on carnets contact the U.S. Council for International Business in New York). This form is expensive to obtain and requires several months' time to apply for but will allow easy passage between countries.

- If you are researching international travel to learn about foreign economic trends and business conditions, contact the Publications Department at the U.S. Department of Commerce and the State Department Publications Office, both in Washington DC. The World Radio TV Handbook is a good resource for information on world TV standards.
- Television standards (NTSC, PAL, SECAM) vary from country to country, so equipment rental and playback of camera footage can present problems. If you plan to take your equipment with you, be sure to include playback capabilities and battery chargers. Also plan on power converters.
- Prepare for local climate conditions at the time you will be traveling.
- Consider hiring local production resources (often required in some countries for large video productions). They can be of tremendous value for problem solving.
- Plan in advance for currency exchange, travelers check purchases and bank card usage in various countries.
- Allow plenty of lead time for health requirements (inoculations) and have medical record with passport. Local city and county health agencies within your state can provide information about travel health regulations.
- And a booklet covering medical advice for the international traveler is available through The Tropical Diseases Center at Lenox Hill Hospital in New York.

Staging

On the day of the shoot, the equipment is delivered to the predetermined staging area. This area is a secure space, out of the way of production and foot traffic where the equipment can be unpacked and checked. Traveling cases, extra lights, cables and stands (grip equipment) can be left until they are needed in the staging area. Instead of taking up valuable space on the set, the staging area acts as the central equipment storage for the production of scenes in that general vicinity.

If the equipment is to be left at the location overnight, a secure room will have to be arranged. If the crew has not been at this location before, be sure to point out where the break area is, bathrooms and the telephone.

Walk through the first scene with the crew. Review the "look" you are after and review the schedule for the production of this first scene and any special technical problems (from your location checklist) facing the crew. This is where your pre-production really pays off. Everyone knows, from prior meetings, what you are looking for and the production requirements of the script. The site survey allowed you to prepare for special technical problems and the lighting requirements. Power has been found and arranged for in advance and equipment and camera all have predetermined locations for the first shot. The crew starts to work on setting up the lights and the details of equipment preparation for recording, and you can now turn to the needs of your client and talent.

You will need the script, shooting script, shooting schedule, prop list, talent list and location key names and clearances (your production notebook).

Working With Crew and Client

Once the staging is in place and the equipment is unpacked, communicate to the crew the schedule and movement logistics between shots/locations. Always plan more time than you think you need, even if each new location is within the same building. If the equipment has to be powered down and moved, that translates to a location change. This procedure adds time to production. And when you change locations, often the talent (and crew) will dash to a phone. This adds time.

I would like to remind you again of the importance of planning the shots/locations for production convenience and efficiency. If you are shooting a scene at one end of a building one day, you do not want to have to go back to that location again the second or third day. Break the script up into logical scenes and locations and plan the movement between scenes for efficiency.

While shooting on board a large cruise ship, we were constantly revisiting locations because the client had not taken the time to review the script and kept adding shots after we had finished script segments. These additional shots were not planned in the script. This revisiting of locations is a morale buster for the crew and affects the efficiency and mood of the production. Try to avoid this problem at all costs. If the script is well organized and the scenes well planned in advance, the shoot will run much smoother, and you can expect peak performances from the crew.

It is a good idea to shoot extra footage while you are setting up at a scene, so you do not have to come back later to do pick-ups. While at the scene, shoot plenty of extra footage, footage that you may not use or that may not be called for in the script. This extra footage can be a real life saver in editing when you need just a few more seconds of a scene to cover an edit. (This is called the S.L.O.P. theory. *Shoot Lots Of Pictures.*) You never know what you may need when it comes to the edit.

Often this extra footage is referred to as INSERT shots. Insert shots are extra close-ups of the machine or process, close-ups of the talent or a particular movement or action.

Plan extra time at the scene to record extra audio—room noise, background sounds or wild sounds (ambiance), again useful for the edit. This "wild sound" can cover edits or close-ups and can help fill in the audio gaps (blank spaces where there is no on-camera sound or narration) while editing when the talent is not talking.

Be sure to have continuity of lighting between shots, and check playback for lighting consistency. Emphasize safety: be sure that cables are taped to the floor so no one trips. Sand bag or tape stands so they do not fall over. Wear gloves while moving hot instruments; watch for power overloads and be sure that all instruments have scrims in front of the lamps so they do not shatter onto the talent.

Power

After staging takes place, one of the first steps in getting ready for the location shoot is meeting power requirements. If extra power is needed at the location (other than what is available through the 20 amp circuits at the scene), you could use extra power from the house breaker box or have an external generator available. If a generator is used, allow at least half an hour for the electrician to run cables and bring in power from the generator. The site survey will determine where to park the generator truck, how large a generator to have and will prepare you for sound problems that are associated with generators.

If you plan to tap into the power of the building, the production gaffer or electrician will go to the breaker box (location of the breaker box was determined during your location site survey), tap into the house power and provide extra power for the location. This usually requires about 20 minutes. Know in advance where you want to run power cables. Grounding and balance will be checked through a volt and amp meter (probe). This can create a liability situation. Be sure all lighting is grounded and balanced. This procedure is usually referred to as managing the "loads."

In larger productions, the person responsible for creating the lighting "look" is the lighting director, and the person responsible for the lighting equipment is called the key grip. The person who does the lighting set-up is often called the gaffer. An assistant to the gaffer is called the best boy. There may be an electrician on the set. On smaller shoots the gaffer does everything—power, lighting and set-ups.

When determining power requirements for the shoot, keep in mind the production equipment power requirements as well as props and lighting. Have the lighting diagrams ready, so the key grip knows where to place lights and have a camera turned on with a monitor available as you light, so you can see the results. Once the major lighting setup is done, call in the talent and "tweak" for special requirements, such as bald spots, wardrobe reflection, jewelry, and talent movement. (Chapter 4 has more details on power requirements and lighting considerations.)

EQUIPMENT

Equipment and Crew Setup

Once the equipment is brought into the building, allow about an hour for unpacking and setup for the first scene. Often the production equipment will be set up on a production cart (crash cart) and might include the recorder, monitor, wave form monitor, audio mixer, and slate (coffee cups, cookies, hats, sunglasses, keys and other miscellaneous "stuff" that always accumulates on a shoot).

Before the lighting is set up, the camera is placed for its first shot (which was pre-determined during the site survey). This position determines the angle and what will and will not be in the shot. This allows for the lighting setup.

Once the crew begins to set up, you as the director can begin working with talent. First block out the shot (determine where they will stand and the range of their movement). Then start rehearsing the scene. This sequence of events on the set will get routine after a while, and you and the crew will really start working together as a team. They will understand the set-up routine at each location, allowing you to concentrate on working with the talent.

Before you start shooting the scene, check out the equipment for proper operation. First setup the camera (for white and black balance) and check the framing in the monitor and adjust. Setup the monitor for proper display of color bars (refer to Chapter 4 for more details on equipment operation and checks).

Once the camera is ready, do a test recording to check sound levels, camera quality and deck operation. Usually we run a minute or so

FORM XXII

VIDEO EQUIPMENT RENTAL AGREEMENT

On _____ (date) _____ (company)

provided to _____ (client)

the following video equipment in good operating condition:

ITEM	SER. #	Est. Value
_____	_____	_____
_____	_____	_____
_____	_____	_____
_____	_____	_____
_____	_____	_____
_____	_____	_____
_____	_____	_____
_____	_____	_____
_____	_____	_____

_____ (client) agrees to take full

responsibility for the safety of the above equipment and the return of said equipment

in good operating condition to _____ (company)

by _____ (time and date).

Any equipment rented to you which has been lost or damaged while in your care
will be charged at the replacement costs, or labor and parts for repair. Total value of
the above equipment rented in this contract is $_____ . Rental cost for the above
equipment during the time specified is $_____ . Security deposit of $_____ is
hereby received. Additional costs for extension of rental are $ _____ /day. Weekly
rental is three times (3x) daily rate.

DATE: _____ (signed) _____

Company

(signed) _____

Client

FORM XXIII

MAINTENANCE OR INSPECTION RECORD

DATE	SERVICE PERFORMED	TIME	PARTS USED	PRICE

MAINTENANCE SERVICE TIME

EQUIPMENT/PROBLEM WORKED ON	SERVICE CATEGORY	DATE	TIME REQUIRED	SERVICE PROVIDED BY

of color bars to test video and audio. This is a good practice at each new location and at the beginning of each new tape. Form 22 shows a typical equipment rental agreement. Forms 23 and 24 will help you keep track of equipment maintenance.

Logging

"Logging tapes" refers to the process of keeping track of camera shots, scenes and takes by writing time code numbers on paper log sheets. The importance of having good logs shows up in the editing process, as detailed in Chapter 9. Logs can save you time and money during the edit and help in the archival process for storing and retrieving camera tapes. Logs can be created manually while you are shooting (paper logs), through a computer software program and a laptop computer, or after you shoot the footage. Time code, the numbering system that is placed on your footage as you shoot or on the tape after the shoot, helps you keep very accurate records of each shot and scene.

A production assistant can log tapes as you shoot. The PA will watch the time code numbers as they appear on the deck and keep track of start and stop points of each shot. Often, if you do not have a large crew, the PA may be required to run audio or hold a microphone or move the camera dolly, so time code logging may not be possible during the shoot. In this case the PA will log tapes after the shoot. Even if you log during the shoot, it is still a good practice to allow time afterwards to "clean-up" the logs and review the logs for accuracy.

Usually a time code log sheet (see Form 25) is made available for the production with lots of extra copies. The log sheet lists the scene number, shot number and take. Start and end points appear along with a section for comments, which may contain your notes on the scene or shot, what the problem was with the take or general production notes that might help you during the edit. The log sheet will also contain the production name, page number and tape number and date.

If you do not have the capability on your recording deck to lay down time code during the shoot, you can opt to have time code recorded on your footage after the shoot. In this case, as the time code is being laid down, a "window dub" is usually made. A "window dub" refers to a copy of all the original footage you shot with a "burned-in" window where time code becomes visible for you to read. Rough edits or off-line edits often use window dubs. With the window dubs the time code is visible, and the off-line edit master contains the time code in a window as well. This is helpful for discussing the edited scenes with the client, because you can refer to time code numbers as you select scenes that need to be shortened or deleted.

On productions that require quick turnaround time, you can make the window dubs as you shoot the footage. By placing a time code reader/generator between the recording deck and a second tape deck, you can record window dubs as you shoot. The time code reader/generator also allows you to see the time code on the monitor you are using in the field, which helps the PA log tapes as you shoot.

There are many time code logging software programs available on the market (refer to Chapter 9 for an in-depth description of these systems). Programs such as the *Log Producer* by Image Logic of Chevy Chase, MD, and *The Executive Producer* by Imagine Products of Carmel, IN (along with a computer or lap top), allow you to generate computer logs in the field either as you shoot or after the production. Computer gener-

FORM XXV

SCENE/TAKE LOG

Page _____ Of _____

Project Title _____ Tape No. _____ Date _____

Time	Scene	Take	Description
_____	_____	_____	_____
_____	_____	_____	_____
_____	_____	_____	_____
_____	_____	_____	_____
_____	_____	_____	_____
_____	_____	_____	_____
_____	_____	_____	_____
_____	_____	_____	_____
_____	_____	_____	_____
_____	_____	_____	_____
_____	_____	_____	_____
_____	_____	_____	_____
_____	_____	_____	_____
_____	_____	_____	_____
_____	_____	_____	_____
_____	_____	_____	_____
_____	_____	_____	_____
_____	_____	_____	_____
_____	_____	_____	_____
_____	_____	_____	_____
_____	_____	_____	_____
_____	_____	_____	_____
_____	_____	_____	_____
_____	_____	_____	_____
_____	_____	_____	_____
_____	_____	_____	_____
_____	_____	_____	_____

Figure 8 – 1
Production assistant logs tapes on location by viewing time code numbers on the field monitor.

ated logs allow flexibility and save time by allowing you to create very accurate edit decision lists that become a graphic representation of your program for the on-line edit. Computer generated edit decision lists can be read by on-line editing equipment. This process speeds up editing time by allowing the editing equipment to automatically track the list instead of the editor typing in each number. This automated process saves large amounts of time in the edit suite. And you're not dependent on someone's handwriting.

The Payoff

The lights are set. You have done your sound check, and the crew is ready to begin recording. Not bogged down with crew, equipment or technical problems, you can focus your attention and energy on performance. Your mind is cleared of the details of production and equipment; you know where you are going in the scene, where the action will start and stop and you are free to concentrate on the performance you expect from your talent. You are ready. Pre-production has paid off. But . . .

What Could Still Go Wrong?

- The talent turns to mush in front of the camera
- You blow an electrical circuit
- The tape jams
- No tape (it was left in a taxi at the airport)
- The prop (usually a computer) does not work
- Someone walks in front of the camera or into the scene

- The phone rings
- The house PA system speaks
- A crew member sneezes during a take
- A crew member talks during a take
- A crew member drops a light during a take
- A crew member forgets to roll tape during a take (fire that crew member!)
- The music is turned up too loud during a take
- A plane passes over
- A train goes by
- A truck goes by
- A car drives by and beeps its horn
- People have shift change outside the room
- The fire alarm goes off—lights are too close to the smoke detector
- No audio
- No picture
- Someone's stomach growls
- The talent forgot their lines
- Someone's beeper goes off
- The crew starts giggling
    This list could go on for pages.

PREPARING THE TALENT

Volumes have been written on directing talent, but not much attention has been paid to preparing the talent for production. This section will discuss working with talent as it applies to pre-production, as well as tips for talent. Several good books about directing talent appear in the appendix. I especially recommend: Steven D. Katz, *Film Directing Shot by Shot*, Michael Wiese Productions; Richard Bare, *The Film Director, A Practical Guide to Motion Pictures and Television Techniques* by Macmillan Publishing; and Albert and Bertha Johnson, *Directing Methods*, A.S. Barnes and Company.

Meeting Talent Needs

The Comfort Zone

Talent, whether they are professional or in-house, need a comfortable area for applying make-up, combing their hair and making phone calls. Plan ahead. Find out where the closest bathrooms are to the scene and where the phones are and have a portable mirror, tissues and touch-up make-up handy. On a longer shoot lasting several hours, bring snacks and provide hot coffee. If the shoot will run through the lunch hour, have lunch catered or otherwise arrange for lunch for the crew and talent. Traditionally, the client pays for the talent and crew's lunch, so advance arrangements should be made. For long afternoon shoots, have snacks and soft drinks handy.

A good producer will anticipate the talent's needs. When the talent arrives on the scene, introduce them to the crew. Provide general information about the equipment and the setup for the scene. Professional talent will be familiar with the equipment, but for in-house talent, all the lights and equipment may be overwhelming.

Figure 8 – 2
An area should be arranged in advance for staging the production equipment on the day of the shoot.

Prompting

If cue cards are used, they should be made in advance. Talk with the talent in advance and decide if cue cards will be needed. Talent also has the option of using a TelePrompter, an electronic cue device that allows the talent to read the script as he or she is looking at the camera. The TelePrompter hangs on the front of the camera. It is an automatic device that is usually controlled by a production person off camera. It takes practice to use a TelePrompter, so prepare the talent for the cueing mechanism.

The talent may also choose to use an audio cue device. This is an earphone that is attached to a small audio recorder hidden on the person. Before the scene begins, the talent reads his parts of the script into the recorder. As the camera rolls, the talent plays back his recorded words through the ear piece. He then speaks the words he hears. This too takes practice.

Communication

Good communication with the talent is important to help the talent understand the production process and the sequence of events of recording video. Describe the ability to edit, and communicate the sequence of recording events (roll tape-speed-action). Once the talent understands what is expected of them, discuss camera angles and talent movement (direction). If staying on marks is important for camera focus and lighting, be sure to explain that to the talent. Let them rehearse their moves with your direction and practice delivering lines to the camera. Be sure to communicate last minute script and schedule changes.

Clothing and Costumes

With today's chip technology video cameras, the concern about clothing is not as important as it was a few years ago. Back then, we had to be sensitive to the talent wearing white or colors that contrasted. However, a few simple rules still apply.

You still need to be sensitive to creating high contrast situations. If a black person, for example, wears a white shirt and you are not paying attention to the lighting, the camera will respond to the white shirt, and detail in the face will be missing. Try not to create such strong contrast. Dark clothing on any skin color can create problems; usually the dark suit will look drab, again lacking detail. To correct that problem, you would have to light the suit very brightly, but keep the brightness off the face so it does not get washed out. This can be tricky. It is best to choose clothing colors that provide pleasing contrasts to the eye but that are not too extreme. Several steps on the grey scale for contrast will work well.

Also, be sensitive to high contrasting stripes and tight patterns. This can cause the picture to shimmer or "move" on the screen. And bright stripes may bleed into other areas of the picture. Bright, reflective jewelry and accessories may cause problems as well. They tend to reflect the light, cause glare and attract the eye away from the subject. Use dulling spray, tape or bounce lighting (not direct lighting) to eliminate the glare.

Background colors, materials and patterns are important to plan. Do not let the backgrounds overpower the talent, become too busy or bright in contrast with the talent. The eye should be attracted to the talent, not the background.

Make-up

Make-up for video production is desirable for both men and women to smooth out skin color and control perspiration. However, the less you use the better.

Try to make the talent look as natural as possible, adding make-up only when absolutely necessary. It is not necessary to strongly enhance features as in theater. Television is a "close-up" medium, and too much make-up can be seen. Extreme care should be given to applying make-up for video talent. Careful application and blending are essential.

Always apply make-up lightly using a pancake, dry water-soluble material or a stick that is creme based. The idea is not to change the subject in any way, but rather to retain the natural appearance through changes caused by perspiration or light reflections.

For men choose a pancake material with the color closest to the talent's natural skin tone. Use a small sponge starting with a very small amount doing "touch-up" on the nose or forehead as needed to control perspiration and even skin color. If more make-up is needed to cover a beard shadow, start with a very small amount of creme stick and spread evenly over the facial area and then press on translucent no-color powder.

You may have to touch up the eyebrows with a brown eyebrow pencil. Don't draw lines or apply too much. Again you are after the natural look on the close-ups.

A touch of hair spray will hold the hair in place.

Problem areas that might arise for make-up and styling include under-eye problems. Add make-up to remove the dark areas or "bags" under the eyes, and be sure the lights are adjusted correctly so that they do not increase this problem. Make-up can be applied to cover shiny spots on the forehead and bright bald spots. To conceal "5 o'clock shadow," apply a light make-up base. For eyeglass reflection, adjusting the lights (the reflection ratio) will remedy the problem. If the talent will appear on camera often and people are used to seeing them in glasses, getting another pair of frames that have no lenses in them may help.

For women street make-up is adequate. Touch up areas changed by perspiration. Add eye shadow lightly and blend carefully. The same goes for lipstick.

Be sure to check the make-up in front of the camera with the full lighting setup on. The combination effect of the lights, talent's costume and natural skin color will all effect how people look in front of the camera. Adjustments may be necessary.

Most make-up artists bring make-up kits to the production. It is advisable to create your own make-up production kit for touch ups if you do not always use a make-up artist. A kit may include the basic pancake powder, lining colors, applicators, swabs, tissue, small mirror, combs, brushes, pins, cleaning creme, hair spray and bib.

A good reference about make-up is *Film and Television Make-up* by Herman Buchman, published by Watson-Guptill Publications.

Working with Non-Professional Talent

The key to working with non-professional talent is communication. Corporate staff does not usually have acting experience or experience in front of the camera. You are asking them to do something that is totally out of their realm. Give them plenty of advance notice, let them know what is expected of them and the details of the schedule. They will have many questions concerning what to wear, make-up, where to be at what time, how long it will take and what to do with the script. Most non-professional talent will not really want to appear in front of the camera; it will be a stressful situation for them, so the more details you can communicate about the production, the more success you will have. It pays off to have a preprinted booklet or memo describing the video production process that addresses their concerns.

Meet with the talent well in advance. Explain the goal of the program you are producing, their involvement and what is expected of them. They were probably chosen for the program because of their skill or expertise with the subject being presented, so take advantage of their knowledge and experience. Let them know that their contribution is important to the success of the program. Share the script and storyboard with them, explain how you plan to shoot the scenes and ask for their contributions for shot ideas. The more you get them involved, the more likely you will get their full cooperation.

Non-professional talent will be anxious and apprehensive. Put them at ease by sharing as much information with them as possible. It's a good idea to have them watch the shooting of an earlier scene, so they can see the production environment and meet the crew. Also show them a tape of past productions you have done with non-professional talent. This will help them understand the process.

Explain to the talent that appearing relaxed in front of the camera, as talk show hosts do, is not as easy as it looks. It takes lots of practice. You are not expecting them to be hosts, rather you are asking them to appear as themselves, experts in their area, and the more natural they are, the better they will appear to the audience. Non-professional talent lend naturalness and credibility to your production. They will not be reading and acting lines. They will be doing their jobs or talking about their jobs, so there is no need for memorizing lines. (In fact, you should discourage them from memorizing their parts. It will not look natural.) Your purpose is to capture natural delivery, sincerity and conviction. You want the talent to project their organization's style and character. Television is a visual experience, so how the talent looks is just as important as what they say. Does the audience trust and believe in the person in front of the camera? If the talent looks nervous the audience will be uncomfortable watching them.

This does not mean the talent can come to the shoot unprepared. Good preparation will give them the confidence to deliver a good, believable presentation. They should practice their presentation in advance but be careful of over-memorizing their lines and losing their spontaneity.

You should have your homework done, know the goal of the program and what you are looking for from the talent. Block your shots well in advance. Decide how you are going to light the set and how you will handle audio. If you are organized and reflect a confident manner, the talent will have confidence in your ability to make them look good. Nothing disturbs the talent more than your having to make decisions while they wait around wondering why they are wasting their time.

It is important that the director be the only person giving them direction. There is only ONE director on the set. Commands and direction from different people on the set and crew members confuse the talent and create the appearance of an unorganized production. Communicate your role clearly to the talent. You are in charge today.

As the director, you are the talent's coach. You should be positive and supportive of their performance. Make them feel good about what they are contributing to the program. Let them feel they are a part of the team. Your pre-production planning should pay off now, and you can focus your attention on performance. Your attitude makes an immense difference in the whole process with the crew and talent. You set the pace and tone for the production and a lot of the success relies on your attitude and expertise.

Tips for Working with Talent

- Give the talent plenty of advance notice, so the talent can prepare and schedule the time.
- If there is a script involved, allow the talent to re-write the script so it sounds natural to them. Putting the material in their own words will create a better performance.
- Communicate! The more the talent knows about the production, what is expected of them and the schedule, the better success you will have.
- Discuss wardrobe selection ahead of time, so they arrive on the set prepared and look right.
- Arrive early, be prepared, have everything ready for the talent, don't make them wait, know what you want and be decisive!
- Create a comfort zone. Anticipate the talent's needs, provide a separate room or area for the talent to prep make-up and hair, practice lines, drink coffee or relax between scenes.
- Explain the production process to the talent. First time talent usually do not know what is involved in the shooting of a video. Explaining

the process from script development to editing will help relieve their anxieties about the production. Have them visit a production shoot if possible.

- Introduce the crew to the talent; try to make the talent feel as comfortable as possible and a part of the team.
- Communicate blocking instructions first and then rehearse lines. Concentrate on delivery first, action second. Do not give non-professional talent too much to do and remember. Plan to shoot in short segments.
- Give plenty of praise. Build their confidence which will show up in their performance.
- Rehearse difficult technical shots that involve camera movement in advance without the talent. Use a stand-in to rehearse difficult shots.
- Use a stand-in to light the set. When the talent arrives, make minor adjustments to the lights.
- Give non-professional talent good directions. Tell them where to stand or sit (and how to sit, legs uncrossed, arms folded on lap or on the arms of the chair) and where to look if they are being interviewed off-camera. Communicate the cue sequence to them (set a pattern for production and stick with it) and be sure to tell them what to do after they deliver their lines (look off camera, freeze or walk off).
- Know when to give up on a take. Don't force the talent to do 20 takes of a shot. If they can't do it in five takes, you probably will never get it.
- Let them know when you or the crew make mistakes, so they know re-takes are not aways their fault.
- Be sure to ask their permission before you mic them, or have them mic themselves with your direction about mic placement. Usually the mic is hidden under a tie or a collor of a blouse so use discretion when dealing with mic placement.
- Don't let the talent just "wing it." Even if they don't have a prepared script, they should practice—out loud—what they are going to say several times before they arrive for the shoot. They should also understand the purpose of the entire video production, so they understand how their part fits into it.

Planning for Post-Production

9

On a recent trip to Orlando I interviewed Oliver Peters about planning for post-production. Peters is a twenty-year veteran of corporate and broadcast television. He has supervised the post-production of many national television series and specials and is currently editor of visual effects and senior technical advisor at *Century III* at Universal Studios.

CONSIDERATIONS FOR POST-PRODUCTION
Time Considerations

One of the biggest considerations for planning for post-production is time. Time relates directly to cost. Often the first question asked about the editing process is "How much will it cost?"—and before the editor or post-production facility can determine the cost they first try to figure how much time it will take to edit the program. This question is often answered by reviewing the script, giving the editor an idea of how long the finished program should be and how many effects are going to be in it.

Editing Facility Capabilities

Producers should become familiar with the capabilities of the editing facility. As Peters points out,

> Many times with a first time customer, we like to get them familiar with what we can and can not do and get an understanding from them of what they expect. They may have a certain effect in mind that they have seen on television so we have to be sure we can deliver what they want. Or maybe there are other special requirements, for instance, if it has to be a laser disk pre-master and they're thinking in terms of an hour-long show, there's a limitation there right away that needs to be addressed. So we try to introduce them to the facility's capabilities and get an understanding of what their requirements are, so there's a good match. This applies to personalities as well, some people click better with others, so getting them in tune with our different editors and their styles will help build a successful session.

Figure 9 – 1
Oliver Peters is the Editor of Visual Effects and Senior Technical Advisor at Century III at Universal Studios.

Establish Deadlines

Once the facility or your editor has gotten a handle on what needs to be done with the project, a time frame and a general budget for editing can be established. The facility can also help you determine if what you are asking for is doable within the time frame you have set. The facility can also point out things that might affect the deadline, such as, if the project will go to laser disk, if several animation sequences are required, or if live music needs to be recorded. All of these elements will add to the post-production time frame. It is important to go over in detail the requirements of the program well in advance of the editing session so there are no surprises that could affect your deadline or budget.

The Approval Process

Your approval process may effect your editing session as well. If the client is going to be on site (at the edit session) and has the final say for approval, then an effect or graphic that may have a complicated build or an animation sequence can be created as the client watches in its final form. But if the client has to take the project to an approval above him, then you might want to go through several tests, or rough edits. In the case of animation, you might want to have several motion tests done and get those approved first before you do the final assembly.

Also be sure to have all the graphics approved in advance. Usually graphics are approved at the storyboard stage, the rough drawing

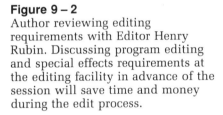

Figure 9 – 2
Author reviewing editing requirements with Editor Henry Rubin. Discussing program editing and special effects requirements at the editing facility in advance of the session will save time and money during the edit process.

stage and the final before it is placed in the program (more on graphics later in this chapter). Advanced approval holds true for music selection as well.

Project Requirements

Other things you need to determine in advance of the editing session are:

Format

What's the shooting format? Is it film or tape? What format within that? Is it 16 mm or 35 mm? If it's tape, is it going to be SVHS, Hi-8, 3/4SP, BetaCam, BetaCamSP? Check with the facility first to ensure that they can handle the tape or film format you will be shooting on. It is not always a good idea to "bump-up" smaller formats for editing because of the quality loss due to the step in generation.

International Distribution

Are you editing a program for international distribution? If so you have to consider the different international television standards such as NTSC (US), PAL and SECAM. Be sure the facility knows in advance that you are planning international distribution so that they can make the appropriate dub master for the standards. Some corporations may want a simultaneous PAL and NTSC production. This will affect your production shooting as well as your post-production requirements.

Nonlinear Editing

Nonlinear editing is becoming a serious consideration. Nonlinear editing changes the mind set of how you work and how you approach the scheduling of the project. Most people that come from a video background, as opposed to a film background, are used to taking their tape from the field, going into the edit suite and starting the editing process right away. With nonlinear editing systems, you have to allow a certain amount of time at the beginning to load the raw footage into the system, whether it's hard drives, or tape based.

Foreign Languages

Producing a program for multiple languages presents many challenges. It is best to have someone on the crew and present during post that understands the language. Not all foreign language scripts match perfectly with English scripts. Foreign versions may take longer to "read," the sentences may last longer which effects the length of the shot. Seldom can you make a straight translation of a script without having to re-edit the program.

If you are doing a foreign language version of a script, you may want to record the narration on two tracks. Do the foreign narration on one track and then go back and have the person who did the track put in key words or phrases in sync on the other track. You may not fully understand it, but if you ever get lost, at least you can figure out what paragraph you're on and the editor can follow along. Often you can find translation services in the phone book, and there are companies such as Henninger Video in Washington, DC, that specialize in translating and even producing foreign language video productions.

Figure 9 – 3
Shown here is the Media 100 from Data Translations, an example of the new digital, nonlinear editing systems that allow editors to "cut and paste" video, audio, and graphics.

It may be more cost-effective to do a translation into a foreign language in that country. They get the lip sync better and they do it all the time. English to French is often done in Canada and English to Spanish in Mexico City.

When translating programs, consider how you lay out your audio. You may want to have a clean version of your program with music and effects on one track and narration on the other so the dialog track can be re-recorded (translated version) without remixing.

Captioning

Captioning is becoming increasingly required for government based video projects. Captioning poses aesthetic and time issues. Aesthetically it's better to put on a Chyron caption or some sort of character generator, rather than have an actual open captioning device that's used for the hearing impaired. You can send companies that provide captioning services for open and closed captioning a tape of your finished program and they can transcribe it almost in real time by just listening to it. A skilled typist on a character generator will take longer and that will impact on the editing time, so there is a trade-off of aesthetics versus speed.

If you know you're going to have captioning in the lower third of the screen throughout the entire program, you have to plan where you are going to put the other name supers and other text that need to appear in that area of the screen.

If closed captioning is required, then you need specialized equipment to properly record the closed caption data into the vertical interval signal (open captioning tends to be something that most post facilities can do, even though it's just character generated), which adds to your post time and cost and planning.

Get Organized for the Edit

Be sure the editing facility really knows what material you are going to walk in with. If you book a Beta Cam shoot and want to edit to D-2, that is pretty straightforward. However, when you walk into the edit session and reveal that 50% of your material is stock footage from old shows on one-inch or VHS, this can cause the facility problems. You lose a lot of time, either in securing machines or in bumping material over to the format that you did have booked. Eliminate these roadblocks as early as possible.

A good facility will help you get organized for the edit session. If your project has a lot of lower third name supers, check the spelling and the titles. If graphics are involved, double check the content and spelling. Be sure the style of the titles is consistent—is manager spelled out every time or is it abbreviated half the time?

SHOOTING FOR THE EDIT

Try to be consistent with your production. Using the same crew throughout the whole shoot will assure consistency in the look of the program and the technical quality.

Using Time Code

Time code, the "sprocket holes" of electronic post-production, is a counting scheme in which each video frame is assigned an 8-digit number that corresponds to hours, minutes, seconds and frames. In NTSC video, there are 30 frames per second. There are two kinds of time code: drop frame and non-drop frame. Since NTSC video is synchronized to a frequency of 59.94 Hz (not 60 Hz), video "time" is said to run "slow" as compared to clock time. This means that in non-drop frame time code a duration of one hour as measured in time code will be 108 frames longer (over 3 seconds) than one hour of actual time duration. Early on, this proved to be a problem for such purposes as accurately timing network television programs, so drop frame time code was developed. Drop frame is a numbering scheme in which a total of 108 frames are "dropped" over a 1 hour period in the count. No actual video frames are "lost"—only certain numbers in the numbering sequence are skipped over. Therefore, in drop frame time code, a one hour duration equals one hour of actual time. Most modern edit systems and time code readers can deal with both types and calculate the proper offsets automatically if you mix tapes of different time code types.

Sometimes there are other time code types to deal with. In pure audio environments, such as a recording studio, time code may be used to synchronize multiple audio decks. Since there is no interface to video required and the audio tape recorders (ATRs) are locked to line frequency (60 Hz), such time code may be synchronized to 60 Hz and not 59.94 Hz. If these recordings are later introduced into a video post session, speed will not be correct and adjustments must be made.

Therefore, when shooting in the field, be consistent with the use of time code and reel organization. If on your first reel to be shot in the field, you set your time code hour digit so it relates to the reel number, (hour one is reel one) be consistent with this setting throughout your shoot.

There can be problems with the way time code is handled in the field. Videographers from a news shooting background have a different way of doing things than people coming from a production background. Production people tend to keep time code continuous, and hour one is reel one, and hour two is reel two and so on. I've run into news cameramen who use continuous running time of day code and the reason they do that is because the reporter can look at a digital wrist watch and take notes of an event based on time of day, and then they know where to go on the tape to find that based on the time code. That is valid for its own reasons, but it also tends to pose preroll problems because if you're editing based on time codes, you may not have enough preroll.

Pre-production planning can help you determine the standard for the facility you will be editing at. They can tell you their standard so you can shoot the tapes in a consistent way that will speed up the editing process.

Computer-based time code capture and organization programs such as *The Executive Producer* by Imagine Products, can be of tremendous help in the editing process. *The Executive Producer,* for example, eliminates the need for delayed or haphazard logging of shots with time code entries on log sheets. It reads the time code output of the field recorder (or later through playback) through an SMPTE time code reader and sends it to a computer (perhaps a laptop in the field) through a standard RS-232 serial port. This data base becomes an organized time code list with field notes and reel numbers.

Labeling

Be consistent with the labeling of tapes; the information is often pretty cryptic. If possible have a production assistant on the crew to take script notes, label tapes, keep track of time code settings and keep track of all the little things that can help a great deal in organizing for the edit. Many companies use an intern for this position and it is something that is easily taught but makes a big impact on the production.

Keep the Script Current

Change the script as your shots change on location. Often the logistics of the location require subtle script changes (a shot added or deleted, a different angle chosen or dialog added for explanation). These changes should be reflected in the final script that is used for editing. Be sure to get the new version reviewed and approved; the changes you make in the field may have significant impact on the final program.

Be Prepared

Be sure that **all** of the material you want to edit is on tape. All graphics, studio cards, slides, voice narration and footage should be recorded on one consistent format, labeled properly and prepared for the edit session. If slides are to be used, plan in advance how you are going to shoot the slides to tape. Will you use the telecine transfer system at the studio during your edit session (this can add a great deal of time to the edit session) or are you going to record the slides to tape with your camera in advance of the edit? If you do, be consistent with your lighting and slide angles and try not to use vertical slides; they are not consistent with the television aspect ratio. You can save a lot of time in the edit suite if all your material is prepared in advance, ready for the edit.

Think about transitions before you shoot. As I mentioned in Chapter 4, know where your transitions are so you can plan for them

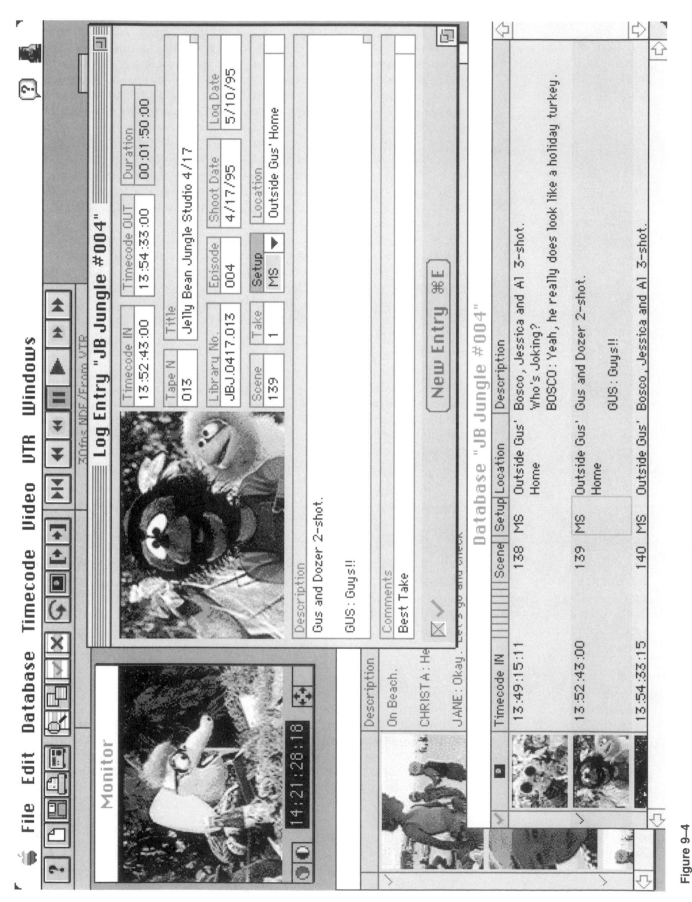

Figure 9–4
An example screen from *The Executive Producer*, a time code software managment system for personal computers. It allows you to grab time code and video frames right off the camera with a personal computer. Photo courtesy of *The Executive Producer*, Imagine Products.

during the shoot. Allow enough time at the beginning and ending of your shots for dissolves and special effects. Compose the shots for the effects you plan to create in post and be sure to shoot enough angles and extra footage so you have editing choices. It is a whole lot cheaper to shoot a few extra seconds on the scene than it is to go back and re-stage and re-shoot the scene because you didn't allow enough choices during the edit.

Good editors have an eye for consistency. They will adjust the colors, brightness and levels so they are balanced for each scene (if possible). However, if your shooting levels are way off between scenes, the editor may not be able to properly balance them and you end up with an inconsistency of colors or brightness between shots and scenes. Taking a waveform monitor into the field as you shoot helps with the levels. Most good videographers have a good, trained eye for levels and can keep pictures very consistent with a good monitor. It pays to pay attention to the levels as you shoot so the editor has good pictures to work with. This will save you a lot of time in post.

Search for music in advance of the edit and have it recorded to the format you will be editing on. Selecting just the right music for a program or transition often takes longer than you think. Set aside time for doing a good job in the music search, especially if you are using library music.

Coordinate as many of the post-production requirements in advance as possible. If animation sequences have to be built and rendered have that portion of the work done in advance, be sure that footage shot at out of town locations by other crews is shipped in well in advance, stock footage retained and all the credits approved. Refer to Forms 26–31 to help organize the post-production process.

"Being prepared well in advance of the editing session saves you money" states Peters, "however, some situations may require you to juggle many balls at the same time . . . you may have the graphics production happening while the on-line editing is going on. What you want to be careful of is you don't end up in a situation where one element bottlenecks the other, you often have to be the kind of producer that can bounce back and forth between two rooms and make the appropriate decisions on the spot. However, it is usually better to focus your attention on one element at a time. But in many cases, elements are interrelated. I don't know what the graphics are going to look like until I see them over the video, so you have to be a little bit fluid in that respect. You have to plan carefully so all of the elements come together and can be done within the deadline. If you're working within a facility that has all of those different options—they can do audio post, they can do editing, they can do graphics—then that makes it much easier. But if you're working in a number of smaller shops where maybe you go to one house for the graphics and a different house to do your audio post, then it's really up to the producer to be very sharp because he doesn't have the umbrella of one organization that can kind of watch out for him, if there are problems, and it's really up to the producer to be that much more savvy because the facilities are really at his mercy and he's the communication link as to what is needed by what deadline. And if the requirements are wrong at one facility, that usually affects all of the work at the other facilities. Audio and graphics for instance—a lot of people are going with DAT now and that's a real favorite format for audio producers, particularly music producers. However if you take it to a post facility that doesn't own a DAT machine, you're in trouble, and that's the kind of simple question up front—that's a key element that can save time.

CAMERA
SHOT LIST

1 _____

2 _____

3 _____

4 _____

5 _____

6 _____

7 _____

8 _____

9 _____

10 _____

11 _____

12 _____

13 _____

14 _____

15 _____

16 _____

17 _____

18 _____

19 _____

20 _____

21 _____

22 _____

23 _____

24 _____

25 _____

FORM XXVII

TAPE LOG

Title _____ Tape # _____

Prod # _____ Subject _____

Date _____ Producer_____

SCENE	SHOT	TAKE	Time In	Time Out	Notes
_____	_____	_____	_____	_____	_____
_____	_____	_____		_____	_____
_____	_____	_____	_____	_____	_____
_____	_____	_____	_____	_____	_____
_____	_____	_____	_____	_____	_____
_____	_____	_____	_____	_____	_____
_____	_____	_____	_____	_____	_____
_____	_____	_____	_____	_____	_____
_____	_____	_____	_____	_____	_____
_____	_____	_____	_____	_____	_____
_____	_____	_____	_____	_____	_____
_____	_____	_____	_____	_____	_____
_____	_____	_____	_____	_____	_____
_____	_____	_____	_____	_____	_____
_____	_____	_____	_____	_____	_____
_____	_____	_____	_____	_____	_____
_____	_____	_____	_____	_____	_____
_____	_____	_____	_____	_____	_____
_____	_____	_____	_____	_____	_____
_____	_____	_____	_____	_____	_____
_____	_____	_____	_____	_____	_____
_____	_____	_____	_____	_____	_____
_____	_____	_____	_____	_____	_____
_____	_____	_____	_____	_____	_____
_____	_____	_____	_____	_____	_____
_____	_____	_____	_____	_____	_____
_____	_____	_____	_____	_____	_____

FORM XXVIII

SHOT LOG

Show Title _____

Date Shot _____

Reel #	Take #	In Time	Out Time	Description
_____	_____	_____	_____	_____
_____	_____	_____	_____	_____
_____	_____	_____	_____	_____
_____	_____	_____	_____	_____
_____	_____	_____	_____	_____
_____	_____	_____	_____	_____
_____	_____	_____	_____	_____
_____	_____	_____	_____	_____
_____	_____	_____	_____	_____
_____	_____	_____	_____	_____
_____	_____	_____	_____	_____
_____	_____	_____	_____	_____
_____	_____	_____	_____	_____
_____	_____	_____	_____	_____
_____	_____	_____	_____	_____
_____	_____	_____	_____	_____
_____	_____	_____	_____	_____
_____	_____	_____	_____	_____
_____	_____	_____	_____	_____
_____	_____	_____	_____	_____
_____	_____	_____	_____	_____
_____	_____	_____	_____	_____
_____	_____	_____	_____	_____
_____	_____	_____	_____	_____
_____	_____	_____	_____	_____
_____	_____	_____	_____	_____
_____	_____	_____	_____	_____
_____	_____	_____	_____	_____

FORM XXIX

EDIT SHEET

Date _____

Writer/Director _____

Production Title _____ Project # _____

Tape No.	Recorder In Hr. Min. Sec. Fr.	Recorder Out Hr. Min. Sec. Fr.	Notes	Video/Graphics	Audio
——	———————————	———————————	———————	———————————	———
——	———————————	———————————	———————	———————————	———
——	———————————	———————————	———————	———————————	———
——	———————————	———————————	———————	———————————	———
——	———————————	———————————	———————	———————————	———
——	———————————	———————————	———————	———————————	———
——	———————————	———————————	———————	———————————	———
——	———————————	———————————	———————	———————————	———
——	———————————	———————————	———————	———————————	———
——	———————————	———————————	———————	———————————	———
——	———————————	———————————	———————	———————————	———
——	———————————	———————————	———————	———————————	———
——	———————————	———————————	———————	———————————	———
——	———————————	———————————	———————	———————————	———
——	———————————	———————————	———————	———————————	———
——	———————————	———————————	———————	———————————	———
——	———————————	———————————	———————	———————————	———
——	———————————	———————————	———————	———————————	———
——	———————————	———————————	———————	———————————	———
——	———————————	———————————	———————	———————————	———
——	———————————	———————————	———————	———————————	———
——	———————————	———————————	———————	———————————	———
——	———————————	———————————	———————	———————————	———
——	———————————	———————————	———————	———————————	———

FORM XXX

PRODUCTION LOG

Client _____

Job No. _____ Tape No. _____ Date _____ Editor _____ Due Date _____

SOURCE

Entry No.	Tape No.	Tape Counter	Time Code	Location
1.	_____	_____	_____	_____
2.	_____	_____	_____	_____
3.	_____	_____	_____	_____
4.	_____	_____	_____	_____
5.	_____	_____	_____	_____
6.	_____	_____	_____	_____
7.	_____	_____	_____	_____
8.	_____	_____	_____	_____
9.	_____	_____	_____	_____
10.	_____	_____	_____	_____
11.	_____	_____	_____	_____
12.	_____	_____	_____	_____
13.	_____	_____	_____	_____
14.	_____	_____	_____	_____
15.	_____	_____	_____	_____

MASTER

Time Code	Tape	Notes
_____	_____	_____

FORM XXXI

EDIT WORKSHEET

TITLE _____ TAPE # _____

PRODUCER _____ PAGE _____ OF _____

DIRECTOR _____ EDITOR _____ DATE _____

TAPE #	INDEX IN	FOOTAGE OUT	SHOT DESCRIPTION	COMMENTS
_____	_____	_____	_____	_____
_____	_____	_____	_____	_____
_____	_____	_____	_____	_____
_____	_____	_____	_____	_____
_____	_____	_____	_____	_____
_____	_____	_____	_____	_____
_____	_____	_____	_____	_____
_____	_____	_____	_____	_____
_____	_____	_____	_____	_____
_____	_____	_____	_____	_____
_____	_____	_____	_____	_____
_____	_____	_____	_____	_____
_____	_____	_____	_____	_____
_____	_____	_____	_____	_____
_____	_____	_____	_____	_____
_____	_____	_____	_____	_____
_____	_____	_____	_____	_____
_____	_____	_____	_____	_____
_____	_____	_____	_____	_____
_____	_____	_____	_____	_____
_____	_____	_____	_____	_____
_____	_____	_____	_____	_____
_____	_____	_____	_____	_____
_____	_____	_____	_____	_____

"Graphics . . . for instance, a lot of people are doing their graphics with independent graphics facilities, and they often give you the graphics on Beta Cam. But if you happen to be posting at a facility that doesn't have BetaCam, that's a problem. So those are areas where you have to make sure everybody is asking all the questions up front".

Working With Audio

Audio recording and mixing can create further problems in the edit session. Be sure that time code matches from the audio facility to the editing facility and that the recording formats are compatible. For instance some of the MIDI recording systems will only handle non-drop frame time code. Also, a lot of audio recording facilities use VHS as their reference format for the picture (as they build your audio tracks and mix), because that's the cheapest available machine, but VHS tape machine quality tends to vary. Be sure that the recording formats are consistent and that, if the audio facility records and mixes your tracks on digital, the editing facility can handle it. A number of the music people are going with the newer audio recording systems such as DAT, but there are not a lot of those machines available in the typical video post environment.

Always use time code-controlled or stable timebase devices. This must start before off-line editing. If exact sync and edit points are essential, speed cannot drift. Do not use audio cassettes, non-time coded open-reel audio, CDs, LPs and consumer VCRs not locked to an external reference. If these sources are used, dub them to a time code-based medium, such as 3/4 inch, Beta Cam, 1 inch, or D2, which will become the real source for the off-line and on-line edit. DATs seem to be stable and are OK to use without time code, if the tracks are easy to match up later.

Be sure to keep the recording tracks on all sources in order and consistent. The two analog tracks can employ Dolby noise reduction. Know what is on all the tracks and whether or not noise reduction was used. When editing, know what the mastering format and post house is capable of. For instance, D2 VTRs have four editable digital audio tracks; however, a lot of post houses are only wired to deal with two tracks at a time. D2s also have an analog cue track (a fifth channel). This can occasionally be useful, but most edit controllers cannot control inserts on it.

> Peters points out . . . "Video producers often like to work in audio recording facilities because audio is their specialty. We tend to think of the video post facility for editing video and the audio studio for recording and mixing sound. If you are dealing with a lot of dialogue for instance, like dramatic TV, feature film, corporate training reenactments and role modeling, that sets up a whole other discipline and you have audio facilities that handle that very well and others that do not handle it very well. For example, if you're editing dialogue, there is a particular talent to editing dialogue and scenarios and reenactments and those kinds of things, so that impacts the whole facility, particularly on the audio side. There is a whole editing discipline of editing feature quality sound tracks, cleaning up directors' cues and then going back and building a whole sound effects sequence and doing whole sound design for the background in that scene. If you're dealing with a company that does a lot of that, they have certain short cuts they can build in, but if they don't do that a lot, it's going to take them a lot longer."

Building a sound track in an audio recording facility is usually referred to as **audio sweetening**, a highly technical and aesthetically complex process. On many video, multimedia and film projects simple audio mixing of voice and music is performed during the edit session at the video facility. However, more complex projects often require audio sweetening or sophisticated mixing and equalization at a sound studio. The edited sound tracks from the video master are transferred onto a multi-track audio recorder along with the time code (called layover). The audio elements are equalized and sound effects, music and special audio effects are mixed with the video voice track. This mix (sweetening) is then placed back onto the edited video master (called layback).

When building a sound track in an audio facility, it is best to work with at least four tracks. In a mono program, this might be: track 1—voice-over, track 2—sound-on-tape, track 3—natural sound-ambiances/SFX, and track 4—music. These would be edited onto an edit master and then mixed in mono to a final mixed master. If extensive sound effects, stereo tracks or overlapping tracks are required, the need quickly grows to 8, 12 and 16 tracks. Additional tracks can be built up onto other copies of the master which are then slaved together for the mix. With D2's preread feature it is also possible to mix down the four tracks onto a single track of the same master tape, thus freeing up more working tracks.

Finally, know what the final delivery requirements are. Should your dubs have noise reduction? Depending on the recording format you are working on and the VHS dub format, Dolby noise reduction may or may not be an option. Will your dubs be stereo or mono? Will the program be presented on a large screen or through a computer speaker for multimedia use? Consider how your audience will see the finished program.

Special Effects

Adding special effects to the program should be planned well in advance. As Peters suggests:

"Certainly one of the things we like to encourage is enough of a preproduction conference with the client so that we can sit down at the switcher and demonstrate what effects we have the capability of doing. What helps an awful lot is if the client has an idea based on something they've seen and they can show you something and say this is the direction I want to go in or this is the specific effect I have in mind. Then you know right away that that's what you need to do. Some effects can be structured, designed in advance. For instance, if the client wants to do a specific effect (like a DVE move) a dozen different times, then it may affect how you organize and schedule the editing session. If there are a bunch of similar effects, you may want to schedule a day just to create these types of effects and then bring them in as you need them for the rest of the session. Designing of effects is real important for saving time in the session."

Be careful that the facility or editor knows exactly what you are asking for. There are so many buzz words and jargon in this business that you have to be certain that you are communicating with the editor. For instance, thinking in terms of what hardware is needed to create an effect, you may have a three dimensional effect in mind, but you may not have the budget for it. The editor can then suggest an alternative, you might be able to get the intent of what you want by painting it to look three dimensional, then moving it around with an ADO.

That is where a demo reel helps. You, as the client can look at the work the post facility has done and ask for similar effects, knowing what they can and can not do, before the session starts. Also if the effect is really critical, sometimes it warrants actually spending money just to do storyboards and then bid on those storyboards as a separate element. This will help the approval process as well. You do not want to spend time and money on developing a series of complicated effects or graphics and have management tell you "That's not what we wanted at all."

The storyboards will help in the budgeting process as well. Editors will be able to tell you how much time it will take to build the series of effects and you can weigh that cost against their effectiveness in communicating the message. Special effects usually take much longer to create than you plan for. Having a good idea of what you want through storyboards, demo reels or tape examples can alleviate cost over-runs.

"Most people underestimate what it's going to take," adds Peters. "If you've got 30 pictures going by in 30 seconds, somebody's got to figure out what those 30 pictures are. Often what's not done is someone sitting down with a tape before the edit session and deciding on what exact pictures are needed, what tape they reside on and the time code number. In the edit session you do not want to eat up time by making decisions, finding shots or trying out effects that should have been decided upon well before the session starts. That's the kind of problem that leads to the 8 and 12 hour days when 4 were budgeted. It's all in the planning and organizing of the material before you get the session."

Communicating The "Look"

The pre-production meeting should also deal with the "look" of the program and the feel and pace of the program.

As I have said, it really helps if the producer knows what style he or she is after and communicates his or her goals well in advance so the post-production facility can be prepared for your program and line up the right talent to accomplish your goals.

An obvious problem with post-production is just the unfamiliarity with the process. A lot of people are not as familiar with all of the pieces that go on and they think one thing is happening, when in reality, something else is. And although we're in the communications business, nobody communicates! That can be overcome by education and you and the facility working together.

Peters has a philosophy he calls the Fixodent post philosophy.

"In other words, maybe there were problems in the shoot and you've got buzz throughout all of the microphones. In that case you generally can't fix it totally in post, unless you do looping for all of the audio, which is rarely ever done for anything other than the highest budget projects. Sometimes that relates to things that could have been done in preproduction, sometimes it's just the quality of people used on location wasn't very good. Or sometimes, particularly in a corporate environment, if you're dealing on camera interviews with top level management, something you don't have the time to go in and do proper lighting, proper sound, and you're kind of stuck with what you get. That's usually something you can't do anything about, you just have to deal with it, and you end up with less than satisfactory results. We then apply the Fixodent philosophy, FIX IT IN POST. Which works sometimes but not all the time."

Post-Production for Multiple Camera Shoots

This book has been devoted to shooting single-camera productions; however, I will include a short segment here for posting multiple camera shoots since they do have some special requirements.

Many producers believe that when they plan on multi-camera production, it will go straight to tape with little or no editing required. This is usually erroneous. If a definite duration is required (such as in a broadcast show or an infomercial) subject matter must get correctly edited to maintain time limits and continuity. And usually after reviewing the material, the producer will want to correct minor imperfections in post. So plan your taping with the most efficient post in mind.

Record not only the production switcher output (line or program master) but also "isos" (isolated cameras). If you have enough VTRs, you should record an "iso" of each individual camera. You can also record "switched isos" if there aren't enough VTRs, but that will require an additional crew member (usually a director) to watch and correctly select the best alternate camera angles during the taping. In order to review the footage before editing, many producers record a "quad split display" to VHS or 3/4 inch during the taping. This tape usually shows the switched program and iso feeds with a time code window, but may only show iso cameras if more than three isos were recorded. Panasonic makes an inexpensive "black box" that creates a compressed quad display. VHS tapes of the quad display and the switched program allows that producer to review the show at his/her leisure and make decisions about content and continuity edits, as well as to find alternate camera angles to fix problems, add audience reactions or otherwise improve the cut and pacing.

When taping, most producers use drop frame time code that is synchronized to the time of day. This allows the production assistant taking script notes to keep track of the time code for all events by simply watching a correctly set digital wristwatch. All recorders should get the same time code from a master generator and there must be plenty of preroll at each pick-up point in the taping before coming to program material because the code will jump ahead with every pick-up edit on the record VTRs (the code generator is free-running with clock time). A knowledgeable PA taking extensive script notes is worth a mint when it comes to post. Although I would always recommend off-line editing if time permits, a talented script PA makes it possible to go straight into an on-line edit session without too many problems.

Working On Film Projects

Film projects that are edited on video have special needs. You must plan for the transfer factor (transferring the film to video), adding time to the edit. And you usually have double system sound, which means if it is a sinc-sound shoot you usually have to synchronize the sound. In most modern telescenes, you can simultaneously transfer the film (to video for the edit) and synchronize the sound at the same time. This process is done at post-production facilities in the telecine and often incorporates a technician called a "colorist" to help with the transfer. The "colorist" can color correct the footage, apply image enhancement and sound synchronization. Most producers choose the Rank Cintel or Bosch telecine. So once it is on video tape, there are no extra steps. This type of editing project will usually take longer and cost more. But if it's a film project to begin with, the budget is usually there.

If you have scenes that involve effects, you may need to consider mechanical or electronic pin registration, so that the image is stable. The film, going through a telescene (for transfer) has a slight amount of weave in special effects applications.

With film shoots, you are a little more subject to how good the director of photography is, because he does not have a monitor to go by. 16 mm rather than 35 mm would be used, and 16 mm is a little less forgiving of good or bad exposure than 35 mm is. You must have a very good director of photography to assure quality pictures that are consistent.

As Peters points out, "A commercial director, depending on his style, will do ten, 15 takes on a line of dialogue that, if he were a corporate video director, even a feature film or an episodic director, he wouldn't do. In a commercial production, the director is trying to mold what the actor is doing and how they're delivering the lines, so it's very easy for a commercial director to chew up a lot of film. Typically an episodic or a feature film director will shoot less film. In my experience for a half hour episodic television show, generally the top end was 50,000 feet of film of 35 mm . . . 1,000 feet every ten minutes worth of stock.

"We transfer probably 50 to 75 percent of what was actually shot. And typically for a half hour show we'd have between three and five hours of raw footage. So a 6 to one or even ten to one shooting ratio for commercial film is standard which is similar to the shooting ratio for video. It can affect post production, for instance, if you're doing film transfers, generally you're doing transfers probably to hour long tapes. If you are shooting video in the field, Beta is probably used, and 20 or 30 minute tapes are used. So the frequency of reel changes in a typical edit session is probably a little more with a video shoot than with a film, which can add to the editing time, however, with the longer reels from film, search time can take longer."

Once the film project is edited on video it usually goes through color correction. Film producers are more attuned to doing a color correction pass than video producers. And the ability to do a very detailed color correction session from tape to tape has greatly improved over the last five to ten years, so you have almost the same latitude as you would coming off of the film originally. You lose another generation, because you are doing another pass on a tape, but because of the technical processing that's involved it is hardly noticeable. However, it is not uncommon for film producers to be thinking about that generation loss and plan and budget creatively (in shooting) with that in mind. An elaborate film shoot will almost always go through some kind of color correction procedure that is either done at the time of initial transfer or done after the entire tape is finished, or a combination of the two. But the final edited master is similar to a straight video edited project that is dubbed and distributed the same way.

OFF-LINE EDITING AND ON-LINE EDITING

Off-line editing and on-line editing are terms that often create confusion in the video industry. Off-line and on-line are best defined by the desired result of each process. Using this approach, the point of the *off-line edit* session is to finalize the creative editing process, the creative decision making process; selecting shots and putting scenes in proper sequence with narration (comparable to editing the workprint in film, or the blue copy for print) and the result should be a finished edit decision list, commonly referred to as an "EDL."

The *on-line edit* session should result in a finished master videotape (comparable to the lab and optical work in film, and the printed piece in print). These definitions are independent of the type of hardware used in each session. Although most producers think of "cuts-only" 3/4 inch or VHS editing as "off-line" and an A/B roll, one-inch or D2 edit sessions as "on-line," it could be the other way around in certain situations.

The intent of off-line is to get the most time consuming part of the editing process completed at the least expensive hourly dollar rate. It is during the off-line session that the right "takes" should be selected and that editor and producer should try out the creative possibilities to see how the scenes best come together. The end result should be a fairly accurate "rough cut" that is the basis for the look of the finished program or commercial. It is very important that the client is heavily involved in the off-line process. The producer should cut as many versions as necessary to get final client approval of the "rough cut" prior to going on to the on-line session. Changes made later in on-line are very costly.

Once a "rough cut" is completed, all necessary edit information must be logged creating the "road map" for the on-line editor to follow. Generally the basis of such information is time code recorded on the master tapes. This time code is superimposed over the video on the cassette copies (called window dubs) used in off-line editing, allowing the off-line editor to properly log all edit information. This can be as simple as numbers written on a pad of paper or as involved as a fully CMX-compatible floppy disc generated during the off-line edit session. Although the CMX-compatible disc is not necessary, it does save a considerable amount of time in on-line editing.

Generally a ten minute video for a corporate image piece, sales or point-of-purchase program will have about 200 edits. This may be a combination of audio and video edits such as "talking-head" shots and video interviews or it may be a voice narration with video inserts cut to a pre-recorded tape or to music. Often the editing time and amount of edits average out for both types of programs. If the producer has only made a cursory review of the source material and on-line edit time is used (misused!) to view various takes, find shots and make things up as the edit progresses, then it would be hard to average more than about ten edits an hour. This means a ten minute video may take at least 20 hours to edit.

If the producer has screened all the source material, selected the takes, determined in and out time code numbers for all the shots and done a "rough" cut or simple off-line edit, and this information is prepared into a list for the on-line editor to follow, the on-line will go much faster and 25 edits an hour would be a good average. This would make the session an 8 hour time frame for the edit.

A true off-line edit with an "EDL" generated would make the on-line session go almost automatically. An auto-assemble session can move along at almost 100 edits an hour because no time is lost to the manual entry of time code numbers during the session.

Factors that affect the on-line session include number and extent of effects used, complex graphic sequences and audio mixing. Digital video effects can be time consuming and costly. It takes time to set up the effect. Simple lower-third supers and dissolves usually add ten to fifteen minutes to a session whereas multiple-image effects (split screens, quad splits, cubes etc.) can add at least a half hour for each of these sequences.

As a rule of thumb, an on-line edit session in which no prior off-line editing was done will probably not proceed any more quickly than at a rate of five to ten edits per hour. An on-line session based on a "paper list" written on a pad and created in a simple off-line session will proceed at ten to 25 edits completed per hour. And finally, an on-line session which can use a finished list provided on a CMX-compatible floppy disc can clip along at over 100 edits per hour. And as we all know, time is money.

Saving Time and Money in the On-line Session

The on-line edit session is often approached as if the producer had all the time in the world, but when the session comes close to the end, everyone starts worrying about the bill. This is often because adequate preparation was not made and there is not enough recognition early on that time is money. Oliver Peters offers some pointers on how to make your next on-line edit session go more smoothly and be a pleasant experience.

- Walk into the session with approved material and an approved script. If you were able to get an off-line edit done and get your client's approval, you are vastly ahead of the game. In most cases, however, non-video clients cannot tell much from a "cuts-only" off-line and must see everything in place to make a judgment. Even before you go to the off-line session have all your raw footage dubbed to viewing cassettes (usually VHS) with visually displayed time code (the "burn-in window" or "window dub"). At your leisure before the session, make sure that you have viewed all footage, selected all takes, timed all takes and selected the proper in and out time codes (preferably to he nearest second) and made a log of these reel numbers and time codes corresponding to your script. If necessary, review these selected takes with your client so that you get their input, approval and understanding before the off-line. Again, good communications is the key.
- Organize all your tapes. If possible, get all your source footage onto a single format. If this isn't possible, then be sure that you know which reels are on which formats and be sure that you have booked all the necessary VTRs for the session. In some cases, if you have source footage on several different videotape formats, it may be cheaper to get them dubbed (before the session) onto a single format than to incur the additional VTR charges during the edit session. The generation loss with such a dub is minimal. Be sure that all reels are properly numbered and labeled and that this information corresponds to your logs and edit script.
- Make sure all your tapes have valid time code and know whether that time code is drop frame or non-drop frame. Consumer/industrial formats should be dubbed to higher formats ("bumped-up") such as 3/4 inch or Beta Cam.
- Determine if you will have to do a lot of dissolves to and from the same tape. If so, a B-roll dub will have to be made. If there are a lot of these, make duplicate dubs of all of your footage ahead of time (dub time is cheaper than edit time), keeping the same time codes. If there are only a few scenes, then it is easier (and cheaper) to do this as part of the edit session.

An interesting feature of the D2 VTRs (often found in on-line suites) is the "pre-read" recording mode. Video is played back on the video confidence heads rather than the normal play heads. In this mode you can reenter the play signal into a switcher, add video to it as in a key or dissolve and re-record the composite back to the same VTR. Although this can save one VTR in the session, it still results in the same generation loss, because the signal is going through the same A-D and D-A conversions (analog to digital/digital to analog). In "pre-read" you get no margin for error; in other words, it becomes difficult to redo the edit if you make a mistake in "pre-read".

As an audio function the "pre-read" mode can be quite useful. D2 VTRs have four digital audio tracks. By building up tracks and submixing them back on the same VTR, it is possible to create complex soundtracks in the edit suite without the use of an additional multitrack audio recording.

- Create all paintbox graphics and artwork ahead of time and provide the editor with the graphics on tape. Usually keyable graphics will require the color artwork on one reel and a hi-con matte (to cut the "keyhole") on a second reel. Two source VTRs are required in the edit for this single graphic.
- Define all character generator artwork beforehand. Determine font styles and sizes, colors, edge attributes and proper spelling. If possible, book cheaper "off-line" time (or evenings) to compose and store lengthy text information. Avoid paying on-line edit time simply to type text. Avoid art cards; but, if you must bring them, they should have white text on black backgrounds. Avoid text with thin typeface and fine detail.

The best display of text over video is created with a character generator, such as the Chyron. These systems properly "cut the hole" for the key over video and fill it with a letter and some edge or shadow. Most character generators offer a wide variety of typefaces, styles and sizes.

- Decide on the amount of digital effects required and, if possible, storyboard them (simple line drawings will do) so that the editor can easily follow what you want. Consultations with the editor before the session are helpful. Again, you are trying to avoid "creative" decision time in the expensive on-line session.

GRAPHIC DESIGN FOR VIDEO

Graphics can help visualize the abstract, illustrate the unviewable and demonstrate the complex. Graphics can create a visual style for a program that will differentiate this program from all others. The color scheme, typeface, logo design and other graphic elements provide additional information through their visual approach, whether it be informality, humor, sophistication, boldness or subtlety. The producer, graphic designer and director must decide which visual approach will provide the most appropriate subject matter for the audience.

Mark McGahan, a computer graphics designer, heads **Design Interactive** in Dallas. McGahan lectures on graphics design at numerous conferences across the country and through these lectures has provided the basis for this section.

Fundamental Graphic Design

Before we can discuss planning for graphics, it is helpful to have a brief exposure to basic graphic design. Your best reference is to watch television with the sound off and to try to analyze what you are watching.

BASIC GRAPHIC DESIGN

Graphics used in video are limited by the medium in areas such as contrast ratio, coloration predominance, screen resolution and color artifacting. The video producer should be aware of these specific limitations in order to plan effective graphics for video and multimedia production.

All visual information and visual style are created through the use of the seven basic elements of graphic design—point, line, polygon (regular and irregular), shade, color, texture, and typography. These elements are arranged in a 3:4 format on the video screen. Static graphics, depending on their arrangement, can relate a sense of regularity or randomness, direction, motion and speed. All objects exist only in relation to the space around them.

Lines are the simplest directional graphic element. Characteristics of lines include length, width, and whether they are straight, curved, flowing or broken. Lines can indicate moods such as relaxation, excitement, stability and can create the illusion of depth.

Other elements of graphics include **shape, circles and ellipses**. These elements can convey a feeling of closure, wholeness, completion. The triangle represents the most stable form in nature, the circle the most complete. Multiple polygons can simulate a third dimensional view on a two dimensional screen.

Shading implies the existence of a light source, and it illuminates a graphic with directional light. Along with converging lines, overlapping shapes, relative size and perspective, shading adds the illusion of fullness, depth, and a third dimension to a flat, two dimensional element. Three dimensions are more interesting and visually informative than two.

Color in graphics brings highly subjective information to the viewer, and since no two people interpret color in exactly the same way, the designer can use color to create a psychological mood or frame of mind in the viewer.

Patterns and textures applied to shape are used to impart surface characteristics that reveal more visual information than can flat or shaded color alone.

Typography can broadly be divided into serif and sanserif. Generally sanserif type such as Helvetica imparts a factual, impersonal message. Serif type, such as Times, can convey a wide range of feelings due to its varying design factors such as contrasts in line thickness, heights and widths of letters and shape of the serifs (or little feet).

Symbols are groups of graphic elements that together convey more information than the individual elements do separately. Symbols can also contain a metaphorical aspect that text alone can not convey. They represent a powerful, direct form of communications.

In laying graphics out we usually refer to two types of composition—**symmetrical** and **asymmetrical**. **Symmetrical** composition is vertically balanced. It is straightforward, formal, stable and boring. **Asymmetrical** composition is more informal, energetic and dynamic in its feeling because the eye is persuaded to move around on the screen, not just up and down on it.

GUIDELINES FOR CREATING EFFECTIVE GRAPHICS FOR VIDEO

NTSC Video Artifacts

Aliased imagery Because video produces comparatively coarse images displayed by horizontal scanning, any objects that have lines or arcs running at a diagonal direction are represented—*or aliased*—by the vertical stepping of the horizontal line segment that make up the diagonal. This will affect diagonal lines, polygons, circles and ellipses. However, this can be countered by the anti-aliasing function built into raster computer graphics systems.

Color dominance The standard video signal modifies the original RGB (red, green, blue) color component and causes a warm shift in the video image because the red end of the spectrum is over driven. As a result, the green tones are less well defined, and the red tones tend to spread horizontally, or bleed.

Chroma crawl The video signal also causes chroma crawl, where two high contrast colors come together and undulating black lines appear.

Legibility Video graphics need to be a minimum of 18 points in order to be legible because video is a low resolution medium.

Color Colors for video graphics should be less than 100 percent saturation or intensity. More subdued colors help prevent chroma crawl or spread and allow objects that have type on them to be more legible.

Background separation Drop shadows separate objects from the background and create more visual interest.

A good graphic should be clear, precise (not too busy), accurate, simple (eliminate the non-essentials), bold, legible and interesting.

Types of Video Graphics

Two-Dimensional Static Graphics

This type of graphic includes textual data, data-driven and diagrammatic information such as bar charts, maps, diagrams, line graphs and organizational charts, as well as graphic illustration.

Three-Dimensional Graphics

Personal computers have made three-dimensional graphic design more accessible to the video producer. The computer software creates a "real" object that exists in the computer. It can be lit by different types of lights. Three-dimensional solid modeling computers use different types of rendering methods, and once an object is in a 3D graphics computer, it can be resized, rotated and lit as well as viewed whenever desired.

Animated Graphic Sequences

Animated segments can be created by sequencing individual graphic frames. Graphics animated through time can demonstrate process. A moving object, even if it is small and moving quickly, commands more visual importance than any larger stationary object. Because video functions through time, your audience expects each frame on the screen to contain some movement.

Three-Dimensional Animation

Generating successful three dimensional animation is a highly complex process requiring the careful integration of a number of procedures. The artist defines key frames, where the objects are placed in critical positions. Often he or she will use wire-frame or low-resolution models to determine the start, pivot, and end points of each major animation movement. Then the surface rendering or skin is placed on the wire-frame. The next step, "tweening," is to produce all of the steps in between the key frames.

Planning for Graphics

Graphics Style

Planning for graphics begins with communicating the style of the graphics you are looking for in your program with the artist. An initial consultation with the computer graphics artist and showing examples of the graphics style you are looking for will help the planning and produc-

Figure 9 – 5
Artist prepares a storyboard, a crucial tool for planning shots, transitions and graphic elements for production.

tion of the graphic elements. Bring examples of type style and art layouts, colors and textures that you like and that you feel will contribute to and enhance your message. Examples can be brought from print ads or other video programs. With this style reference the artist can begin to start forming a specific "graphic look" for your program.

The artist will be concerned with what part the graphic elements or segments will play in the overall program; what the graphics need to do or what concepts they have to show. What type of audience are you addressing? Are there just a few charts or are graphics an integral part of the overall "look" of the program? Will opening graphic sequences set the "tone" of the program for further graphics, lighting and packaging? Will workbooks or printed support materials be needed and will the program's graphic theme carry through to the printed page? Does the graphics budget include creation of printed support materials, packaging and printing?

The artist will need a clean list of graphics that are to be generated with correct spelling and suggested ideas for layouts. A graphics production schedule will be worked out, a budget set (try to negotiate a fixed rate, not hourly) and review dates for each phase of the production process will be scheduled.

Determine early the type of graphics to be created. Will there be specific type faces needed, how many elements are there in total, are there 2-D graphics needed, 3-D graphics and animation? If there are logos involved, color examples should be supplied for reference and camera ready art work of the logos is usually needed to create the computer generated logo for video. Be sure to check with legal about the proper use of the logo (often companies have very strict rules about using logos, size, against certain color backgounds etc.). Try to communicate as much as possible early with the artist or graphics production house.

For 3-D animation develop a schedule with milestones for review, revisions and approvals. The animation production sequence

VIDEO WORKS   PART 1.   JET LABS INC.

1) ــــــ ـــــــ

2) ـــــ ـــــــ

3) ـــــ ـــــ

4) ـــــ ـــــ

5) ـــــ ـــــ

6) ـــــ ـــــ

7) ـــــ ـــــ

8) ـــــ ـــــ

9) ـــــ ـــــ

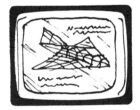

10) ـــــ ـــــ

11) ـــــ ـــــ

12) ـــــ ـــــ

13) ـــــ ـــــ

14) ـــــ ـــــ

15) ـــــ ـــــ

16) ـــــ ـــــ

Figure 9–6
Example of a storyboard for planning
shots for production.

usually follows the development of a storyboard for the design, modeling of the elements, a motion test (that may be wire frames or low resolution), color tests with full resolution of key frames of the animation for review and full animation. If 3-D animations are to start and/or end static, make sure that "holds" are put into animation, sufficient for editing. Often animators only render a few frames at the beginning and end of the animation and this is insufficient for editing.

Be sure that all of the edit elements have been created such as mattes and fills for graphics, additional logos for use as bumpers and character generations of all word slides.

If your graphics and animations are produced at a different place than you are editing, make sure that the tape formats and time code are compatible with the post house.

Be sure to make frequent reviews of the graphics being created, daily checks if possible. Don't let the designer work for long periods unsupervised without your input or you may not get what you expect. And be sure to check your graphics on a composite video monitor, not on RGB as they are being created. RGB monitors will always look better. The graphics may fall apart in NTSC. Also evaluate graphics that are to be keyed over video in the edit. Check for color compatibility and readability and the quality of the key.

After the final edit be sure to make clear agreements about the disposal of graphic elements and files. Are the data files to be archived? Will tapes be held with masters? Do you retain possession of this material or are these the property of the design house?

Graphics Tips

- Always apply the **KISS** principle (keep it simple stupid!)—add clarity not confusion.
- Each screen should be self-contained, with a balance between content, space, and complete idea. Only use key words.
- Use progressive disclosure. Control what information the viewer sees.
- Ragged right lines are easier to read than right justified. Avoid hyphenated words.
- Organize along eye movement path—top to bottom, left to right. Avoid placing new information on the lower left side.
- Text display techniques such as labeling, highlighting, and illustrations assist students in (a) the task of focusing on important points, and (b) selectively processing the text.
- Lists do not work well in video. If you have to list items do not go beyond three or four items.
- Graphics illustrations are useful to maintain viewer interest, but are better utilized for retention—as memory cues or to summarize information.
- Do not have the narrator read the graphics word for word.
- Keep illustrations as realistic as possible—they must be recognizable without supportive text. Eliminate nonessential details. Critical attributes can be highlighted with arrows and color.
- Assist the viewer with content organization by visually structuring the graphics with consistent headings, subheadings and colors.

- Text presented in all CAPS tends to be less legible and gives the screen a very solid appearance.
- Color can be used to distinguish between different kinds of information, highlight and offer contrast. However, keep this use to a minimum.
- Provide a consistent "look" with graphics for video and printed support material.

A Quick Test to Check Your Graphics

1. Focus—what area demands the viewer's attention.
2. Originality—creative, self-expression, not copied. Idea is new.
3. Simplicity—elimination of nonessentials.
4. Balance—apparent equality of weight on either side of center line.
5. Consistency—overall agreement of the parts.
6. Harmony—pleasing relationship between all of the elements.
7. Unity—sense of oneness.
8. Fitness—suitability of design for its purpose.
9. Rhythm—planned visual movement.
10. Variety—enough difference to prevent monotony.
11. Contrast—enough difference between elements.
12. Proportion—is the relationship between things usually in size?

GETTING READY FOR THE DUBS

Even before copies of the program are made there is planning to be done. You will have to consider: are you making the copies or will you contract for this service with a duplication facility? How many copies will you need? Will they need to be labeled and packaged? Mailed? Returned after viewing? Who will manage this mail/return/scheduling/quality check responsibility?

In planning for program duplication consider:

- The duplication master should be well marked with bars, tone and directions for when the program should start (at bars? after bars?). Allow several seconds (15) for the leader on the tape and be sure to indicate the length of the program.
- Will the copies require custom length tapes or off the shelf tapes? If it is a series of several training programs or modules be sure the tapes are well marked.
- Be specific with your instructions to the duplicator. Provide the instructions in written form.
- Be sure the levels of both audio and video are consistent between programs. This will save duplication and cost of mixing.
- Are you going to put all the programs on one tape to save money? If you take this approach, the individual programs are hard to find. Individual tapes for each program in the series or modules work better but will add more cost.

191

FORM XXXII

DUBBING RECORD

Client _____ Date _____

Department _____ Phone _____

DUB (Master) _____ To (Copy) _____

Title	Format	Length	Format	No. of Copies

Comments:

Date Completed and Notified   Date of Pick-up   by

_____   _____   _____

_____   _____   _____

_____   _____   _____

_____   _____   _____

FORM XXXIII

DUPLICATE COPY REQUEST

Date Due: _____

Cost Center Names: _____

Cost Center Number: _____

Contact Person: _____

Date Submitted: _____

Date Required: _____

Deliver To: _____

Product Title: _____

Number of copies desired: _____

Format Desired: _____

Figure 9 – 7
Before the program is complete, plan for the duplication process. Craig Spencer of the Video Workshop prepares video dubs.

- How do you find a good duplicator? Check references of duplicators, call around and see who other producers are using in your area. Finding a duplication facility is based on price and good service. Competition is keen, so shop around.
- Does the service provide a warranty on its work? What methods of quality control do they have? What type of test equipment do they have? Do they time base the dubs? This is really important when making VHS copies.
- What type of tape are you going to use? Different levels of grade of tape create different levels of quality.
- What is their normal duplication turn around time? Can they deliver "rush" service?
- Where will you store your master? Duplication facilities often offer this service, usually at a price.

Customer Service: What Producers Want from Duplicators

Producers want to look good in front of their clients, and the duplicator can make them look good. Producers want to feel confident knowing that their duplication requests will be handled professionally and that their recommendations won't backfire on them and cost them a client. Forms 32 and 33 show examples of dub request forms.

Carl Levine, Director of Television at Unitel Video and Windsor Digital in New York, explains,

"Do the duplication facilities provide standards conversions, special handling and labeling? Can they provide mixed format duplication at regular rates and at the quantities you need? Are you charged for the sub-master? Do they make a sub-master? Do they evaluate your masters and do a dropout count? What is the RF envelope? How well will it track? Do they provide freight expediting?

"It all boils down to customer service. You may be able to save a few cents down the street, but quite frankly, what is more important is knowing that your job will get done correctly, and you won't be embarrassed in front of your client. That is worth the extra few cents."

Duplication is a key point in producing any program. If it is not duplicated properly, all of the creativity and work you have invested in the project will be lost. It is important to know what the actual viewer will receive and see. Good duplication adds to the success of the show.

Levine points out,

"Reputation is a two-way street. The producer has his reputation to worry about, so he counts on the reputation of the duplication facility. Duplication is a highly competitive business, so duplicators are making their presence known through exhibiting at trade shows and targeted advertising. Good duplication facilities emphasize matching technical expertise and service to client needs. What most companies are stressing today is service. With such competitive pricing and low profit margins, there is no room for make-goods. This runs into the service area. You have to provide quality and service if you want to keep the producer coming back. Producers are as sensitive to price as everyone else, but I have found that they are more concerned about getting the job done right the first time. This confidence is worth the few extra cents a producer might pay."

Quite often the quantity of the duplication order will be another decision factor in facility selection. Some facilities are better equipped to handle larger runs, say 5000 to 50,000, and some facilities can better handle the smaller 1 to 1000 copies. So the numbers quite often dictate the facility.

Computers and the Production Process

10

Just a few years ago most video producers probably couldn't tell the difference between booting a computer and booting a football. Today it would be difficult to find a producer who doesn't use a computer during some part of his or her production. There is not one aspect of the video production process that computers can not enhance. The wide use of computers in video has created a new industry where equipment and technology no longer change over a series of years but over a series of days.

Computers can make you a better camera operator, writer, gaffer, director, editor, production manager and producer. They allow us to do our work faster, cheaper and better than ever before. Yet many people still use computers for writing scripts and little else.

I'm indebted to Mr. Randy Baker of **Baker Productions** in Orlando, an excellent cameraman, director and producer, for the conversation we had that formed the basis of this section. This chapter will review the production process and discuss where computer software programs can assist in that process. It represents only an overview, however, because we couldn't possibly include every new application coming on the market daily. We won't dwell on specific programs, because the use of the application and how it relates to the production process should really be what you focus on. Most of the software mentioned in this review is available on several computer platforms.

PRE-PRODUCTION

Needs Analysis

The first step in producing training and communications programs, as we have detailed in Chapter 2, should always be a needs analysis. In the past a producer might go into the initial project meeting armed with pad and pen, ask a series of questions about the project, and leave the meeting, often forgetting to cover a few important points.

Today that important meeting can be better handled through the use of a laptop computer loaded with needs analysis templates for

Figure 10 – 1
Randy Baker (behind camera) of Baker Productions in Orlando, FL, lines up a shot in the field.

every question you could ever want to ask of any production. Before each meeting you can simply customize the template for that particular project and get all your questions answered. This organized approach can help you develop a welcomed sense of trust with your clients early in the game.

These templates are easy to create using simple word processing programs that allow you to create custom templates. **Microsoft Word For Windows**, for example, has several templates already installed including templates for outlining material, proposals, reports, and cover sheets. **Scriptwriting Tools** available through Morley & Associates of La Canada, CA, offers templates for creative treatments, storyboards and questions for research and on-camera interviews. The template approach offers a basic structure that can easily be customized for your particular needs following the simple prompts and menu instructions.

Proposals

Writing the video production proposal is an important step in the production process, that can be greatly simplified by using computer software and templates designed for that chore. Major word processing programs such as **Word for Windows** and **Word Perfect**, or desktop publishing programs such as **Pagemaker** or **Publisher**, contain dozens of templates that can be modified to create outstanding proposals and cover sheets. Many third party vendors are now supplying add on templates that work with the word processing programs to give you an even wider variety. **Random House's Winning Forms for Word** is one example.

New stand alone programs, such as **Winning Proposals**, are now becoming available that will guide you through creating proposals, grants and even dissertations.

Concept

The needs analysis defines your clients needs and helps form the objectives and goals, but it is up to you to put all that into a concept that will be successfully received by the audience. There are dozens of story development software programs on the market that can help you create concepts. These programs are designed primarily for the film industry but can be applied to video programs. These programs include story analysis tools that help you define story structure, outlines, characters, plots and resolutions. Some let you have access to thousands of plots while others let you compare your plot and outline to those of famous movies. Most are set up to walk you step by step through the writing process including concept development.

The problem with all these programs is that they are meant for writing screenplays, not corporate videos. If you are lucky enough to be able to incorporate three-scene story structure into your corporate video, you're in luck. However, they can help even if you're not and are fun to work with.

Two good resources for computer programs for the film and video industry are **The Whole Shebang** located in Hoboken, NJ, a company that sells several production related software programs for the Macintosh, and **The Writer's Computer Store** in Hollywood.

There are a few idea-generating programs out that help you unlock your creative juices by taking you through creativity exercises. These programs are great when you are stuck on a particular problem with a concept or script. An example would be **Corkboard, The Idea Proces-**

sor available form The Whole Shebang. Another example of this type of program is **Inspiration**, from Inspiration Software, based on the "mindmapping" concept. This program turns the computer screen into a blank slate and lets you enter ideas and concepts. It organizes the ideas, lets you edit and rearrange and modify your ideas and provides a graphic link for the ideas you generate.

Script Development

The advantages of using computers to write your treatments and scripts are so numerous it doesn't make sense to do it any other way. With computers you have the advantage of advanced editing capabilities on any written document. You can cut, paste, copy, move, check your spelling, grammar, sentence structure, import pictures, graphs, databases, other documents, and even include audio and video segments.

Scriptwriting software generally falls within three areas, each with its own advantages and disadvantages.

1. Word processing programs.
2. Stand alone scriptwriting programs.
3. Script formatters (which work in conjunction with popular word processing programs).

The type of scriptwriting software you need and use will depend on your needs, computer power and money.

1. The majority of high end word processing software contains enough customized features to allow you to do basic formatting for split screen and screenplay type scripts. These full-function programs include spell check, thesaurus, and style sheets and are very user friendly, especially those set to operate in graphical user interfaces (GUIs), such as Windows or Macintosh. If you are working in a word processing program already, you do not have to learn new program commands and structures to write your scripts. It is very easy to create your own custom script formats with title pages, client and project information, split audio and video pages and scene numbering systems. Corrections are easy with the editing capabilities of today's word processing, and they are very flexible and easy to use. The most commonly used of these word processing programs include ***Word for Windows, Word Perfect, Ami Pro*** and ***Word Star.***

The obvious problem with this type of software is its limitations in regard to formatting. You can set up a split screen format, but you can't make it disclose scene or shot numbers, mark revisions and omissions, remember character names or continue scenes to the next page. However, if you can put up with these minor inconveniences, you can save a great deal of money by using word processing programs to format your scripts.

2. Stand alone scriptwriting software was designed to do one thing—write scripts. Most will handle feature film, sitcom, and stage play formats, while a few will also allow split screen formats. These programs combine word processing power with formatting intelligence, allowing you to write, format, edit, and print scripts. The drawbacks to these systems are their high cost, the large amount of memory they take up in your hard drive and lengthy learning curves. Most programs require learning a whole new command language that can slow your writing down and cause formatting problems. They are not as flexible to use as the word processing programs (very few can really be customized for your particular need or style). Some of the most popular scriptwriting programs include, *Movie Master, Scriptware, Final Draft, Script Master* and *ShowScape by LAKE Compuframes.*

Dramatica, a new software program soon to be released by Screenplay Systems, Inc. of Burbank, is designed to aid writers in the process of story creation and analysis. The program will define what elements are present in all well-structured stories, how these elements are related, and how they interact. The software program promises to help writers actually analyze and *write* better scripts.

3. In between the word processors and the stand alone scriptwriting software are the script formatters. These programs work with the most popular word processors and give you the formatting tools and capabilities at a fraction of the cost of the full-blown stand alone scriptwriting software. Adding these programs to your word processor lets you keep the power, flexibility and all the special features of your word processor software without adding the cost and complexity of single-purpose writing programs. Since they work on the word processor you already know, the learning curve is dramatically shortened. They are very flexible in creating customized formats and are easy to use. An excellent example, *Scriptwriting Tools*, is an enhancement package that makes it easier to both learn and use Microsoft Word 6.0 for writing scripts and script related documents. It includes templates for several versions of screenplays and two-column format-scripts, plus templates for multimedia, storyboards, creative treatments and questions for both research and on-camera interviews.

Scriptor, available through Screenplay Systems in Burbank, places page breaks automatically so sentences and paragraphs are not broken-up, which could create a problem for the narrator. *Scriptor* also provides a page numbering and scene numbering system, and does script breakdowns for scheduling and provides a style and vocabulary feature. Other examples of script formatters are *Warren Script Applications, Script Perfection and SuperScript.*

Like scriptwriting software, there exists a number of storyboard formatting software programs that are integrated, stand alone or add on type programs. Again the one you chose to use will depend on your need, budget and the amount of memory you have. LAKE Compuframes offers a storyboard program that is linked to *ShowScape*, their scriptwriting program. The script and storyboard work together and can be linked together through talent, crew assignments, props and scenes. You do not need to be an artist to create storyboards. Example storyboard programs called *StoryBoard Quick* and *Storyboarder* have built-in pre-drawn characters (through clip art), locations and props. With a click of the mouse you can move pre-drawn characters around within a full color scene, move props or bring in graphics and photos through PICT files from other graphics programs. *StoryBoard Quick* also offers you a choice of aspect ratios for television, feature film or wide screen formats.

For more aggressive productions and more extensive storyboards, there are a few interesting pieces of software like *Virtus WalkThrough* created by the Virtus Corporation that lets you create virtual environments for storyboards, but only if you have enough RAM, ROM, time and money. This computer-aided visualization program lets the user draw a structure (set or room) and the software develops a three-dimensional color drawing that allows the user to walk around within the environment, experiencing the scene in three-dimensional space.

Before we leave the realm of scriptwriting software, you should also be aware of the importance of being able to do research for scriptwriting with your computer. Besides the myriad on-line services offering information, you can now order software and **CD-ROMs** which contain an amazing array of reference material. For instance, one inexpensive program will give you complete access to the New York City Public Library's reference section. Or a CD-ROM like *Great Cities of the World* will give you an instant database of information about cities like New York or Paris. You can even look up a telephone or fax number from a national CD-ROM telephone disk or access information on a particular article by name or even by words within the article from thousands of professional journals and magazines.

Production Management

Professional production management applications offer easy to use scheduling and breakdown software that provides a complex depth of features that save time for the film and video producer, production manager, production assistant or assistant director. Some of the features of this software allow you to scan your script, extract scene numbers, determine if the scene is an interior or exterior setting, if it takes place in the daytime or at night, counts and numbers each page, and tells you who your entire cast is and what scenes each is in.

You can break your script down into dozens of predefined or custom categories (for props, vehicles, stunts, costumes, audio, lighting, talent). You can also sort and print a variety of reports and lists such as shooting days, shooting schedules, shot lists breakdown sheets, call sheets, cast lists, prop and costume lists and general production forms. With *Movie Magic Scheduling/Breakdown* software program, available from Screenplay Systems, you can create as many as twenty-six different

Figure 10 – 2
The computer is becoming an important tool for pre-production, production and post-production. This photo shows a new generation post-production facility, utilizing the computer for graphics, animation, audio production and video editing.

breakdown categories or create your own custom categories for your production. You can bring storyboard images into your breakdown sheets and create schedules that are linked directly to your script using their *Scriptor* program.

In scheduling and breaking down a script consider a good calendar creating program such as **Calendar Creator Plus**. Calendar programs can allow you to customize and print an assortment of calendars for production and shooting schedules, approval and deadline milestones as well as make individual calendars for client, crew, location and talent.

Production Assets

The best producers are the ones with access to the most information. What used to be called artificial intelligence is today called knowledge assets. We already discussed how a simple inexpensive program could contain a complete reference library, but that's just the tip of the iceberg. Today you can find an amazing amount of information aimed at the film and video industry literally right at your finger tips. For instance you can access a program that provides you with over 1200 stock footage houses throughout the world—all on a few floppy disks.

There now exist programs to track music libraries (**Network Music** offers a CD-ROM library tracking system for their music library), clip art and stock images (**Corel Draw** offfers a stock image and photo library consisting of 200 CD-ROMs with over 20,000 images that can be used in multimedia program development; **Four Palms Royalty Free Digital Video** of Reston, VA, offers effects and royalty free video clips and **Timescape Image Library** of Studio City, CA, offers a CD-ROM reference of their production ready stock image library), production equipment rentals and products (**Prolog5** from Testa Communications of Port Washington, NY, offers equipment and companies on a CD-ROM), production companies and resources (**Video On-Line** is an on-line service provided by Video Copy Services of Atlanta), production talent and resources (**The Source** from The Source Maythenyi, Inc. of Boca Raton, FL, offers N.E.D., the National Electronic Directory of Directors, Music/Sound Designers and their companies), talent clearance (**Second Line Search** of New York offers talent clearance, research and budgets) and just about any other source material you may need in the course of doing production . . . all on floppies, CD-ROMs, and databases.

For those who work in production or post-production facilities such as a corporate video facility, there exist professional facilities management software such as **ScheduleALL** from VizuAll, Inc. of Miami, FL, **Video Management System** from Hinton/Wells Communications in Atlanta, **Media Management Information System** from Droege Computing Services of Durham, NC, and **Studio Management Software** from NDG Phoenix of Vienna, VA. These software programs are very comprehensive and allow you the capabilities to manage and schedule your entire production facilities. They offer the manager quick access to facility scheduling, budgeting, project management, library and labeling, invoicing, personnel management, equipment information, client information and job tracking.

Sales and Marketing

For the independent producer or production company, personal information managers can save your business. This software is perfect for all of us who are not sales and marketing oriented. It lets you keep track of who you talked with, who you are going to talk with and who you should be talking with. You can create a database of potential clients, set up a sales and marketing schedule to court those clients and track progress of each account and even prompt yourself when it's time to check back in on that account.

Business and marketing plan software are available although not specifically yet for the film and television industry. The idea behind this software is that it walks you through a step by step series of questions that help you formulate your business and marketing plans both on a short term and long term basis.

Business and Legal

If you are an independent or freelancer who is just starting his or her own production business, you should also check into the abundance of business software designed to help you start and run a small business. Software exists to help you run every aspect of your business from general accounting, legal forms, contracts, insurance, permitting and taxes. None exists just yet exclusively for the film and video industry, but these general purpose business software programs can help in the everyday business of running a business.

Budgeting

Perhaps the second most widely used piece of software for production is budgeting. Over the years popular spreadsheet programs have been utilized to prepare and break down budgets for both large and small productions. These programs allow users to break down and define every phase of production and the associated cost.

Unless you do a few budgets by hand, you will never begin to appreciate how much time, energy and frustration budget programs can save you. With a good video and film production budget program you can talk with your client on the phone and be typing in budget considerations as you speak. Because every item of every production process is listed on the budget form, it acts as a check off sheet assuring that any budget consideration, no matter how small, isn't missed. At the end of the conversation you not only have a final budget price, but a detailed breakdown about how much you'll spend on each particular phase of the production process such as scriptwriting, equipment rental and charges, production personnel, travel, post-production services including narration, music selection, rough editing and final editing and duplication costs. The better programs available that are really designed for the feature film industry but offer many features for corporate video and film production like *Movie Magic Budgeting* are flexible, easy to use and offer non-technical budget presentations, libraries of databases for rates, crews and talent charges, sub-groups for handling multiple versions of a budget, prepare budgets for foreign currencies and offer many pre-designed budget forms to match your accounting system. These types of software programs speak the language of video and film production using categories and units we are familiar with.

There are stand alone spreadsheet programs, accounting and financial business packages, and specific film and TV budgeting and film and TV accounting programs. Other examples of budgeting programs include *InstaBid* from The Production Source Inc., *Turbo Budget* from

Quantum Films of Los Angeles, and the *MacToolKit Production Budgeter* from Mac Toolkit of Santa Monica, CA.

The Association of Independent Commercial Producers (AICP) has developed a standardized set of forms known as the *AICP bid forms* that are widely used throughout the industry. These forms are easily customized and the formulas can quickly be set up on standard spreadsheet programs such as *Excel* or *Lotus*.

Some business software is available that is very industry specific. These programs will help you finance your project, set up limited partnerships and even private offerings.

Site Surveys and Sets

Through the use of computers, location scouts are taking their craft to a new height. They outfit themselves with small laptop computers and digital still cameras. This allows them to take location stills of the various areas outlined in the script and dump those scenes from the digital still cameras directly into the script or storyboard they have on their laptop computer. This approach greatly improves the approval process with clients and provides a more accurate storyboard, which makes shooting faster and easier and in the long run saves lots of money.

A few production designers are beginning to use simple CAD programs (computer-aided design and drafting) to design and lay out sets before construction. They say it's easier to get approval from a client by showing him 2D or 3D computer generated images of what the set or sets will look like before construction begins, plus it streamlines the construction process by having detailed blueprints to build from. An example of this advanced type software program would be *CyberSpace* from Autodesk, a California-based computer software developer.

PRODUCTION

In the Field

Use of computers doesn't stop once you are in the field shooting. For instance, a simple label program like *Avery Label Pro* can be used to print labels for the production book and field tapes. It can save time in the field to have pre-printed labels; they look professional and there is less of a chance that you will forget any necessary information on the label.

Advances in software along with the compact size of laptops and notebooks have dramatically changed doing remote teleprompting in the field. Today it's not uncommon to see one or two computers on the set of any given production.

There are now software programs for the videographer that work from hand held personal information managers such as *Sharp's Wizard* or *Casio's Boss*. These programs give videographers complete control over information in the field such as sunrise/sunset times, depth of field, angle of view and other critical factors that can help them become better shooters.

For continuity and tape logging there are programs such as *Log Master*, from Comprehensive, *The Executive Producer* from Imagine Products Inc. in Carmel, IN, and *Log Producer* from Video Logic in Chevy Chase, MD. These are excellent computerized videotape logging systems that help you organize the production, save time in the editing process and catalog tapes for future reference. The mundane task of logging tapes and off-line editing can be streamlined and turned into a rather simple, quick procedure using logging software. *The Executive Producer*, for example, simplifies the logging and off-line editing process by creating fast and accurate tape logs. It allows you to make a paper edit that generates an EDL (edit decision list) that can connect directly to an on-line editing system to speed the on-line process and save money. *The Executive Producer* coupled with Imagine's *The Executive Librarian* becomes a convenient tape library logger, client database or scheduler.

Some programs such as *Log Master, Log Producer* and *The Executive Producer* allow you to read and log time code information directly from the field recorder into your laptop computer. This type of software allows you to walk away from your shoot at the end of the day with a completed EDL (edit decision list) paper edit of your best takes. Or you can log your tapes after you finish shooting with software such as *Edit List Manager* from Future Video Products in Laguna Hills, CA, and *Dubner's Scene Stealer.* This program recognizes NTSC/PAL video signals and detects and grabs each scene. These digitized black and white scenes can be reviewed with time code numbers and any annotated notes you want to include, in essence providing you with a visual storyboard of every scene on your tape. This visual log can be played back on the computer or printed out as a hard copy and when used with *The Executive Librarian*, becomes an extensive visual database for creating a library and catalog of images and scenes. Although rather expensive (around $1500), this type of software can save hours of time when you are logging or cataloging large quantities of tape for long form programs and documentaries. As with most software, the faster the computer you have the faster this software works.

There are also programs that let you design lighting plots for both studio and field productions. These programs can design complex multicamera soap opera type plots or simple three light setups—all in an easy to use inexpensive format.

We are seeing more and more digital video cameras used in the field. These cameras can be programmed with a simple ICU card that each videographer can set up to his or her own parameters. A videographer completes shooting, takes out his or her ICU card, and the next videographer can plug in. It's that simple.

POST-PRODUCTION

Editing

As we saw in Chapter 9, the area affected most by the rise of computers in the production process is in post-production. Computer-based linear and nonlinear editing systems are growing every day. Computer-based non-linear editing is transcending traditional boundaries as we know them. It has brought near broadcast quality editing systems to video producers, broadcast television, corporate video and even the consumer market at affordable prices. A few short years ago a typical A-B roll, linear editing system with a DVE (digital video effects) CG (character generator) and paint and animation system couldn't be purchased for under half a million dollars. Today the same package including non-linear editing performance could be on your desk for around fifty thousand dollars.

206

So now instead of editing back and forth to videotape, we can edit our program in a digital non-linear format, on a hard drive. Starting with the audio and video recorded in the field, we transfer the analog footage to the computer hard drive through video compression creating digital files. This allows us to access the video footage and audio tracks randomly, eliminating the time consuming chore of shuttling through tape. We can view scenes and shots instantly and assemble the program in any order and make changes to the edited program quickly. We can add titles, graphics and video transitions and edit and mix audio with the computer. Random access editing is similiar to creating a document through a word processing system on your computer. When we are satisfied with one of the various versions of the edited master, we then "print to tape." **But be warned!** It is not as simple or as cheap as the non-linear manufactures would lead you to believe. The learning curve for non-linear editing is steep and the total system costs are often more than actually advertised. Be prepared to spend a lot of time learning systems and spending more than the magazine ads proclaim.

A pioneer in computer-based editing systems is Avid Technology, offering several systems. The **Media Suite Pro** by Avid is a low cost, Macintosh-based system that offers random access editing at project-selectable 30 and 60 field resolution with EDL output. This system is fairly easy to use.

D-Vision from D-Vision Systems, Inc. of Chicago, offers low-cost, non-linear, off-line quality editing on the PC Windows-based environment. It can be purchased as a complete system or in components allowing you to purchase only the items you need to create an editing system. The **D-Vision On-Line** system offers broadcast quality, non-linear editing on the PC platform as well.

D-Vision is also working with a consortium of video and computer companies to develop the OpenDML standard. The Open Digital Media Language is an extension of Video for Windows that will allow interfacing of hardware and software from third party developers allowing you to plug in your own choices of dozens of video and audio boards to create a very flexible editing system. Often called Open Architecture, it allows you to use standard hard drives and monitors and share files while working over a standard network.

The **Video Cube** by IMMiX of Grass Valley, CA, is an elegant digital video workstation offering high quality, on-line, non-linear, random access editing that has four CD quality stereo channels and allows you to preview and perform edits and special effects in real time. Devel-

Figure 10 – 3
The Grass Valley Desktop Video Nonlinear Editing System represents a good example of the new merging of computers and video technology for video production. Photo courtesy of Grass Valley.

oped by video folks, this digital editing system has a very nice control panel that operates and "feels" like a video editor as opposed to moving the mouse around and making computer key strokes to make edits. The system offers a video training tape to ease the learning curve and offers good quality video output.

A new player on the field, the **Media 100** by Data Translation, Inc., is the first 100% digital, on-line, non-linear video production system for editing high quality video programs directly from the Macintosh and PC. These systems are near broadcast quality offering fast, non-linear editing and special effects at prices never seen before. Expect to see a lot more of these systems come on the market with increasing features and reduced prices.

Graphics

Low cost computer generated graphics offering character generation, still graphics, 2/D-3/D graphics and animation and 3/D modeling on the desktop are becoming commonplace in video facilities throughout the country. Computer graphics software programs allow artists to draw in 2/D or 3/D imaging, paint, manipulate images, re-touch photos and animate using low cost personal computers. These computer graphics programs allow total control of image creation and print to tape capabilities allowing the small production company or the corporate in-house video facility to effectively and economically handle graphics and animation projects that might otherwise have to be sourced out.

Audio

Computers have made their impact on audio as well. Digital audio workstations that are available for the PC and Macintosh are disc-based, non-linear, audio mixing and editing systems that allow the audio engineer full audio manipulation and editing capabilities with the touch of a mouse. Multi-track audio mixing, audio sweetening and audio editing are now done on the personal computer adding flexibility, speed and lower production costs. Couple this with MIDI (musical instrument digital interface) and the sound studio today is a computer-based system for creation, recording, manipulation, and editing.

An excellent example of this type of computer-based audio editing system is the **SAW, Software Audio Workstation** software from Inovative Quality Software of Las Vegas. **SAW** is a professional audio production tool for manipulation and recording on the PC. It offers high quality recording, signal processing and editing for complete audio sessions on the desktop.

Validation

Validation of your training programs can be simplified using a desktop publishing system with templates for different types of tri-fold brochures and cards. Now you can offer clients a chance to send out with every videotape a self-addressed stamped validation form that is attractive, easy to read and takes only minutes to fill out and drop in the mail. In return clients will get a better understanding about how effective their videos are and if they are meeting the defined needs and objectives. This enables clients to justify the use of video to their superiors, which can mean more work for your company.

It seems like at every meeting or professional conference I go to there is a new piece of computer software that promises to make the video producer's job faster, easier and more cost effective. In conjunction with television programming you will see the software market narrow in on specific niche areas such as television production. In the not too distant future you will find integrated software that will hand hold you step by step from conception and story ideas to packaging and validation—loaded with modules for writing, storyboarding, shooting, audio, music, labeling, etc.—set up and ready to work on the digital editing, graphic and audio work stations that sit on the top of your (very large) desk. The conclusion here is that if you are not into computers . . . get into computers. Your job will soon depend on them.

Appendix
Resource List

The author would like to acknowledge the information and support of the following authors, manufacturers and suppliers have provided in the development of this book by offering this production resource list:

Stock Footage and Music Libraries

Film/Video Stock Libraries

Airboss Stock Library (military), 4421 Bishop Lane, Louisville, KY 40218 (502) 454-1593

Action Sports Adventure, 330 W. 42nd St., New York, NY 10036 (212) 594-6838

American Production Services, 2247 15th Ave. West, Seattle, WA 98119 (206) 282-1776

Archive Films, 530 W. 25th Street, New York, NY (800) 876-5115

Cameo Film Library, 10620 Burbank Blvd., N. Hollywood, CA 91601 (818) 980-8700

Cascom Inc., 806 4th Ave., South Nashville, TN 37210 (615) 242-8900

CBS News Archives, 524 W. 57th, New York, NY 10019 (212) 975-2875

Cinema Arts Inc., P.O. Box 70, South Sterling, PA 18460 (717) 676-4145

Cinenet Cinema Network, 2235 First Street, Simi Valley, CA 93065 (805) 527-0093

Clip Joint, For Film, 833 B. N. Hollywood Way, Burbank, CA 91505 (818) 842-2525

Comstock Stock Photography, 30 Irving Place, New York, NY 10003 (212) 353-8686

Dreamlight Images East, 163 E. 36th St., Suite 1B, New York, NY 10016 (213) 850-1996

Energy Productions Timescape Image Library, 12700 Ventura Blvd., 4th Floor, Studio City, CA 91604 (818) 508-1293 or (800) IMAGERY

Film Bank, 425 South Victory Blvd., Burbank, CA 91502

Firstlight Productions Inc., 15353 N.E. 90th St., Redmond, WA 98052 (206) 869-6600

Footage.net, stock footage on-line, INFO@FOOTAGE.NET., (508) 369-9696

Great American Stock, 2290 Cantina Way, Palm Springs, CA 92264 (619) 325-5151

Hot Shots & Cool Cuts Inc., 330 W. 42nd St., New York, NY 10036 (212) 967-4807

The Image Bank/Film Search, 111 Fifth Ave., 4th Floor, New York, NY 10003 (212) 529-6700

Imageways, 412 West 48th Street, New York, NY 10036 (800) 862-1118

Los Angeles News Service, 1341 Ocean Ave. #262, Santa Monica, CA 90401 (310) 399-6460

Merkel Films (sports), Box 722, Carpinteria, CA 93014 (805) 648-6448

National Aeronautics & Space Administration, Lyndon B. Johnson Space Center, 2101 NASA Road 1, Houston, TX 77058-3696 (713) 483-8602 (Still Footage) (713) 486-9606 (Research Video)

National Geographic Film Library, 1600 M St. N.W., Washington, DC 20036 (206) 898-8080

NBC News Archives, 30 Rockefeller Plaza, Room 922, New York, NY 10112 (212) 664-3797

Paramount Pictures Corp. Stock Footage Library, 5555 Melrose Ave., Hollywood, CA 90038 (213) 956-5510

Producers Library Service, 1051 N. Cole Ave., Hollywood, CA 90038 (213) 465-0572

Second Line Search, 330 W. 42nd St. Suite 2901, New York, NY 10036 (212) 594-5544

The Stock House, 6922 Hollywood Blvd., Suite 621, Hollywood, CA 90028 (213) 461-0061

Stock Video, 1029 Chestnut Street, Newton, MA 02164 (617) 332-9975

Streamline Film Archives Inc., 432 Park Ave. South, Room 1314, New York, NY 10016 (212) 696-2616

Timescape Image Library, 12700 Ventura Blvd., 4th Fl. Studio City, CA 91604 (800) imagery

Universal City Studios, 100 Universal City Plaza, Universal City, CA 91608 (818) 777-1695

Video Tape Library, 1509 Crescent Heights Blvd., Suite 2, Los Angeles, CA 90046 (213) 656-4330

WPA Film Library, 12233 South Pulaski, Alsip, IL 60658 (708) 385-8528 or (800) 777-2223

Music Libraries

Associated Production Music, 6255 Sunset Blvd., #820, Hollywood, CA 90028

Chameleon Music, P.O. Box 339, Agawam, MA 01001-0339 (800) 789-8779

City Tunes Production Music, 311 Austin Road, Mahapac, NY 10541 (914) 628-7231

DeWolfe Music Library, 25 W. 45th Street, New York, NY 10036 (212) 382-0220

Dimension Music & Soundeffects, Inc., P.O. Box 992, Newman, CA 30264-0992 (800) 634-0091

Energetic Music, Inc., P.O. Box 84583, Seattle, WA 98124 (800) 323-2972

FirstCom Music, 12747 Montfort Drive, Suite 220, Dallas, TX 75240 (800) 858-8880

Fresh Music Library, 80 South Main Street, Hanover, NH 03755 (800) 545-0688

Gene Michael Productions, 1105 N. Front St., Suite 29, Niles, MI 49120 (800) 955-0619 or (616) 684-0633

Impact Music, P.O. Box 67, Dale, WI 54931 (800) 779-6434

Killer Tracks, 6534 Sunset Blvd., Hollywood, CA 90028 (800) 877-0078

Manhattan Production Music, P.O. Box 1268, Radio City Station, New York, NY 10101 (212) 333-5766 or (800) 227-1954

Musi-Q Productions, Inc., 3048 Coral Springs Drive, Coral Springs, FL 33065 (800) 749-2887

The Music Bakery, 7522 Campbell Road, Suite 113-2, Dallas, TX 75248 (800) 229-0313

Network Music, 15150 Avenue of Science, San Diego, CA 92128 (800) 854-2075

Sonic Science, 119 Spadina Ave., Suite 767, Toronto, Ontario, M5V 2L1 (800) 26-SONIC, (416) 351-9100

Production Software

Multimedia

Graphics/Animation

Arts and Letters, Computer Support Corporation, 15926 Midway Road, Dallas, TX 75244 (214) 661-8960

Animator Pro, 3-D Studio, Autodesk Incorporated, 2320 Marinship Way, Sausalito, CA 94965 (800) 879-4233

CorelDraw, Corel Systems Corp., 1600 Carling Ave., Ottawa, Ont. Canada K1Z 8R7 (800) 836-DRAW

Crystal Graphics Incorporated, 3110 Patrick Henry Drive, Santa Clara, CA 95054 (800) 979-3535

ElectricImage Animation System, ElectricImage Corporation, 117 E. Colorado Blvd., Suite 200, Pasadena, CA 91105 (818) 577-1627

Fractal Design Corporation, 335 Spreckels Drive, Aptos, CA 95003 (408) 688-5300

Freehand, Aldus Corporation, 411 1st Ave. South, Seattle, WA 98104-2871 (206) 628-4526

Illustrator, Photoshop, Adobe Systems, Inc., 1098 Alta Ave., Mountain View, CA 94039 (415) 961-4400

MacPaint, Claris, Inc.

RIO, AT&T Software Systems, 2701 Maitland Center PKWY, Maitland, FL 32751 (800) 448-6727

Tempra, Mathematica, Inc., 402 S. Kentucky Ave., Lakeland, FL 33801 (800) 852-MATH

TIPS, Truevision, Inc., 7340 Shadeland St, Indianapolis, IN 46256 (317) 841-0332

Xaos Animation Tools, 600 Townsend Street, Suite 270E, San Francisco, CA 94103 (800) 833-9267

Authoring Software

Director, Authorware Professional, Macromedia Incorporated, 600 Townsend Street, San Francisco, CA (800) 326-2128

Hypercard, Claris Corporation, 5201 Patrick Henry Drive, Santa Clara, CA 95052 (408) 987-7000

Icon Author, AimTech Corporation, 20 Trafalgar Square, Nashua, NH 03063 (800) 289-2884

Quest, Allen Communications Wayside Plaza II, 5225 Wiley Post Way, Salt Lake City, UT 84116 (801) 537-7800

Toolbook, Asymetrix Corporation, 110 110th Street, Bellevue, WA 98004 (800)448-6543

Production

Avery Labels, 150 N. Orange Grove Blvd., Pasadena, CA 91103

Collaborator II, Character Development, Story Creation, Structure and Analysis, The Writer's Computer Store, 11317 Santa Monica Blvd., Los Angeles, CA 90025-3118, (310) 479-7774 (very comprehensive collection of production software)

Corkboard, The Idea Processor, The Whole Shebang, 205 Seventh Street, Hoboken, NJ 07030 (201) 963-5176

Dramatica, Screenplay Systems Inc., 150 East Olive Ave., Suite 305, Burbank, CA 91502 (818) 843-6657

Easy Log, Limelight Communications, 2532 W. Meredith Dr., Vienna, VA 22181 (703) 242-4596

Edit Lister, Log Master, Comprehensive Video Supply 148 Veterans Drive, Northvale, NJ 07647 (800) 526-0242

Edit List Master, Future Video Products, Laguna Hills, CA 92653

The Executive Producer, The Executive Librarian, Imagine Products Inc., 581 S. Rangeline Road, Suite B-3, Carmel, IN 46032 (317) 843-0706

EZ Write Marketing Plan Writer, Force Marketing, One Place Commerce, Suite 350, Nums Island, Quebec, Canada H3E 1A4 (800) 363-9939

Idea Fisher, Idea Fisher Systems, Inc., 2222 Martin Street, Ste. 110, Irving, CA 92715 (714) 474-8111

Inspiration, Inspiration Software Inc., 2920 S.W. Dolph Court, Suite 3, Portland, OR 97219 (503) 245-9011

Log Producer, Easy Caption, Image Logic, 6807 Brennon Lane, Chevy Chase, MD 20815 (202) 452-6077

Production Prompting Systems, Comprompter Inc., 141 S. 6th Street, La Crosse, WI 54601 (608) 785-7766

SAW, audio workstation software system, Inovative Quality Software, 2955 E. Russell Rd., Las Vegas, NV 89120-2428 (702) 435-9077

Scene Stealer, Dubner International, Inc., 13 Westervelt Place, Westwood, NJ 07675 (201) 644-6434

Scriptor, Movie Magic Budgeting, Movie Magic Script Breakdown & Scheduling, Dramatica, Screenplay Systems, 150 E. Olive Ave., Suite 203, Burbank, CA 91502 (818) 843-6557

Scriptwriting Tools, Morley & Associates, 1923 Lyans Drive, La Canada, CA 91011 (818) 952-8102

Showscape Storyboard Software, Script Master, Lake Compuframes, P.O. Box 890, Briarcliff, NY 10510 (914) 941-1998

Storyboard Quick, Storyboarder, The Writers' Computer Store

Storyline Computer Software, Truby's, 1739 Midvale Ave., Los Angeles, CA 90024-5512 (800) 33-TRUBY

Turbo Budget, The Writers' Computer Store, 11317 Santa Monica Blvd., Los Angeles, CA 90025-3118

Warren Script Applications, Stephanie Warren & Associates, 3204 Dos Palos Drive, Los Angeles, CA 90068 (213) 874-7963

Write Pro, Fiction Master, Write Pro Inc., 43 South Highland, Ossining, NY 10562, (914) 762-1255

Facility Management

CreativePartner, software for image and sound networking, E motion, 2650 East Bayshore Road, Palo Alto, CA 94303 (800) 385-6776

Media Management Information System, Droege Computing Services, Durham, NC

NSI'S Tape Library System, Nesbit Systems Inc., Five Vaughn Drive, Princeton, NJ 08540 (609) 799-5071

Schedule All, Schedule All, 20377 N.E., 15th Court, Miami, FL 33179 (800) 334-5083

Studio Management Software, Library Management Software, NDG Phoenix, Vienna, VA

Video Management System, HintonWells Media Products, One Paces West, Suite 1260, 2727 Paces Ferry Road, NW, Atlanta, GA 30339

Vidicaption, open captioning system, Image Logic, 6807 Brennon Lane, Chevy Chase, MD 20815-3255 (301) 907-8891

Production Resources

Audio Plus Video/International Post, standards conversion, 240 Pegassus Ave., North Vale, NJ 07647 (201) 767-3800

Cohen Insurance, production insurance, 225 West 34th Street New York, NY 10122 (212) 244-8075, 9601 Wilshire Blvd., Beverly Hills, CA 90210 (310) 288-0620 ("What you should know about production insurance" booklet)

Crews Control, crew location and contacts, (800) 545-CREW

Central Bookings, crew location and contacts, (800) 822-CREW

Devlin Videoservice, standards conversion, 1501 Broadway, Suite 408 New York, NY 10036 (212) 391-1313

Motion Picture, TV and Theatre Directory, Motion Picture Enterprises Publications, Inc., Tarrytown, NY 10591 (212) 245-0969

Prolog5, CD-ROM-based equipment directory, Testa Communications, Port Washington, NY

Second Line Search, talent clearance, New York, NY

The Source, National Electronic Directory of Directors, Music/Sound Designers, The Source Maythenyi, Inc., Boca Raton, FL

Video On-Line, on-line equipment resource, Video Copy Services, Atlanta, GA

INTERNATIONAL PRODUCTION RESOURCES

Eurocrew Ltd., London 01144-71-284-4465 (resource for NTSC crews in Europe)

International Teleproduction Society, Inc., 990 Avenue of the Americas, Suite 21E, New York, NY 10018 (TV facilities trade association)

National Association of Broadcasters (NAB), 1771 N Street, N.W., Washington, D.C. 20036 (research, technical, legal information)

Royal Television Society, RTS North America Inc., KAET-TV, Arizona State University, Tempe, AZ 85287-1405

Leo Baca, **Carnet Representative**, U.S. Council for International Business, 1212 Ave. of the Americas, 21st Floor, New York, NY 10036-1689 (212) 354-4480

State Department Publications, Room B648, U.S. Dept. of State, 320 21st Street, N.W., Washington, D.C. 20520 (202) 647-2518 (background papers on countries—general economic, social and cultural information)

Publications Department, U.S. Dept. of Commerce, 14th Street & Pennsylvania Ave., N.W., Washington, D.C. 20230 (202) 377-5494 (foreign economic trends and overseas business reports)

Independent Television News (ITN/WTN) ITN House, 48 Wells Street, London W1P 4DE (071) 637-2424 (crews and services worldwide)

Visnews, Visnes House, Cumberland Avenue, London NW10 7EH (081) 965-7733 (crews and services worldwide)

Medical Advice for the Traveler (booklet), by Kevin M. Cahill MD, Director, The Tropical Diseases Center, Lenox Hill Hospital, New York, NY

UNIONS, GUILDS AND ORGANIZATIONS

Alliance of Motion Picture and Television Producers (AMPTP), 14144 Ventura Blvd., Sherman Oaks, CA 91423 (818) 995-3600

American Film Institute, J.F.K. Center, Washington, DC 20566

American Federation of Musicians, 1501 Broadway, Suite 600, New York, NY 10036 (212) 869-1330

Association of Independent Commercial Producers (AICP), 100 East 42nd Street, New York, NY 10017 (212) 867-5720

Directors Guild of America, 7950 Sunset Blvd., Hollywood, CA 90046 (213) 656-1220

International Television Association, 6311 N. O'Connor Road, Irving, TX 75039

National Association of Broadcasters, 1771 N. Street NW, Washington, DC 20036

Producers Guild of America, Inc., 8201 Beverly Blvd., Suite 500, Los Angeles, CA 90048 (213) 651-0084

Screen Actors Guild, 5757 Wilshire Blvd., Los Angeles, CA 90036

Society of Motion Picture and Television Engineers, 595 West Hartsdale Ave., White Plains, NY 10607-1824

The Songwriters Guild, 6430 Sunset Blvd., Suite 317, Hollywood, CA 90028 (213) 462-1108

Writers Guild of America, WGA - East, 555 W. 57th Street, New York, NY 10019 (212) 245-6180

U.S. Military Contacts

Air Force: Chief TV/Movie Liaison, (213) 209-7525

Army: Chief of Public Affairs (213) 209-7621

Coast Guard: Public Affairs Liaison Office (213) 209-7817

Marine Corps: Director, Public Affairs Office (213) 209-7272

Navy: Director, Navy Office of Information West (213) 209-7481

Film Commissions

Office of Alabama Film
Commission,
340 N. Hull Street
Montgomery, AL 36130

Alaska Motion Picture and TV
Production Service
3601 C Street, #722
Anchorage, AK 99503

Phoenix Motion Picture/
Commercial Coordinating
Office
251 W. Washington Ave.
Phoenix, AZ 85003

Arizona Motion Picture
Development Office
1700 W. Washington Ave., 4th
Floor
Phoenix, AZ 85007

Arkansas Motion Picture
Development Office
1 State Capitol Mall
Little Rock, AR 72201

Northwest Arkansas Motion
Picture Association
P.O. Box 476
Siloam Springs, AR 72761

California Film Office
6922 Hollywood Blvd., #600
Hollywood, CA 90028

San Diego Motion Picture and
TV Bureau
110 West C. Street #1600
San Diego, CA 92101

San Francisco Bay Area Film/
Tape Council
P.O. Box 77024
San Francisco, CA 94107

Colorado Motion Picture
Commission
1313 Sherman Street, #523
Denver, CO 80203

Connecticut Film Commission
210 Washington Street
Hartford, CT 06106

Delaware Development Office
99 Kings Highway, P.O. Box
1401
Dover, DE 19903

Mayor's Office of Motion Picture
and TV Development
District Building, Rm. 208
Washington, D.C. 20004

Florida Motion Picture Bureau
Collins Building
107 West Gaines Street,
Tallahassee, FL 32399

Metro-Dade Office of Film and
TV Coordination
73 W. Flagler St., Room 1900
Miami, FL 33130

Georgia Film and Videotape
Office
285 Peachtree Center Ave.
Marquis Two Tower
Atlanta, GA 30303

Mayor's Film Office, County of
Hawaii
Department of Research and
Development
34 Rainbow Dr.
Hilo, HI 96720

Idaho Film Bureau
Capitol Building, Room 108
Boise, ID 83720

Illinois Film Office
100 W. Randolph St, Room 3-400
Chicago, IL 60601

Indiana Film Commission
Indiana Department of
Commerce
One North Capitol, Suite 700
Indianapolis, IN 46204

Iowa Film Office
Iowa Development Commission
600 E. Court Ave.
Des Moines, IA 50309

Kansas Film Commission
503 Kansas Ave., 6th Floor
Topeka, KS 66603

Kentucky Film Office
Berry Hill, Louisville Rd.
Frankfort, KY 40601

Louisiana Film Commission
P.O. Box 94185
Baton Rouge, LA 70804

Maine Film Commission
167 Maine Ave.
Portland, ME 04103

Office of the Mayor
100 N. Holliday Street
Baltimore, MD 21202

Maryland Film Commission
45 Calvert Street
Annapolis, MD 21401

Massachusetts Film Bureau
100 Cambridge Street
Boston, MA 02202

Detroit Producers Association
3117 Woodslee
Royal Oak, MI 48073

Minnesota Motion Picture and
   Television Board
100 N. 6th Street, Suite 880C
Minneapolis, MN 55403

Mississippi Film Commission
P.O. Box 849
Jackson, MS 39205

Missouri Film Commission
P.O. Box 118
Jefferson City, MO 65102

Department of Commerce
Montana Travel Promotions
1424 9th Ave.
Helena, MT 59620

Nebraska
Telecommunications Center
P.O. Box 95143
Lincoln, NE 68509

Nevada Motion Picture Division
McCarran International Airport,
   2nd Level
Las Vegas, NV 89158

New Hampshire Film and
   Television Bureau
Box 856
Concord, NH 03301

New Jersey Motion Picture and
   Television Commission
One Gateway Center, Suite 510
Newark, NJ 07102-5311

New Mexico Film Commission
1050 Old Pecos Trail
Santa Fe, NM 87501

North Carolina Film Office
430 N. Salisbury Street
Raleigh, NC 27611

North Dakota Economic
   Development Commission
Liberty Memorial Building,
   Capital Grounds
Bismarck, ND 58505

Ohio Film Bureau
P.O. Box 1001
Columbus, OH 43266-0101

South Carolina Film Office
P.O. Box 927
Columbia, SC 29202

Texas Film Commission
P.O. Box 12728
210 E. 5th Street, B-6
Austin, TX 78711

Tennessee Film, Entertainment &
   Music Commission
320 6th Ave. N 7th Floor
Nashville, TN 37219

Utah Film Development
6290 State Office Building
Salt Lake City, UT 84114

Vermont Film Bureau
134 State Street
Montpelier, VT 05602

Virginia Film Office
Department of Economic
   Development
1000 Washington Building
Richmond, VA 23219

Washington DC
Mayor's Office of Motion Picture
   & TV
717 14th Street NW
Washington, DC 20005

West Virginia Film Industry
   Development Office
2101 Washington Street East
Charleston, WV 25305

Calgary Economic Development
   Authority
P.O. Box 2100, Station M
Calgary, Alberta CANADA T2P
   2M5

Edmonton Motion Picture and
   Television Bureau
2410 Oxford Tower
10235-101 Street
Edmonton, Alberta CANADA T5J
   3G1

Ontario Film Development
   Corporation
81 Wellesley Street
Toronto, Ontario CANADA M4Y
   1H6

Ottawa-Hull Film and Television Association
19 Fairmont Ave.
Ottawa, Ontario CANADA K1Y 1X4

Toronto Film Liaison
18th Fl, East Tower, New City Hall
Toronto, Ontario CANADA M5H 2N2

City of Montreal Film Commission
155 Notre-Dame Street E.
Montreal, Quebec CANADA H2Y 1B5

Quebec Cinematographique
2836 Rue Allard
Montreal, Quebec CANADA H4E 2M2

The Caribbean/Bahamas
Bahamas Film Promotion Bureau
P.O. Box N-3701
Nassau, Bahamas

Jamaica Film Office
35 Trafalgar Road
Kingston 10, Jamaica W.I.

Puerto Rico Film Institute
355 Franklin Delano Roosevelt Ave.
Hato Rey, Puerto Rico 00918

Virgin Islands Film Promotion Office
P.O. Box 6400
St. Thomas, U.S. V.I. 00804

Books

Anderson, Carol J. and Veljkov, Mark D., *Creating Interactive Multimedia*, Glenview, IL: Scott Foresman and Company, 1990

Anderson, Gary, *Video Editing and Post-Production,* Boston, MA: Focal Press, 1993

Bergman, Robert and Moore, Thomas, *Managing Interactive Video/Multimedia Projects,* Englewood Cliffs, NJ: Educational Technology Publications, Inc., 1990

Browne, Steven, *Videotape Editing,* Second Edition, Boston, MA: Focal Press, 1994

Cartwright, Steve R., *Training With Video*, Boston, MA: Focal Press, 1986

Cartwright, Steve R., *Secrets of Successful Video Training,* Boston, MA: Focal Press, 1990

Chamness, Danford, *The Hollywood Guide to Film Budgeting and Script Breakdown,* Los Angeles, CA: S.J. Brooks Co., 1986

DiZazzo, Ray, *Directing Corporate Video,* Boston, MA: Focal Press, 1993

Floyd, Steve, *The IBM Multimedia Handbook*, New York, NY: Brady Publishing, 1991

Gates, Richard, *Production Management for Film and Video,* Boston, MA: Focal Press, 1992

Katz, Steven, D., *Film Directing, Shot By Shot,* Studio City, CA: Michael Wiese Productions, 1991

Kehoe, Vincent, J-R, *The Techniques of the Professional Make-Up Artist,* Boston, MA: Focal Press, 1985

Kennedy, Thomas, *Directing Video,* Boston, MA: Focal Press, 1989

LeTourneau, Tom, *Lighting Techniques for Video Production, The Art of Casting Shadows,* Boston, MA: Focal Press, 1987

Lowell, Ross, *Matters of Light & Depth,* Philadelphia, PA: Broad Street Books, 1992

Mager, Robert F., *Preparing Instructional Objectives,* Belmont, CA: Fearon Publishers, Lear Siegler, Inc., 1962

Maier, Robert, *Location Scouting and Management Handbook,* Boston, MA: Focal Press, 1994

Mathias, Harry, Pattersson, Richard, *Electronic Cinematography, Achieving Photographic Control Over the Video Image,* Belmont, CA: Wadsworth Publishing Company, 1985

Media Arts Catalog, Books on film/video production, AV/Corporate video, Theatre/Performing, Boston, MA: Focal Press

Miller, Pat P., *Script Supervising and Film Continuity,* Boston, MA: Focal Press, 1990

Morley, John, *Scriptwriting for High-Impact Videos,* Belmont, CA: Wadsworth Publishing Company, 1992

Multimedia Resource Catalog, Information Resources for Multimedia Professionals, Future Systems, Inc., P.O. Box 26, Falls Church, VA 22040-0026

Smith, Coleman, *Mastering Television Technology, A Cure for the Common Video,* Richardson, TX: Newman-Smith Publishing Company, Inc., 1988

Sneed, Laurel C., *Evaluating Video Programs, Is It Worth It?,* Boston, MA: Focal Press, 1991

Van Nostran, William, *The Scriptwriters Handbook,* Boston, MA: Focal Press, 1989

Vaughan, Tay, *Multimedia, Making It Work,* Berkeley, CA: Osborne McGraw-Hill, 1993

Wiese, Michael, *Film & Video Budgets,* Studio City, CA: Michael Wiese Productions, Inc., 1990

Wodaski, Ron, *Multimedia Madness!,* Sams Publishing, 1994

Zettl, Herbert, *Sight Sound Motion, Applied Media Aesthetics,* Belmont, CA: Wadsworth Publishing Company, Inc., 1973

Manufacturers

3-M Optical Recording, 3M Center, Bldg. 223-5N-01, St. Paul, MN 55144-1000 (612) 733-2142

Avid Technology, Metro Tech Park, 1 Park West, Tewksbury, MA 01876 (508) 640-6789

Canon USA, Inc. 610 Palisade Ave. Englewood Cliffs, NJ 07632 (201) 816-2900

Carpel Video (video accessories), 429 E. Patrick Street Frederick, MD 21701 (800) 238-4300

D-Vision, Touchvision Systems, Inc., 8755 W. Higgins Road, Suite 200, Chicago, IL 60631 (800) 8-DVISION

Data Translation Incorporated (Media 100), 100 Locke Drive, Marlboro, MA 01752 (508) 481-3700

ImMix (Video Cube), P.O. Box 2980 Grass Valley, CA 95945 (916) 272-9800

JVC Professional Products, 41 Slater Drive, Elmwood Park, NJ 07407 (201) 794-3900

Lowell-Light Incorporated (lighting), 140 58th Street, Brooklyn, New York 11220 (718) 921-0600

Matrox Video Products Group, 1055 St. Regis Blvd., Dorval, Quebec Canada H9P 2T4 (514) 685-2630

Mole-Richardson Company (lighting), 937 N. Sycamore Ave., Hollywood, CA 90038 (213) 851-0111

O'connor Engineering Labs (tripods), 100 Kalmus Drive, Costa Mesa, CA 92626 (714) 979-3993

Panasonic Communications & Systems, 2 Panasonic Way, Secaucus, NJ 07094 (201) 348-7000

Sennheiser Electronics Corporation (microphones), 6 Vista Drive, POB 987, Old Lyme, CT 06371 (203) 434-1759

Shure (microphones/mixers), 222 Hartrey Ave., Evanston, IL 60202-3696 (708) 866-2200

Sony, 3 Paragon Drive, Montvale, NJ 07645 (201) 358-4107

The Grass Valley Group, Inc., P.O. Box 1114, Grass Valley, CA 95945 (916) 478-4120

Tiffen MFG Corporation (camera filters), 90 Oser Ave., Hauppauge, NY 11788 (516) 273-2500

Vinton Broadcast Inc. (tripods), 44 Indian Lane E., Towaco, NJ 07082 (201) 263-4000

Index

About the Disk...

This product contains the online versions of the forms found in *Pre-Production Planning for Video, Film and Multimedia* by Steve R. Cartwright. The forms are delivered as Microsoft Word® 6.0 templates for the PC. These templates consist of text fields and check boxes that can be filled in online and then printed. Additionally these forms can be printed and then filled in on paper.

System Requirements/OS Platform

Windows   Microsoft Word 6.0 or higher

- Operating System: Windows 95, 98, 2000, or NT
- Computer/Processor: Personal or multimedia computer, 486 or higher
- Memory: 8 MB of memory for Windows® 95 or 98; 16 MB for Windows NT
- Hard Disk: 6 MB of available hard-disk space required
- Drive: 3.5" floppy
- Display: Super VGA, minimum 256-color

MAC OS   Microsoft Word 6.01 or higher

- Operating System: Macintosh, System 7 or later; Power Mac—System 7.1.2
- Computer/Processor: 68020 or higher processor or Power Macintosh
- Memory: Macintosh—4 MB of memory minimum, 8 MB recommended; Power Mac—8 MB of RAM with virtual memory on
- Hard Disk: On a Macintosh, minimum installation 4.5 MB, typical 10 MB, complete installation with all optional components 23 MB. On a Power Mac, minimum 7.5 MB, typical 13 MB, complete 27 MB.
- Drive: 3.5" floppy
- Display: Any Macintosh-compatible monitor

Installing the Product

Place disk in your A: drive. Copy all the .dot files (a: *.dot) into your Microsoft Word sub-directory entitled "Templates". If you are unsure where the "Templates" sub-directory resides on your computer, open Microsoft Word, click on the Tools menu, click on Options, and click on File Locations.

For further instructions, refer to the **Readme.doc** file found on the disk.

Beyond providing replacements for defective product, Butterworth-Heinemann does not provide technical support for the contents of this disk. Send any requests for replacement of a defective disc to: Focal Press, Customer Service Dept., 225 Wildwood Avenue, Woburn, MA 01801-2041 or email **techsupport@bhusa.com**. Be sure to reference item number **DI-02713**